A Dream of Peace

Modern American Literature
New Approaches

Yoshinobu Hakutani
General Editor

Vol. 9

PETER LANG
New York • Washington, D.C./Baltimore • Boston
Bern • Frankfurt am Main • Berlin • Vienna • Paris

Ronald Grant Nutter

A Dream of Peace

Art and Death in the Fiction of John Gardner

PETER LANG
New York • Washington, D.C./Baltimore • Boston
Bern • Frankfurt am Main • Berlin • Vienna • Paris

Library of Congress Cataloging-in-Publication Data
Nutter, Ronald Grant.
A dream of peace: art and death in the fiction of John Gardner /
Ronald Grant Nutter.
p. cm. — (Modern American literature: new approaches; v. 9)
Includes bibliographical references and index.
1. Gardner, John, 1933–1982 —Criticism and interpretation. 2. Death
in literature. I. Title. II. Series: Modern American literature
(New York, N.Y.); vol. 9.
PS3557.A712Z79   813'.54—dc20   96-22420
ISBN 0-8204-3368-3
ISBN 1078-0521

Die Deutsche Bibliothek-CIP-Einheitsaufnahme
Nutter, Ronald Grant:
A dream of peace: art and death in the fiction of John Gardner /
Ronald Grant Nutter. –New York; Washington, D.C./Baltimore; Boston;
Bern; Frankfurt am Main; Berlin; Vienna; Paris: Lang.
(Modern American literature; Vol. 9)
ISBN 0-8204-3368-3
NE: GT

Cover design by James F. Brisson.
Cover photo courtesy of Jim Gardner.

The paper in this book meets the guidelines for permanence and durability
of the Committee on Production Guidelines for Book Longevity
of the Council of Library Resources.

© 1997 Peter Lang Publishing, Inc., New York

All rights reserved.
Reprint or reproduction, even partially, in all forms such as microfilm,
xerography, microfiche, microcard, and offset strictly prohibited.

Printed in the United States of America.

To

**Zadok William Nutter
7/2/90–7/14/90**

who, in his twelve days of life, helped teach me that
Death is more than just words on a page,
and Peace more than just an intellectual idea.

CONTENTS

	Preface	ix
	Introduction	1
1	A Story of a Death	9
2	Some Intellectual Antecedents	31
3	Of Pattern-Making and Art	59
4	Pilgrimages Toward Death	77
5	Isolation by Guilt	99
6	Pilgrimage Toward Life	119
7	Freedom and Responsibility	133
8	Self-Reliance and Redemption	147
9	Death, Guilt and Ritual Beginnings	169
10	Magic, Celebration and Novelty	185
11	Whitehead, Gardner and Peace	203
	Notes	223
	Bibliography	225
	Index	233

PREFACE

It goes almost without saying that the writing of a book cannot be completed without the help and support of others. This book is no exception. It owes its existence to the encouragement and assistance offered by many along the way.

This project originated in the late 1980s as a doctoral dissertation, then languished for a number of years while I was on the faculty at Alderson-Broaddus College in West Virginia. An unexpected set of circumstances in 1995 led me to Ludington, MI, where I now live, write, and occasionally teach at West Shore Community College. Thanks to the initial interest of Heidi Burns of Peter Lang Publishing, I returned recently to the Gardner manuscript.

There have been many mentors along the way. In particular, I want to thank C. Robert Wetzel, Tracy Miller and Terry Dibble for helping to engender in me a love of literature and of ideas; Robert C. Roberts and Robert K. Johnston for their friendship and the exemplary manner by which they demonstrate that a life of faith and a life of open-minded critical scholarship are not mutually exclusive; and Clark Williamson, J. Gerald Janzen and Walter Wiest for introducing me to the ideas of Alfred North Whitehead. Of especial help to me during my time at the University of Pittsburgh were Paul Bové, Michael Helfand, Alex Orbach and Ron Curran. My eternal gratitude goes to James D. Bratt and Fred Clothey, both of whom taught me much and were always supportive. Most recently, Jon Erickson has shown patience and skill in reading the manuscript, thus helping me to avoid some infelicities of language as well as some grammatical barbarisms.

My sincerest thanks, of course, go to my wife and son. Truth be told, I am neither gifted enough as a writer nor insightful enough as a husband to discern and communicate the manifold reasons for which I owe Laura my thanks. I can but give her my love and my life. That will have to be enough. As for my son, Chapin, he is the joy of my life. In ways he will not know for years to come, he has filled a void that I didn't even know existed before July, 1990. A little like Henry Soames in Gardner's *Nickel Mountain*, there is a sense in which my life began in December, 1993, with Chapin's birth. You've taught me to crawl, son, now teach me to sing.

Ron Nutter, Ludington, MI

INTRODUCTION

John C. Gardner, an American writer of considerable appeal, died in a motorcycle accident in 1982. His name is beginning to fade among lovers and scholars of American literature, however, and that is unfortunate. Gardner was a writer just beginning to develop a maturity to his work that promised fiction of great depth and insight. Less charitable critics may challenge that assessment, but will, if fair-minded, grant the brilliance of the man and the ambitious scope of his work. Even the harshest of his critics cannot help but be impressed with the prodigious volume of Gardner's writing, which includes not only fiction, but also plays, libretti for operas, scholarly works on Middle English literature and life, texts on creative writing, and works of literary criticism.

The fact that Gardner is even known today is testament to the support shown for his work by David Segal (Cowart, 1983:4). It was Segal who accepted Gardner's first novel for publication, *The Resurrection* (1966), while he was with New American Library. Segal "took his enthusiasm for Gardner with him," as David Cowart notes, when he went to work for Harper & Row, resulting in the publication of *The Wreckage of Agathon* in 1970. Having moved to a third publisher, Knopf, Segal initiated the process for the publication of *Grendel* in 1971 and *The Sunlight Dialogues* in 1972.

While Gardner's first two novels stirred little excitement, the publication of *Grendel* met with great success. Having gone through many hardback and paperback editions, this brief work—the story of Beowulf told from the monster's point of view, a blurb for the book proclaims—is still popularly read. The excitement generated by *Grendel* was vindicated with the publication of *The Sunlight Dialogues*. Unlike *Grendel*, this later novel was intimidating in its length and complexity, demanding much of its readers. The public appeared to love it, however, judging from its bestseller status and acceptance by a major book club, the Literary Guild.

Segal died before the actual publication of *Grendel* and *The Sunlight Dialogues*, but there was no longer a need to worry about his protégé. Gardner was now in demand and would never again have difficulty finding a publisher (Cowart, 1983:4–8). His next novel, *Nickel Moun-*

tain, was published in 1973 and became his most popular novel to date. Work on this novel began in the early 1950s when Gardner was a very young man. Critics have noted some failings of the novel, most all of which being the result of the fact the novel was written over a period of many, many years. Regardless, the publisher was forced into a second printing within a month after the first printing of 27,000 copies was exhausted. A further indication of the novel's popularity was its being chosen by the Book-of-the-Month Club, which itself was forced into a second printing of the novel just to satisfy its own club member's demands. Other Gardner offerings followed, including some of his scholarly work in Old and Middle English literature, and collections of short stories. His next novel would not come until the publication of *October Light* in 1976. Sometimes referred to as his "Bicentennial book," Gardner saw the novel awarded the 1977 National Book Critics Circle Award for fiction. In addition to seven hardcover printings within a year and two printings as a Book-of-the-Month Club selection, it was also published as a paperback by both the Quality Paperback Book Club and Ballantine.

It was becoming clear to readers that certain philosophical issues were prominent in Gardner's fictional world. Order vs. chaos, as a theme, is present in all of his work as he prods readers to think through the question: From whence does our sense of physical and moral order come, and what is the ontological status of that order? The question centers around whether that perceived order mirrors the orderliness of an actual world or is simply imposed by human imagination longing for orderliness and stability. This was a common theme in the fiction of the 1960s and 1970s. Thomas Pynchon, Donald Barthelme, Robert Coover and others have made their literary careers by an almost exclusive interest in such questions. Gardner's treatment, however, was of a different tone, though most did not realize it until some years later.

The late 1970s was a pivotal time for Gardner. Whether because of his growing popularity, or ancillary to it, Gardner's personal life was to endure a number of severe blows, including the break-up of his marriage of more than 20 years, accusations of plagiarism in his books about Chaucer, and a personal bout with colon cancer leading to surgery and several anxious weeks of hospitalization. Perhaps the biggest blow came with the publication of *On Moral Fiction*, which led to strident criticism—and sometimes very personal vilification—of Gardner. It is also around this same time that Gardner published in a magazine a short story titled "Redemption," which is included in his collection *The Art of Living and Other Stories* (1981), in which he discusses the burden of guilt felt by a young boy after a farm accident. It is a story with close parallels to Gardner's own experience as a youth.

Gardner continued to publish novels, including *Freddy's Book* in 1980 and *Mickelsson's Ghosts* in 1982, as well as the posthumously published *Stillness and Shadows* in 1986. These later works elicited little excitement among most critics, which may reflect the changed attitude of critics toward Gardner after the publication of his "literary critical work," *On Moral Fiction*. Indeed, its publication made Gardner's name a lightning rod of opinion as he named names in accusing contemporary literary artists of abdicating what he believed to be their responsibility "to improve life, not debase it. . . . to hold off, at least for a while, the twilight of the gods and us." (1978:5) While most discussions of the book center around Gardner's admittedly ill-tempered attacks on his peers, the book nonetheless does raise serious questions about the nature and function of art. Gardner insists:

> True art, by specific technical means now commonly forgotten, clarifies life, establishes models of human action, casts nets toward the future, carefully judges our right and wrong directions, celebrates and mourns. It does not rant. It does not sneer or giggle in the face of death, it invents prayers and weapons. It designs visions worth trying to make fact. . . .
> (The artist) lights up the darkness with a lightning flash, protects his friends the gods—that is, values—and all humanity without exception, and then moves on. (100–01)

Many contemporary critics and writers rejected Gardner's thesis, claiming it to be a reactionary moralism catering to a political movement toward conservatism by Americans in the late 1970s. John Barth, with support from writers like Bernard Malamud and John Updike, led the way with just this sort of criticism of Gardner.[1] Such protests miss the point. The heat of the debate, fed by the hurt feelings of writers criticized in *On Moral Fiction*, clouded people's opinions. This resulted in little recognition of what Gardner was, in fact, attempting to say. To begin, he saw his audience as far wider than that of professional writers and literary critics. But because of the book's harsh reception those who have sought to give thoughtful critical readings of Gardner's work have been forced to expend far too much time and effort having to address the rancor surrounding *On Moral Fiction*.

What has been needed, and with the passing of time is now possible, is an empathetic reading of Gardner's work articulating the positive contributions of Gardner rather than a rehash of that to which he was opposed. Such an approach will render a basic insight into his work: Gardner sees literature not as merely the subject of parlor room debates reserved only for those who proclaim themselves the literary elite—though Gardner certainly had his share of heated debates with literary luminaries. Rather, Gardner views literature as a thoroughly human activity inextricably intertwined with the broad ethos of a culture. And it is in this sense, as will be argued later, that Gardner's vision of literature ultimately has parallels with religion.

Gardner is a survivor of a childhood accident which led to the death of his brother, as well as a survivor of a life-threatening cancer which augers the ultimate hold that nature's way has with all creatures. Socially, he is a survivor of two marriages, both of which failed largely through his own actions. But Gardner is also an artist, and to the extent he is able to (1) assess accurately his and other's actions, (2) share honestly his most intimate and deeply-rooted feelings, emotions, and judgments, and (3) communicate effectively his insights using the tools and techniques of his artistic craft, he then is able to present to a reader a "vivid and continuous dream" of men and women seeking to make their way in a world which is often mysterious and, on occasion, very cruel.

Not surprisingly, the reading of his novels make plain that the dominant theme which Gardner constantly explores has to do with questions concerning death and guilt. One could argue that many fictional genres (e.g. Westerns and Mysteries) have characters threatened by death and/or die, but these genres treat the death of a character so matter-of-factly that the impact of the deaths are mitigated in the reader's mind. Gardner's novels are quite different. Death and guilt are brooding presences in his texts, exerting social and psychological pressures from which characters attempt to escape, not always successfully. Fiction is where Gardner the survivor and Gardner the artist merge; it is also where readers are given a glimpse of that psychological wound Gardner insists is a generative element of the creative process, as exemplified in the fictive exploration of the dimensions of his own sometimes tragic past.

Gardner's fiction, in addition to exploring issues of human death and guilt, also explores corollary topics having to do with, among other concerns, the question of human freedom and human responsibility, as well as the relationship between an individual and the community in which that individual lives. What becomes clear in his writing is that there are no unambiguous answers to these questions. The fact that these areas of concern admit of no definitive resolutions is expressed artistically by his use of what Dean McWilliams, citing the work of M. M. Bakhtin, calls "dialogical" fiction. What McWilliams is referring to is the tendency of fiction to fall into one of two contrasting views: "The first of these is centripetal and monological: all meaning is absorbed into and controlled by a single, all-encompassing value system. The other is centrifugal and dialogical: meaning explodes outward into a multiplicity of contending worldviews, all of which are given a fair hearing." (1990:7)

With some exceptions, Gardner's novels use an omniscient point-of-view allowing many different characters to present their own full-bodied perspectives—their emotions and feelings, not just their words—for the reader's consideration. It is out of this panoply of viewpoints that the reader is given an opportunity to weigh and assess the fictional advocates, and hopefully grow in knowledge and wisdom as a result. His tendency toward the ambiguous ending is well acknowledged, but the reason for not tying up all the loose ends in a neat little package is that Gardner is not interested in playing the role of a schoolmarmish arbiter of correct thought and action. Rather, he wants readers to come to realize the labyrinthine complexities of life's most enduring questions. Gardner does not stipulate a set of rules for people, opting instead for a range of possible responses. No one set of rules, he believes, is fully adequate and comprehensive enough for men and women having to live their lives caught in the tension between conflicting forces. He speaks in an interview, for example, of the tension between contrasts in his own personality and of how it might fictionally be expressed:

> ... I am on the one hand a kind of New York State Republican, conservative. On the other hand, I am kind of a bohemian type. . . . So every time I find the situation which is a kind of perfect expression of that war in my own personality—because I feel very strongly on both sides, like I really believe firmly, you know, gotta obey the laws, what's going to happen to the

society if we let the anarchists take over? And on the other hand, I hate people who are always obeying laws that they don't understand—when a plot comes along and that's the essential feeling in it, that's the one I go with. (Edwards, 1977:43)

While not advocating any particular code of behavior or specific answers as guaranteeing that one's life will be successful and happy—in his world there simply are no guarantees—Gardner does offer general guidance about ways one might generally improve one's chances of achieving satisfaction in life. It is guidance Gardner doesn't simply talk about in his fiction, but *embodies*. And to "get at" these ideas it will be necessary to look not just at his fiction, but also at the work of two philosophers who were very influential: Susanne Langer and Alfred North Whitehead. It will also help our exploration to look at some of the work done in Ritual Studies; it will make clearer how Gardner associates "religion" more with concepts of transcendence and transformation than with church and liturgy.

A brief word about the organization of the book might be in order. The first and second chapters attempt to introduce some of the basic ideas that will be addressed throughout the book. Beginning with a short story with strong autobiographical content, an emphasis is placed on the psychological impact of an accident fatal to his younger brother that left Gardner with a tremendous burden of guilt. Robert J. Lifton's work is revealing on this matter. Concepts of religion and the use of ritual are also addressed in the first chapter. Chapter Two discusses Gardner's views on the craft of writing, and also highlights the formative influences of various thinkers, particularly Langer and Whitehead.

Chapters 3–8 focus on Gardner's novels. After opening with some general comments about his fiction, the chapters take a thematic approach. Two of his novels have only slight mentions in this book. I chose not to use the posthumously published *Stillness and Shadows*— which is actually two stories, the one an expansion of a short story, "Stillness," which is also autobiographical, while the other is a sort of philosophical mystery novel for which he apparently had high hopes for success. I feel uncomfortable commenting on books that Gardner himself did not believe were ready for publication. The other novel I've avoided is *Freddy's Book*, a work of moral fantasy. I liken it to Gardner's morally serious novel for youth, *In the Suicide Mountains*, only think it inferior. My purposes lead me to believe a concentration on Gardner's more realistic novels is needed. The one exception, I suppose, is *Grendel*. But *Grendel* is such an important book in Gardner's corpus, whereas *Freddy's Book* is not, that it had to be included in any serious discussion of Gardner's work.

Chapters 9–11 are the more theoretical and abstract chapters. Extensive use is made of anthropological work in ritual as well as philosophical work in "process thought," which is the approach of Whitehead. At times, the Whitehead discussion gets very, dare I say, arcane. However, I feel confident the student of Whitehead's thought will have no difficulty, and I hope the student unfamiliar with but willing to learn about Whitehead will find the experience demanding yet invigorating. It is all needed for an understanding of the key concept of Whitehead's that is present in Gardner's fiction, the concept of "peace."

I have spent many years now reading and thinking about Gardner's novels. The effort required has been exasperating at times, but I count it as one of the blessings of my life to engage this talented man of titanic moods and sentiments. It has enriched my life. And, at a horrendously turbulent time when my 12-day-old son Zadok died, some part of me was soothed and comforted by Gardner's evocations of "peace," that intuition of a permanence immanent in the changes and tragedies of life.

CHAPTER I:
A Story of a Death

"*One* day in April—a clear, blue day when there were crocuses in bloom—Jack Hawthorne ran over and killed his brother David."

Thus begins a short story by John Gardner titled "Redemption." The story continues, describing the reaction of family and friends to the farm accident. Although the 12-year-old is never directly blamed by anyone, Jack Hawthorne comes to feel a great weight of guilt over the death of his younger brother. His father takes David's death particularly hard, with fits of melancholy and contemplations of suicide, all of which exacerbate Jack's feelings of guilt.

We are told that Jack's father would vacillate, raging between God's injustice at one moment, and then doubting God's existence the next moment. (1983:26) Jack has similar doubts. When his younger sister brings lunch to him while he works in a field he immediately begins to eat. When she asks if he is going to say grace, he says no. Then, looking up at her, he sees the alarm in her face. Trying to make the best of an awkward moment, he tells her that he had already said a blessing, only not out loud. Only then did she relax and smile. It is some moments later before he realizes what her look of alarm had meant: if he is unwilling to say grace then perhaps it is the case that there is no heaven, no end to their father's pain, and nothing but a sodden grave for David. (34) Already feeling guilt from the death of his brother, and guilt over his father's depression, now he had nearly taken from his sister that which gives her hope—a belief in a loving God who would nurture her father toward renewed health, and a heaven in which her brother, David, is living.

Seeing how his actions have caused harm to his family, Jack Hawthorne turns more and more to his study of music. Originally attracted by its solitariness when practicing his French horn, he comes eventually to be attracted to music's form—its seeming permanence and perfection in the midst of what is clearly, from his perspective, an imperfect and out-of-balance world. His music becomes his refuge, allowing him plaintive expression by the farm's cavernous haymow as well as an escape from the "herding warmth" of his family. And one of these days, he thinks to himself in the midst of his musical reveries, it just may happen that they will awake and he will be gone. (36) It is unclear—no doubt purposefully so—whether the reference to their finding him gone has merely to do with his leaving the farm. It may also be a broad hint suggesting Jack's own contemplations of suicide.

This short story, found in his collection *The Art of Living and Other Stories*, is an important text in understanding Gardner's fiction. As those familiar with Gardner's life no doubt already recognize, the farm accident described in the story closely parallels an event in Gardner's own life. As his mother, Priscilla, remembers it, young John—known to his family as "Bud"—was to use the family tractor to return a wagon to a neighbor and bring back a cultipacker. When his younger brother, Gilbert, asked his mother if he could go along, she quickly agreed. "The thing I had to live with ever after," the mother later said, "was that I didn't ask, How are you coming *back*? That didn't occur to me at all—that they were dropping off the wagon at the other farm and bringing back this cultipacker; which is a huge roller. Weighs tons." (P. Gardner, 233) Gilbert and Sandy, John's younger sister, rode in the wagon on the way to the neighbor's, but had to ride on the tractor during the return trip. Four-year-old Sandy rode on John's lap while Gilbert was on the crossbar behind him and couldn't be seen. The tractor apparently ran out of gas while coming down a knoll and jerked, causing Gilbert to lose his balance and fall to the ground. There, he was crushed by the cultipacker.

Priscilla learned of the accident when "Bud came running into the house crying, I've killed Gilbert! I've killed Gilbert!" (234) Gilbert died soon after. Gardner's family tried to assure John there was nothing he could have done. His mother recalls: "I told Bud, *Nobody* could have stopped that cultipacker except God, and He doesn't work that way. He doesn't interfere. When a big thing of nature hits you it hits you, and there's nothing that can be done to interfere." (235) Nonetheless, like Jack in the short story, John Gardner, too, felt responsibility and guilt for the accident.

Those who study Gardner's fiction will be forever in the debt of John Howell for a number of reasons, not the least of which is for a very insightful essay, "The Wound and the Albatross: John Gardner's Apprenticeship." In this essay he highlights and expounds on Gardner's notion of a wound being necessary to drive a person toward art. Gardner clearly emphasizes this in *On Moral Fiction* when he writes about the connection between creativity and obsession, and about how the tensions expressed in a work of art act as an objective release for tensions at work in the artist. "Art begins in a wound," Gardner writes, "and is an attempt either to live with the wound or to heal it." (181) He goes on to remark that it is the wound itself which impels an artist to continue to create works of art, while it is the "universality of woundedness" that makes these creations of art of significance to men and women coming to terms with their own wounded lives.

Just before his death, while completing *On Becoming a Novelist*, a text intended for those thinking about becoming writers, Gardner refers again to the positive role a "wound" might play in an artist's work. After saying a writer needs "an almost daemonic compulsiveness" to drive him, Gardner goes on to suggest: "A psychological wound is helpful, if it can be kept in partial control, to keep the novelist driven. Some fatal childhood accident for which one feels responsible and can never fully forgive oneself; a sense that one never quite earned one's parents' love . . . are promising signs." (62) Clearly, Gilbert's accidental death provided just such a wound for Gardner, driving him compulsively to an artistic release of tension.

Another reason for the story's importance is that it touches many of the dominant themes one finds throughout Gardner's fictional work. The one theme omnipresent in his fiction is the question of human death. In all of his novels the protagonists are either facing death themselves (e.g. James Chandler in *The Resurrection*, Agathon in *The Wreckage of Agathon*, and Henry Soames in *Nickel Mountain*) or struggling with guilt as the result of another's death (e.g. James Page in *October Light* and Peter Mickelsson in *Mickelsson's Ghosts*). Some of Gardner's characters, like Henry Soames and James Page, lack formal education and are inarticulate when facing life's challenges. Though their responses are visceral and emotional, a kind of wisdom—though inarticulate—does come through. Gardner uses other, extremely articulate characters, like Peter Mickelsson and James Chandler, both professors of philosophy, in order to set a stage for a free-flowing philosophical investigation of the whole question of human death. Interestingly, the philosophy professors would appear to have no advantage, and indeed may be spiritually handicapped in Gardner's fictional world.

Gardner's emphasis on the theme of death is understandable when one recognizes that the question of death is especially acute to a survivor of an incident in which a death occurs. Robert Jay Lifton, a psychiatrist who has done extensive work in the study of survivors, has developed a framework by which to understand the psychological characteristics of a survivor. In the case of Gardner it helps us to understand how a farm accident like the one in which he was involved would exert an enormous influence on both his life and his writing.

After defining a survivor as "one who has come into contact with death in some bodily or psychic fashion and has remained alive," Lifton goes on to note several distinctive themes tied to a survivor, including:

- a *death imprint*, which leads to an almost morbid concentration on matters of death;
- a *survivor guilt*, which asks why he or she survived, and feels guilt as a result of the belief that someone else may have died in their place;
- a *psychic numbing*, allowing one to continue living in the midst of death by maintaining a diminished range of emotional affect;
- *conflicts of nurture and contamination* as the survivor both accuses others of offering counterfeit nurturing when they try to help and believes him or herself to be dirty and contaminated, beyond the pale of redemption; and
- the *need for a conceptual schema* by which to make sense of the tragedy and all that happens subsequently. (1979:169–78)

Each of these themes is exemplified in "Redemption," as well as in Gardner's personal life.

The *death imprint* refers to the survivor's conjuring up of death images as he continues unceasingly to think about death. It is an indication of the survivor's inability to come to terms with the death encounter, perhaps because of its suddenness, absurdity or grotesqueness. The death imprint forces the survivor to recognize the myriad threats to his or her own life in a particularly intense way. Over time, the trauma may come to be seen as positive despite the pain, for the survivor may eventually see it as an aid in gaining special knowledge and inner growth from having "been there and returned." (1979:170)

Jack Hawthorne has plenty of time to think while doing his farm chores in Gardner's short story, and thus he has plenty of time for the accident to play and replay in his mind. As the accident repeatedly is visualized he reacts with his entire body as it flinches from the vision of his brother being crushed. In the midst of these visions he would shriek, perhaps in hopes of driving the vision away from him. Later, the reader is informed:

> from nowhere, the black memory of his brother's death rushed over him again, mindless and inexorable as a wind or wave, the huge cultipacker lifting—only an inch or so—as it climbed toward the shoulders, then sank on the cheek, flattening the skull—and he heard, more real than the morning, his sister's scream. (33)

Gardner would often refer to similar episodes in his own life when he would suddenly have a flashback of Gilbert's death. "Every day I used to have four or five flashes of that accident," he has said in an interview. "I'd be driving down the highway and I couldn't see what was coming because I'd have a memory flash." (Ferguson, 1979:65) Gardner has another fictional rendering of the accident in the posthumously published *Stillness and Shadows*, the first half of which is a novel based on the breakup of his marriage to his first wife, Joan. In this text Gardner, a thinly disguised character named Martin Orrick, takes note of the uncontrollable flashbacks he experiences as well as his ongoing sense of guilt:

> Causes and effects are not neatly separable, as we sometimes find them in fiction. Martin Orrick's nature helped the accident to happen, and the accident helped to shape his nature, each feeding on the other as past and present do, or ends and means, or—as Orrick would say—the brain's two lobes. In any event, part of what Joan's mother called his "darkness" had to do with this: One day, in a farm accident, Martin—that is, Buddy—ran over and killed his brother Gilbert. It was an ugly and stupid accident which, even at the last moment, Buddy could have prevented by hitting the tractor brakes; but he was unable to think, or rather thought unclearly, and so watched it happen, as he would watch it happen in his mind, with undiminished clarity, again and again until the day he died. . . . [His father] . . . loved all his children and would not consciously have been able to hate Buddy even if Buddy had been, as he seriously imagined himself, Gilbert's murderer. But of course he could not help seeming to blame his son, though in fact he blamed no one but himself. (80)

It should also be noted that "the extraordinary power of this imagery—its indelible quality—has to do not only with death but with guilt." (Lifton, 1979:170) The notion of *survivor guilt*, the belief that the survivor should have been able to do something to prevent the death, or that the other died in the survivor's place, is exacerbated when the death involves a close relative or friend. The fundamental question for the survivor is, "Why did I survive while he (she or they) died?" Influenced by the imaging consciousness, that question can easily evolve into "Why did I survive while *letting* him (her or them) die?" (171) Thus the survivor begins to ravage himself with guilt: first for having failed to enact a rescue, and then for not having died in place of the actual victim.

Jack Hawthorne had always told himself stories while driving the family tractor, usually of sexual conquest or heroic battle. After the accident his stories are transformed to fantasies of self-sacrifice, plaintive tales in which he manages to redeem his life by sacrificing it to save others of more worth. Such guilt, while it may be taken to psychological extremes, nonetheless does serve a useful social role. When an incident involves the death of a friend or close relative guilt usually merges with feelings of shame, which may suggest "an evolutionary function of guilt, its importance for human ties in general and for maintaining individual responsibility for *sustaining* other's lives." (Lifton, 1987:237) In short, guilt may play a necessary role in developing notions of family and community responsibility. Indeed, Gardner's notion of "moral art" may be seen as one attempt on his part to sustain the lives of others through the action of literature. (Gardner, 1978:5)

Another feature of the survivor concerns the conflicts centering around *nurture and contamination.* Part of the reason behind a survivor's overt rejection of help is the recognition that help offered by others is a sign of how "helpless" the survivor is. This, in turn, spills over into the survivor's sense of his or her contamination, a belief that he or she is now polluted and corrupt, which easily may evolve into uncontrollable rage and anger. (Lifton, 1979:176) Jack, in "Redemption," is described after the accident as remaining aloof from his family and other workers on the farm. He is repelled by the family chatter and the absent-minded humming when friends and neighbors would drop by to visit. He is particularly indignant with what he considers the pretense of all those gathered, everyone acting as if all is well. Well-intentioned comments made to him by concerned neighbors are met with Jack's quiet anger. For his part, Jack views himself as not worthy to be a part of the family, as trapped in a situation from which he cannot escape. No longer able, in his own mind, to make meaningful contact with members of his family, he finds he has "all the time in the world to cry and swear bitterly at himself." (28) Seething while working a field on a tractor, he rages that he had never loved his brother, nor anyone else, as well as he should have. Indeed, he convinces himself that he has never even been capable of love, that he was bad by nature and spiritually defective. In a word, Jack believed himself to be Evil. As a way of coping he would make a production of confessing his worthlessness, granting himself no quarter in describing his bestial self. This does help—at least for a time. Eventually, he comes to realize that he is acting his usual manipulative self, burying himself in shame in an effort to buy love. The end result is a shackling despair as he comes to realize more and more the utter foulness of his nature. Then, as did his father, Jack begins to consider the idea of suicide.

While it is always suspect to take a fictional text and simply assume it is the writer's own experience, it nonetheless should be noted that Gardner has often admitted a tendency toward suicide. "There are times when you feel you ought to be dead," he has said. (Singular, 1979:34) And while there are those who believe Gardner did, in fact, kill himself on his motorcycle in 1982,[1] other factors would mitigate against such a claim. For one, he was preparing to marry again at the time of his death. For another, he had a just-finished manuscript with him, ready to be published, when the accident occurred. Further, he had written a fantasy for young adults, *In the Suicide Mountains*, which explicitly argues against suicide as a response to life's problems. There was another reason for living, which had to do with Gardner's sense of family and community responsibility: "Whenever I thought I was going to leave the house and kill myself," he has said in an interview, "there was always one thought in front of me: People who commit suicide pretty much doom their kids to commit suicide." (Singular, 1979:34)

According to Lifton *psychic numbing*, or diminished capacity to feel, serves a useful purpose for a survivor in the midst of and immediately after a death experience. It allows a survivor to continue functioning by disabling his or her ability to symbolize the incident, thereby numbing the psyche's conscious experience. (1987:240) By doing so, it avoids an overload of emotions and feelings which may incapacitate a survivor. The usefulness of this numbing is readily outlived, however, if allowed "to give rise to later patterns of withdrawal, apathy, depression, and despair." (239) The difficulty arises when the impairment of symbolization *never* allows the survivor to confront, symbolically in consciousness, all the images and issues related to the traumatic event. Those who have seen the film *Ordinary People* recognize this as exactly the psychological hurdle "Connie" had to overcome through therapy. One must eventually allow the incident to be a part of one's conscious experience in order to "cast out the demons" and have a chance to grow from the experience.

According to his mother, Gardner did talk about the death of Gilbert immediately after the accident, though even then he wouldn't talk about it very much. In later years he would never discuss the incident. His mother recalls that "for years he wouldn't let us mention Gilbert. I remember in Carbondale one time he said, I don't talk about him at all." (P. Gardner, 1984:233) Part of his inability to talk about the accident may have to do with gender expectations in his family. In the short story Jack Hawthorne's father and uncles are described as gentle, but not expressive men. Thus, it would be normal for Jack, working as he does with such people, to keep his feelings and emotions to himself after the accident. If this fictional account is an accurate portrayal of his own father and uncles—and Priscilla Gardner claims the story "is almost literally non-fiction" (235)—this lack of direct expression may have played a factor in Gardner's later inability to talk about the incident. Putting aside idle speculation, Gardner's inability to speak of Gilbert's death for many years, even with his own family, is a clear indication of an inability to symbolize the incident in such a way as to openly confront it. But Gardner was not without resources. In spite of the fact that he had played a part in the tragic death of his brother, and in spite of the fact that he felt personal responsibility and guilt for that death, and in spite of the additional fact that he felt unclean and unworthy of acceptance by his family and neighbors, he did have at least one resource by which to keep going, day by day.

In "Redemption," Jack Hawthorne avoids human contact and turns instead to his French horn to fill the emptiness of his life. By immersing himself in his music he not only avoids those human contacts which exacerbate his feelings of guilt and corruption, but is able to produce something in a mixed-up world of tragedy and pain that is beautiful and good, comforting and—seemingly—permanent. Music allows him, for a moment, to believe in the possible existence of a possible thing which neither judges nor condemns him, a time and place of transformation, approaching sacrality, in which he can feel cleansed and renewed. But only for a moment. Gardner, too, played the French horn as a child, and was quite good. In time he began to take lessons at a preparatory school affiliated with the Eastman School of Music in Rochester, NY. (Cowart, 1983:3) And, like Jack in "Redemption," Gardner also wrote stories and poems as a youngster. Indeed, he would in later years tell of how he entertained his family and the farm hands with his stories. If they were good enough the others would complete his chores while he busied himself creating another story to please his "audience."

The fact that Gardner was able to draw upon the arts as a resource is largely due to the fact that his parents actively nurtured an appreciation of music and literature. Gardner's mother was an English teacher while his father, in addition to being a full-time farmer, was a part-time preacher and sometime actor in the local community. His father loved to read the classics, Shakespeare and the Bible. In a home filled with books, Gardner was often put to bed with a recital of poetry from his father. One of Gardner's fondest memories was of his father and mother reciting together while doing farm chores. "While my father was milking the cows," he recalls in an interview, "my mother would come out and read something to him—*Lear*, say—leaving out the part of whomever my father felt like being that day, and he'd answer his lines from the cow." (Ferguson, 1979:56)

There is another factor that led to Gardner's appreciation and use of the arts: his Welsh background. Gardner was fond of telling people that he was Welsh on his mother's side, and he was clearly pleased to be part of a people with a long heritage of accomplishment and pride. Part of what it was to be Welsh in America was to participate in two annual festivals: one consisting of poetry and drama contests known as *Eisteddfods*, and a second known as a *Cymanfa Ganu*, which is a songfest in which those Welsh gathered would sing songs of the Old Country. In later years, responding to a question on why he maintained such an intense interest in music, Gardner acknowledged the importance of this Welsh influence:

> I'm half Welsh, that had a lot to do with it. I grew up in churches that sang and sang. . . . And they're storytellers and poets and have been for generations. Also I lived in Batavia, which is near Rochester, so very early I

got familiar with real music—we went to concerts and operas. I loved those operas there. My father used to let us off on Saturday afternoons to listen to Texaco opera. (Edwards, 1977:45)

Gardner even provides a description of a *Cymanfa Ganu* in one of his short stories, "Come On Back," which is also contained in the collection *The Art of Living and Other Stories*. This story revolves around a man's recollections as a young boy experiencing his first *Cymanfa Ganu*. The narrative is told from the first-person point of view and is clearly autobiographical in nature, as attested to both by its content as well as the fact that the person narrating the story is, as a youth, called "Buddy" by the others. Buddy, or Bud, of course, was Gardner's childhood name while growing up. Without going into too much of the story's details at this time, it describes a boy's learning of his Welsh heritage, and the importance placed on music by his Welsh relatives. The narrator recalls as a young boy being left behind while his parents were off to a songfest, of which there were many in the area. Acknowledging the predominant role singing has in the lives of the Welsh, the narrator concludes with the saying: whenever three Welsh meet together it is a choir. "Everywhere my parents drove," he added, "they sang, almost always in a minor key and always in harmony; and every time relatives got together they sang, in almost as many parts as there were people." (221) The story moves toward a climax when the narrator joins his parents and relatives in his first *Cymanfa Ganu*, and there experiences all of the tensions that had arisen within the family in the course of the story melt away in the unity of song. "It seemed our bones and blood that sang," the reader is told, "all heaven and earth singing harmony lines, and when the music broke off on the final chord, the echo that rang on the walls around us was like a roaring Amen." (236)

Gardner was once asked why he had such a "messianic complex" about art, in answer to which he explained in words we no doubt understand better than did his inquisitor at the time: "It's made my life, and it made my life when I was a kid, when I was incapable of finding any other sustenance, any other thing to lean on, any other comfort during times of great unhappiness." (Singular, 1979:39) What I am suggesting is that despite his inability to talk about the accident directly, Gardner's childhood immersion in literature and music, poetry and drama, gave him the resources by which to avoid the more debilitating effects of psychic numbing. His music and storytelling allowed him to confront some of the issues related to the death of his brother in the sublimated form of art. His music and stories allowed him, in other words, a mode of expression by which he was able indirectly to voice the fear, guilt, anger, and cries of supplication that he could not bring himself to do overtly and directly with his friends and family. It is instructive to note that one of Gardner's first reactions to the accident was to write a poem titled "My Brother":

> In two feet water my brother would wade
> He'd do it,
> All knew it.
>
> No wilder imp was ever made.
> 'Twas true!
> God knew!
>
> My little brother, sweet though wild
> Was better far than any child.
> With my small brother, Gilbert Day
> Oh yes he lived the mischief way.
>
> Every minute sweet and kind
> My brother,
> Ask mother.
>
> Blessed *was* the tie that bind
> One another
> With my brother.
>
> With a will he shot at work and play
> Laughing, singing, always gay.
> But once he laughed and played too far.
> His jolly songs no longer are.
>
> (MSS, 1984:232–33)

We read that Jack Hawthorne tells stories in "Redemption" to exorcise those demons that plague him. This notion of "bibliotherapy" is prominent in Gardner's work, both implicitly when he speaks of writing as "a way of thinking about things" (Harvey, 1978:79) and explicitly, as when he discusses the process of writing "Redemption." He says:

> You really do ground your nightmares, you *name* them. When you write a story, you have to play that image, no matter how painful, over and over until you've got all the sharp details so you know exactly how to put it down on paper. By the time you've run your mind through it a hundred times, relentlessly worked every tick of your terror, it's lost its power over you. . . . It's a wonderful thing. Which isn't to say that I think writing is done for the health of the writer, though it certainly does incidentally have that effect. (Ferguson, 1979:65)

A few weeks before his own death he spoke again about the writing of "Redemption" saying:

> I had had a lot of trouble with my head: things like, I'm driving down the road, and I see this guilt scene, this old traumatic experience so vividly that I can't see the road, as hard as I try to concentrate, I can't break out of this vision. That's very dangerous: I had to hit the brakes and pray. That would happen to me quite often. So this guy said, "Write the story"; and when he said it, I could have killed him. How *terrifying* it was; such an immensely painful experience. And when you write a story, you have to see it over and over in your mind: copy down details, take out the ones that aren't important, and you finally get it. And it really did work . . . it's amazing. You actually do see your way through it. You keep staring at it and staring at it, and copying down like a scientist. . . . And when you're all done, you're OK. (Stanton, 1983:21)

Another expression of this notion comes from a public debate held with William Gass, his friend and literary adversary. In an October, 1978 debate at the University of Cincinnati Gardner argues:

> You write a book to understand and get control of in yourself things that you haven't been able to control and understand in the world. When you have the kind of problem that will come to you in repeated dreams, you work it out on the page. Maybe it's an illusory understanding, but I think it helps you live. I think with each book you write you become a better person. (LeClair, 1983: 27)

The fifth of Lifton's characteristics of a survivor, the *need for a conceptual schema* by which to make sense of another's death, is exemplified in Gardner's strong advocacy for art which he describes as "moral." The whole issue of "moral art" as raised in Gardner's book *On Moral Fiction* is, without doubt, the most controversial aspect of his career as a writer. The book's publication resulted in a spirited—and at times vituperative—debate about the role of literature in human life and society. It is important we recognize that Gardner's position on "moral art" is tied up with his notion that true art is not simply a matter of parlor room debates reserved for those who proclaim themselves the literary elite. Rather, literature and the other arts are closely tied to the ethos of a culture, and as such have life-giving qualities that allow one to look into the abyss of human death and still celebrate a world in which heroic action and human dignity are possible. As one who has stared into the abyss, Gardner has no romantic illusions. He is fully aware of the entropic end toward which we inexorably move. As he writes:

> [G]ood artists are the people who are, in one way or another, creating, out of deep and honest concern, a vision of life-in-the-twentieth-century that is worth pursuing. And the bad artists, of whom there are many, are whining or moaning or staring, because it's fashionable, into the dark abyss. . . . It seems to me that the artist ought to hunt for positive ways of surviving, of living. You shouldn't lie. If there aren't any, so far as you can see, you should say so, like the *Merdistes*. But I don't think the *Merdistes* are right. . . . I think the world is not all merde. I think it's possible to make walls around at least some of the smoking holes.
> . . . [W]hat's moral in fiction is chiefly its way of looking. The premise of moral art is that life is better than death; art hunts for avenues to life. The book succeeds if we're powerfully persuaded that the focal characters, in their fight for life, have won honestly or, if they lose, are tragic in their loss, not just tiresome or pitiful. (Ferguson, 1979:46, 48)

He makes much the same point in *On Moral Fiction* when he argues art that is both moral and true:

> clarifies life, establishes models of human action, casts nets toward the future, carefully judges our right and wrong directions, celebrates and mourns. It does not rant. It does not sneer or giggle in the face of death, it invents prayers and weapons. It designs visions worth trying to make fact. . . .
> (The artist) lights up the darkness with a lightning flash, protects his friends the gods—that is, values—and all humanity without exception, and then moves on. (100–01)

Because he grew up in a home full of books with parents who valued literature, Gardner was sensitive to the literary trends of the 1950s and 1960s. Existentialist fiction, with its probing questions about human death and human value, particularly attracted him. He came thereby to know the writings of Jean-Paul Sartre, one of two intellectuals he has said "really thrilled me." (Harvey, 1978:75) The first college at which he attended was DePauw University in Greencastle, IN. There, still under the influence of a dynamic teacher from high school, he chose to study chemistry. (P. Gardner, 1984:236) That interest waned, however, and he began to take more interest in the Literature and Philosophy courses being offered. Though he had read Plato previously, he admits he never really understood Plato until he took a philosophy course in college. He studied other philosophers as well, including one who became a particularly important discovery in his life:

> And when I came to [Alfred North] Whitehead my head went off because—not so much that he's a great philosopher, although he is, but—I felt he said what I would say. That is to say his world-view, incredibly, was like the world-view I had developed . . . so that a lot of times when I'm working with a philosophical question or problem of some kind, I think, "What would Whitehead say?" and then I try that out, dramatizing it. (Harvey, 1978:74)

Thus, philosophy was leading Gardner to the writings of Whitehead while his interest in literature was exposing him to the existentialism of Sartre. In spite of the fact that he is a gifted writer, Sartre was a source of ambivalence for Gardner "because he's a horror intellectually, figuratively, and morally, but he's a wonderful writer and anything he says you believe, at least for the moment, because of the way he says it." (75) Passages from Sartre are contained in some of Gardner's short fiction, as well as in *The Wreckage of Agathon* and *Grendel*. In the latter he says he "got the idea of presenting the Beowulf monster as Jean-Paul Sartre, and everything that Grendel says Sartre in one mood or another has said, so that my love of Sartre kind of comes through as my love of the monster, though monsters are still monsters—I hope." (75) The upshot is that there were two thinkers who really excited the young John Gardner: Whitehead and Sartre. Critics in recent years have noted Gardner's reliance on Sartre, but no one yet has fully recognized the extent to which Whitehead also influences his thought. In asking the question of what Gardner was *against*, one has to speak of Sartre; when asking the question of what Gardner was *for*, one needs also to speak of Whitehead.

A philosophical question Gardner had to confront as a youth—and continue to confront throughout his life—was whether there is meaning and purpose to human existence. To answer such a question, or even phrase it for that matter, requires some sort of conceptual notion of the world, i.e. an ethos and a world-view. In short, a context has to be assumed and articulated for the question to be understood and answered. And to give a positive answer to the question of meaning is to imply that a person is able somehow to transcend his own physical finiteness. Lifton addresses this issue as well when he remarks on twentieth-century man's inability to symbolize human meaningfulness transcending death. In other words, moderns seem unable to conceptualize what he calls "symbolic immortality." (1987:13ff) He cites five "modes" of symbolic immortality, each of which may provide a person the means by which to confront and accept his or her physical death. These modes include: (1) the *biological mode*, or survival through children, grandchildren, etc.; (2) the *theological mode*, or belief in an afterlife in heaven, or life in God in some fashion; (3) *immortality through works*, the idea that one's accomplishments will survive; (4) *immortality through nature*, the notion that we are a part of nature and that nature is everlasting; and (5) the mode of *experiential transcendence*, an activity or act of an individual in life (e.g. meditation, the thrill of skydiving, the use of drugs, or the pursuit of aesthetic perfection) which allows one a feeling or intimation of transcending one's finiteness.

Returning to "Redemption" one last time, Jack's father, in the grips of his melancholy, suddenly and secretly leaves. The suffering family is abandoned for several weeks. No one knows where he is, and it becomes a further source of guilt for Jack. In time, however, the father returns. Jack witnesses a tearful reunion as he sees his father drop to his knees, his face buried in his mother's lap, asking forgiveness from his family. Jack then sees his family open up their arms and accept his father's return. It is too much for Jack. How is it, he might ask, that his father can abandon them and then be warmly received back into the family so readily and easily while he cannot? After being prodded, he joins in the hugging of his father, but in his frustration and rage the only articulate thought he can bring to the fore—though silently—is that he hates his father.

After his father's return the story then concentrates on Jack's wholesale embracing of music. A new character is introduced, a 70-year-old Russian French horn master named Arcady Yegudkin, from whom Jack begins to take lessons. Yegudkin is also a survivor. During the Russian

Revolution the Bolsheviks had loaded Yegudkin and hundreds of others on a train, then dumped them in the country and opened fire on them. All of the bodies were pushed into a ravine, but the soldiers were not particularly careful to make sure all were, in fact, dead. A badly-wounded Yegudkin survives the incident and, as we might expect, exemplifies those themes Lifton associates with being a survivor of an act of brutal and grotesque horror. He, too, like his young student, comes to live a life of isolation, caring only for his music. It is one model presented to Jack Hawthorne by which to attain "symbolic immortality."

One day, a fine French horn is delivered to Yegudkin's studio while Jack is there. After unpacking it, the old master fingers it a while, then begins to play. Gardner then describes a transcendent moment in which, inside Yegudkin's cork-lined studio, the Russian master elicits musical notes of a kind Jack had never heard before. First playing single notes, then chords of two notes and then three, Yegudkin begins playing runs. Like a bird trapped and looking for escape, the runs begin at the bottom of the register and then fly to the horn's top E. Then, manic, it drops a bit and runs again, this time bursting through the E and into the trumpet range. When he suddenly stops, "the room still rang, shimmered like a vision." (40) Entranced by his teacher's performance, Jack asks if he will ever be able to play like that. Yegudkin laughs out loud, making clear in his manner the brute impossibility that Jack would ever play as well. Knowing he meant no malice, and recognizing the blunt truth of the matter, Jack nonetheless is startled by the blow. There are tears in his eyes as he leaves his teacher that day. And the story ends with Jack heading for the bus, his French horn under one arm and his music under the other. "The crowd opened for him," we are told, and "he plunged in, starting home." (41)

We are given two strong images in this story of how one may come to terms with death and guilt. In the one, a master technician isolates himself from the tumble of human affairs and gives his life over to experiential transcendence through music. Another model, and one I believe Gardner more often highlights throughout his fiction, is the image of the father, repentant, on his knees in front of his family seeking to come home, and a family accepting him in an act of grace. Jack explores the possibilities of the former, but the story leaves him in the midst of a crowd, amid the tumble and confusion of humanity. And we are told he plunges in. That plunge, indeed, is the first step to his starting home, the first step to an acceptance of that grace his family has offered all along but which he, because of the psychological dynamics involved with being a survivor, has been unable to accept. It would seem not too strong a statement to say that Gardner spent his entire adult life and professional career trying to work his way back home to a community where he would be loved and accepted.

It is this notion of community which is a constant touchstone of value in Gardner's work—a community of fallible, finite, sometimes fearful and sometimes courageous men and women, confronting the mysteries of life in all its joys and brutalities, who share their dreams and tell their stories and keep each other warm around the hearth at night, reaffirming in each other that the life they share in community is their taste of immortality. This is not to suggest that Gardner accepts only one mode of symbolic immortality as efficacious, only that he emphasizes those modes which accentuate the natural and social integration of men and women together in community rather than purely personal expressions of symbolic immortality.

As the reader no doubt has noticed, with words like "immortality," "guilt," "redemption," and "grace" being bandied about, one must address certain religious themes as they are used by Gardner. In his writing, the term "religion" is not used often by Gardner, and when it is mentioned it is usually in negative terms. As often as not, the term "religion" is used by Gardner to stand for an entrenched set of doctrines which exert a controlling influence, usually manipulative, over the lives of people. In *The Art of Fiction* Gardner argues that when a writer advocates truths in his fiction that have already been established within a society as doctrine, but without having tested the contemporary worth of those doctrinal truths, "the effect of his work, admirable or otherwise, is not the effect of true art but of something else: pedagogy, propaganda, or religion." (130) By contrast, Gardner also speaks of the rhetoric of great drama which "can raise our joy or grief to a keen intensity that transcends the mundane and takes on the richness and universality of ritual. What begins in the real, in other words, can be uplifted by style to something we recognize, even as we read, as at once the real and the real transmuted." (116–17) For Gardner, when religion is in league with story-telling seeking to understand the sort of world in which we *do* live and the values by which we *should* live, it is an important—indeed necessary—human activity. When, however, religion becomes weighted with the detritus of hide-bound tradition and unyielding doctrine it becomes static, and thereby removed from life.

A definition of religion which comes close to Gardner's own understanding is that of the cultural anthropologist Clifford Geertz. In his often anthologized essay, "Religion as a Cultural System," Geertz attempts to get away from purely doctrinal and/or essentialist definitions by describing religion as:

> a system of symbols which act to establish powerful, pervasive, and long-lasting moods and motivations in men by formulating conceptions of a general order of existence and clothing these conceptions with such an aura of factuality that the moods and motivations seem uniquely realistic. (1973:90)

If one compares this definition with Gardner's earlier statement about the nature and function of art that is both moral and true (p. 21) the similarities appear obvious. While Gardner speaks of art and Geertz of religion, the two see religion/art as a means of providing both a "model of" as well as a "model for" reality and human action. Geertz argues that religion synthesizes a people's ethos as well as a people's world view, and that it does so by means of sacred symbols. By ethos, he speaks of "the moral (and aesthetic) aspects of a given culture, the evaluative elements. . . . the tone, character, and quality of [a people's] life." (126–27) By world view he means "the cognitive, existential aspects. . . . [a people's] picture of the way things in sheer actuality are, their concept of nature, of self, of society. It contains their most comprehensive ideas of order." (126–27) Expressed symbolically, the meanings of religion sum up "what is known about the way the world is, the quality of emotional life it supports, and the way one ought to behave while in it. Sacred symbols thus relate an ontology and a cosmology to an aesthetics and a morality." (127)

Gardner's fiction, it is clear, deals at length with issues of ethos and world view. Often labeled a "philosophical writer," his emphasis on the need for "moral" fiction accentuates the evaluative role art plays in articulating a people's quality of life. There is an aspect of what Gardner does, however, that goes beyond what Geertz does as a social scientist. In his definition, Geertz states an ethos and world view are "clothed" in such a way as to make the moods and motivations of a people *seem* uniquely realistic. Such a definition begs the question: Well, are these moods and motivations true? Is the ethos represented true? The world view? "Such questions cannot even be asked," Geertz concludes, "much less answered, within the self-imposed limitations of the scientific perspective." (123) As given, Geertz's definition makes no qualitative distinction between religions. As a social scientist, he provides no criterion by which to judge one religion as being more or less true than another. He simply says a religion is a cultural system and as such is either efficacious as an expression of ethos and world view, or it is not. This is a troubling notion for many to accept, because its logical correlate is that Nazism, as a cultural system in the Germany of 1933-45, is as deserving of its status as a religion as is Christianity, Judaism, or any other faith which informs a people's ethos and world view.

Being a literary artist, Gardner is not restrained in quite the same way as he would were he a social scientist. Scientists attempt to remain disengaged from the phenomena they study while the artist is required to be engaged at a very personal level with his medium and that which his medium expresses. For Gardner, art—particularly literary art—not only plays a role in forming a people's ethos and world view, but is also a tool by which *the truth* of a people's ethos and world view are constantly tested and validated, or invalidated as the case may be. As he explains it in *The Art of Fiction*:

> The fact remains that art produces the most important progress civilization knows. Restating old truths and adapting them to the age, applying them in ways they were never before applied, stirring up emotion by the inherent power of narrative, visual image, or music, artists crack the door to the morally necessary future. . . . The true writer's joy in the fictional process is his pleasure in discovering, by means he can trust, what he believes and can affirm for all time. (80-81)

Gardner, it should be noted, is the first to admit he has begun a story thinking one way about the truth of an issue or a value, and in the process of writing, testing and stretching that issue or value, come to change his view. That is what true art does in Gardner's scheme of things. Gardner takes note of three possible approaches to telling the truth in fiction, namely (1) stating that which is a matter of fact, (2) allowing tone and coherence to convey that which is not a lie, and (3) "discovering and affirming moral truth about human existence." (129) Gardner advocates the latter as the highest level of fictional truth to be attained. But this kind of truth, he quickly adds, is not a starting point for the literary artist but his goal. Whatever beliefs and values he may hold to as he begins a story, the artist must test them by means of the process of writing fiction to see if they will stand. Thus, the true artist will leave herself radically open to change. For Gardner, asking the question "Is it true?" is a necessary part of what it is to be an artist.

Geertz has his reasons for declining to make normative judgments about any particular religion. He wants to put aside "the tone of the village atheist and that of the village preacher" in order that "the social and psychological implications of particular religious beliefs can emerge in a clear and neutral light." (1973:123) Such scientific objectivity is canonically held as a positive good within the academy and is, indeed, an important value when seeking to understand another's ethos and world view. Nonetheless, a continual stance of scientific objectivity is clearly unworkable; at least we would consider the behavior of a person adopting such a stance as somewhat bizarre. Such an individual would appear cold, uncommitted, and incapable of making decisions at those times when social life demands that decisions be made. Such a stance, for good or ill, is quite remote from the give and take of daily decision-making required of men and women. Geertz recognizes this and notes the need for some "authority" to be established in a cultural system in order that the ethos and world view expressed in that cultural system have "an aura of factuality." This authority, this conceptual "archimedean point," becomes the guarantor of a people's "knowledge" of the world, and of the emotions and values appropriate in such a world. Geertz cites the axiom: "He who would know must first believe." (110)

The ontological status of such authority and knowledge is a problem Geertz never fully resolves. Rather, Geertz merely suggests that the question of authority and knowledge is tied in with the practice of ritual, for it is in ritual, he argues,

> that this conviction that religious conceptions are veridical and that religious directives are sound is somehow generated. It is in some sort of ceremonial form . . . that the moods and motivations which sacred symbols induce in men and the general conceptions of the order of existence which they formulate for men meet and reinforce one another. In a ritual, the world as lived and the

world as imagined, fused under the agency of a single set of symbolic forms, turn out to be the same world. (112)

Regardless of what definition of ritual one may adopt, there are two dynamic principles at work: (1) rituals are a way of affirming one's identity, both as a distinct individual and as a member of a group with social obligations, and (2) rituals are a way of personal and social transformation; indeed, rituals can provide a meaningful time and space allowing an individual to be made over into a new being. This new being may come to experience the world in a new way and may also come to play a new role within his or her own society. Identity and transformation are the twin faces of effective ritual.

Formal rituals, usually identified with liturgical rites, is an engagement of the senses, as Frederick Clothey has noted. In order to understand formal ritual one must attend to that which is *done*, that which is *said*, and that which is *seen*. (1983:7-12) Ritual symbols convey meaning through the senses of hearing, smell, taste, touch, and sight. As symbols they are condensations of meaning which, taken together, act as overdeterminations of conceptual feelings and thoughts. However, we restrict the field of ritual too much if we attend only to the ritual aspects of formal liturgical rites. Ronald Grimes makes an important contribution to the study of ritual when he emphasizes that ritual has to do not just with religion. Rather, it "suffuses our biogenetic, psychosocial, political, economic, and artistic lives as well." (1982:35) Ritual is very much a part of our lives, helping to give us a sense of ourselves and of our place in the overall scheme of things, as well as providing the occasional—at times planned and at other times unplanned—experience of transformation.

A fuller discussion of ritual will have to wait until a later chapter, but it is important to note here that Gardner's fiction is full of ritual activity. Indeed, much of the power of Gardner's vision—the power of his "dream," to use his own word—is his fictional use of community rituals of eating, celebration, reconciliation, birth, death, and marriage in testing human values and conceptions of existence. It should be observed, however, that Geertz tends to emphasize only the ceremonial aspects of ritual. While the ceremonial is certainly an important aspect of ritual, Geertz's limiting of ritual to the ceremonial tends to emphasize only that aspect of ritual which validates and reinforces the status quo.

Another anthropologist, Victor Turner, places more emphasis in his work on the transformative aspects of ritual. This emphasis on the more dynamic process of transformation leads Turner and his followers to think of ritual as a kind of social performance. Drama becomes a primary metaphor for the sorts of ritual performances Turner describes. This is a particularly apt metaphor when looking at Gardner's fiction. Motifs of transformation have long been a common theme in literature, and it is this power of transformation, achieved in part through communal ritual activity, that comes through Gardner's fiction most clearly.

Being a survivor, Gardner is forced to deal with death and guilt at a very personal level. In order to come to terms with the accidental death of his brother he had to articulate an ethos and world view in which death and guilt play a natural, indeed necessary, role. Resources he comes to rely upon, as we shall see, are the philosophical notions generally associated with Whitehead's "philosophy of organism" and a profound understanding of the role "community" plays in the life of an individual. The medium by which Gardner would think through these issues and arrive at conclusions—the medium, in other words, by which he would attempt to *see* the world rightly—is that of literature and the writing of fiction. "For me," Gardner has said, "literature, writing, is a way of thinking about things." (Harvey, 1978:79) It is the writing of fiction that helps him to formulate a fictive world which is able to hold at bay those Grendel-like monsters ready to mock human strivings for meaning and significance. By his use of fiction Gardner attempts to create a vivid and continuous dream in the mind of the reader. The obvious question is: a vivid and continuous dream of what? It will become clear that Gardner intends his fiction to be an occasion of his own personal growth, as well as an occasion of growth on the part of the reader. It is his hope that his art, the narrative stories he has to tell, will be an occasion for the development of a perspective on life that Whitehead, in his *Adventures of Ideas*, has referred to as "peace," a notion with strong affinity to the concept of "wisdom" in Hebrew scripture. Peace, as described by Whitehead and fictionally presented by Gardner, does not exist isolated from the ebb and flow of life. Rather, it is experienced and understood in the context of a community's ethos and world view, a community's religion, tested and re-tested over time.

CHAPTER II:
Some Intellectual Antecedents

At the time of his death John Gardner was a member of the creative writing faculty at the State University of New York at Binghamton. In the Fall, 1984 memorial edition of *MSS*, a journal originally begun and edited by him, several of his students share personal recollections of Gardner as a teacher, a writer, and a friend. The image that comes through is of one who is extremely giving of his time and energy when working with inexperienced writers, constantly giving encouragement while at the same time working to help them see where their fictions need rethinking and rewriting.

Mel Konner, an author of several books, including two novels and a book of stories, was unknown and unpublished when he wrote Gardner in 1979 asking for advice—and help—in finding a publisher for his work. It wasn't the first time Konner had written such a letter to a successful author, all futile attempts to make contacts with a mentor. Despite his having sworn off such letters, he decided to try once more. As he explains it, he decided to write the letter because of an interview he had read in which Gardner "declared that, although it took him away from his own writing, he absolutely had to help younger writers, or else 'burn in hell for a thousand years.' " (177) Several months passed, and Konner began to believe that his effort was wasted. Then came a response. In five closely-typed pages Gardner both celebrated his excitement with the story Konner had sent and cited several sections of the story to be reworked. Konner was ecstatic that a writer of Gardner's stature would take the time to respond as he had. What followed was an ongoing correspondence between the two as Gardner worked at helping Konner make his fiction as strong as possible. The story, "Winter in Bolton," was finally published in the Fall/Winter 1981 edition of *MSS*, and a new writer was introduced to a reading public.

We will probably never know for sure exactly why Gardner spent so much time and energy helping young writers. His mother recalls his being asked that question in an interview, with his answer being: "Well, we have a word for that in the Presbytarian (sic) Church. We call it stewardship, and that's something I can share." (P. Gardner, 1984:240) It could well have to do with his own difficulty in getting published.[1]

During those years, perhaps as a form of therapy, Gardner began a journal in which he would write down his own thoughts on contemporary fiction's strengths and, more importantly, its weaknesses. Tempered by an anger that saw certain writers being valorized in literary circles while he was being ignored, he used the journal to vent his frustration. When he did become a popular writer and was being asked by editors if there were other manuscripts they could see, Gardner made available to a publisher this record of his own sometimes bitter feelings toward the literary establishment. Though the manuscript went through an editorial process the angry tone was to remain, and in 1978 *On Moral Fiction* was published.

Though several essays from the book have been excerpted for literary journals, with the title essay winning the prestigious Pushcart Prize, the book made more enemies than converts. Whatever literary/philosophical argument was being presented advocating what he termed "moral fiction" was ignored as critics and authors took note of Gardner's seeming petulance in criticizing contemporary writers of fiction. David Cowart argues that it was not his criticism of minor writers like Vonnegut, Brautigan and Barthelme that drew people's ire, but his brutal handling of literary heavyweights like Bellow, Barth, Updike and Pynchon.[2] (1983:15) In time, Gardner came to regret the tone of the book. However, committed as he was to his own view of what fictional art ought to be, he never backed down from the general thesis presented in *On Moral Fiction*. If one accepts the argument that his career as a writer was forever damaged as a result of the publication of *On Moral Fiction*, and it seems clear he did suffer professionally as a result, then one is left to wonder if it would have been different had Gardner found a literary mentor early in his career, thus avoiding the ill-tempered attacks on his peers contained in the book. In any case, Gardner clearly felt some sort of obligation to help young, unpublished writers get their start in the business. One way he sought to help them was through teaching.

Sheila Schwartz and Joanna Higgins were two of his writing students who are among those sharing memories of Gardner in the memorial issue of *MSS*, and both mention a "black book" kept on reserve in the library to which his students could refer. This book was a collection of notes Gardner had written through the years on the process of writing fiction. In these pages he could be insistent on the most picayune points of technical skill, yet he could also write inspiring, often poetic, sections describing the professional, social and moral obligations of an artist to his audience. These notes—the equivalent of scripture to many of his students—were published posthumously in 1983 as *The Art of Fiction*. If one really wishes to understand what Gardner means by "moral fiction," it is this volume rather than the earlier *On Moral Fiction* that should be studied.

Gardner wants his students to understand the technical aspects of writing fiction. He has little sympathy for the sloppily romantic pose that it is pure inspiration which produces great art, and even less for the Formalist position caricatured in the *Punch* cartoon which has a pretentious young woman telling her aunt, "One doesn't write *about* anything, one simply writes." Writing is a craft, Gardner argues, and he displays a clear understanding of his craft in *The Art of Fiction* as he identifies several forms of clumsiness to which a writer may fall victim. Among other mistakes, he cites the use of the passive voice in excessive and/or inappropriate ways, improper introductory phrases using infinite verbs, confusing and distracting shifts in diction, sentences lacking variety in their construction, sentences that lack focus, sentences containing faulty rhythm and unexpected rhyme, passages that are weighed down with unnecessary explanation, and more. (99) In his cataloguing of mistakes he gives whole sections over to techniques in helping a writer improve skills of handling imitation, vocabulary, point of view, timing, and the use of suspense, style, etc. In one section given over to the sentence, Gardner explains on page after page the variety of rhythms a writer can use in a sentence, and how certain rhythms, if properly used by an artist, can set an emotional tone to help move a story along. All of these techniques of the craft are to help bring about one end which, according to Gardner, is the end of all good fiction: a vivid and continuous dream. "Whatever the genre may be," Gardner writes:

> fiction does its work by creating a dream in the reader's mind. . . . [I]f the effect of the dream is to be powerful, the dream must probably be vivid and continuous—*vivid* because if we are not quite clear about what it is that we're dreaming, who and where the characters are, what it is that they're doing or trying to do and why, our emotions and judgments must be confused, dissipated, or blocked; and *continuous* because a repeatedly interrupted flow of action must necessarily have less force than an action directly carried through from its beginning to its conclusion. (31)

Gardner emphasizes the techniques of writing with his students in order that they eliminate those clumsy errors that interrupt the flow of action he insists must be continuous. The vividness of the dream is dependent on a writer's use of details in a story. Whether it be the verisimilitude of Realist fiction, the narrative voice allowing a Coleridgean "willing suspension of disbelief" in the other-worldly tales of science fiction writers, or the authorial "wink" calling attention to the lies of a teller of yarns, the reader must regularly be presented with closely observed details that uphold that fictive vision, that what is said to be happening in the fictional text is really happening. (26)

Gardner discusses at length in *The Art of Fiction* the importance of getting the physical details of a story just right. If one carefully inspects her experience when she reads, he suggests, the reader will realize that it is the physical details that usher one into "a kind of dream, a rich and vivid play in the mind." (30) It is because of the efficacy of getting the details just right, he argues, that a reader finds himself not just reading words on a page, but on shore preparing to board a whaling ship, or in an English graveyard with an escaped prisoner, or amongst a throng of bearded Puritan men standing before a prison door. If the story be both vivid and continuous the reader is engaged not passively but actively, concerned about the choices a character might make, listening in suspense for whatever danger may be behind this door, that curtain, enlivened by a character's successes, saddened by a character's failures. Great fiction grabs the reader, Gardner says, engaging a reader's mind and emotions in such a way that the problems and experiences of the characters are felt as *real*. Vicariously, the reader immersed in fiction that is both vivid and continuous actively engages both in the lives of fictional characters and the situations which are fictionally presented, and as a result the reader learns about the ways of the world in much the same way as one learns in real life. Gardner would no doubt be in agreement with the philosopher Paul Holmer, who writes:

> An unsuspected consequence of the reading of literature is that it enlarges that everyday capacity for explanation that we already command. By thinking and feeling with persons in literary contexts, not so much the authors themselves, but with the fictional characters and by the help of the individual poetical lines, we extend pathos, passion, desire, wishes, and we become, ideally, more competent ourselves. Literature adds to reality, it does not simply describe it. It enriches the necessary competencies that daily life

requires and provides; and in this respect, it irrigates the deserts that our lives have already become. (28)

Literature that is technically well done, that maintains a vivid and continuous dream in the mind of a reader, is for Gardner a means of serious questioning about one's self and one's place in the world. Such literature has also been seen through the centuries as a vitally important source of human wisdom. As Gardner concludes:

> Thus the value of great fiction, we begin to suspect, is not just that it entertains us or distracts us from our troubles, not just that it broadens our knowledge of people and places, but also that it helps us to know what we believe, reinforces those qualities that are noblest in us, leads us to feel uneasy about our faults and limitations. (31)

Gardner has claimed he borrows the notion of "dream" from Robert Louis Stevenson. (Ferguson, 1979:50–51) It is during a debate with William Gass, however, that he gives important clues as to just what he means by "dream." Gardner tells a University of Cincinnati audience that "when I create a character, I want to make a life-like human being, a virtual human being." A few moments later, explaining his theory of art, he argues that a writer tries to create a vivid experience for the reader. If successful, the reader emerges from it realizing he "has been in a vivid and continuous dream, living a virtual life, making moral decisions in a virtual state." (LeClair, 1983:22, 24) Gardner's notion of the reader's dream being "vivid and continuous" has its most obvious source in the philosophical work of Susanne Langer. The term "virtual" is the tip-off. Langer's theory of art is expressed in her volume, *Feeling and Form*, where she seeks to articulate the "virtual space" symbolically expressed in several of the arts. Painting she refers to as "virtual scene," architecture as "virtual place," music as "virtual time," and dance as "virtual power."

In order to understand what she means by "virtual" we must first take a brief look at how she believes symbols come to express meaning. At various times she has defined a symbol as "any device whereby we are enabled to make an abstraction," (1953:xi) or as "an instrument of conception." (1972:289) In *Philosophy in a New Key*, however, she makes an important distinction between those symbols she calls *discursive* and those which are *presentational*. Discursive symbols are largely made up of words we use in our ordinary conversations in order to communicate the variety of abstract conceptions with which we work daily. One characteristic of the words we use in language is that they "have a linear, discrete, successive order; they are strung one after another like beads on a rosary; . . . we cannot talk in simultaneous bunches of names." (80) In order to express an idea in language, in other words, one must use one word after another in a well recognized and accepted syntactic pattern. Over time, language (including abstract math and logical rules of inference, as well as ordinary discourse) has come to be recognized as the prime means by which we seek, conceptually, to understand the physical world. Under the influence of thinkers associated with the Vienna Circle and the Cambridge School an extreme philosophical formulation of this notion developed: the positivistic notion that the *only* meaningful thought is language that can be verified either analytically or empirically. Its corollary was that that which was not meaningful thought (i.e. whatever cannot be verified) was merely feeling, an expression of one's psychological state rather than a verifiable statement about the world. (87) This extreme position is pretty much discarded today. But, as Langer notes, it has taken the work of philosophers like Cassirer, Dewey, and Whitehead to help establish the notion that "the field of semantics is wider than that of language." (87)

She drives home the point by arguing there exists another form of symbolism which cannot be directly transposed into the discourse of language: presentational symbolism. It is clearly recognized that a person may view a painting and undergo some sort of meaningful experience. Later, that person may even be able to describe the experience. Langer suggests, however, that the original experiencing of that work of art is an experiencing of the presentational symbolism of the painting, and as such it is closer to what we might call an intuitive understanding of the painting. To then talk about that experience, thus transposing the experience into discursive symbolism, is in some measure to distort the original experience. Perhaps the major difference to be noted between discursive and presentational symbolism is that the former, in order to be meaningful, must follow accepted laws of syntax, thus giving it its linear quality, whereas the latter may be presented all-at-once. In other words, discursive symbolism, necessarily, is a successive articulation of symbols, while presentational symbolism is a simultaneous exhibiting of symbols. As such, discursive symbolism is a rational process tied closely to the modes of logical reasoning, while presentational symbolism is a rational process able to evoke and prehend meaningfulness from the integration of mind and the physical senses of vision, touch, taste, smell, and hearing.

Langer argues for a physiological foundation for the development of presentational symbolism. If our physical senses were completely undisciplined and unrestricted they would convey to us a chaos of pure sensation. She borrows from William James to say that the world conveyed to us by "that sheer sensitivity to stimuli" would be "a blooming, buzzing confusion."[3] (89) In order to function successfully, a sentient creature must be selective in that which it experiences. "Out of this bedlam our sense organs must select certain predominant forms." (89) This selection is popularly viewed as a conscious process of mind, but Langer suggests this initial process of selection at the sensory level, though a process of mind as she comes to define it, is pre-conscious. As she argues:

> [T]his unconscious appreciation of forms is the primitive root of all abstraction, which in turn is the keynote of rationality; so it appears that the conditions for rationality lie deep in our pure animal experience—in our power of perceiving, in the elementary functions of our eyes and ears and fingers. Mental life begins with our mere physiological constitution. (89)

In explaining why she extends mentality to pre-conscious sensory experience she makes the point that a mind working "primarily with meanings must have organs that supply it primarily with forms," and then goes on to explain:

> The nervous system is the organ of the mind; its center is the brain, its extremities the sense organs; and any characteristic function it may possess must govern the work of all its parts. In other words, the activity of our senses is "mental" not only when it reaches the brain, but in its very inception, whenever the alien world outside impinges on the furthest and smallest receptor. (90)

To speak of presentational symbolism as a rational process able to evoke and prehend meaningfulness from the integration of mind and the physical senses of vision, touch, taste, smell, and hearing is to suggest that the arts—both fine and practical—are an appropriate mode of symbolic expression. Whether it be the fine art of an opera engaging the senses of hearing and sight, or a holiday meal appealing to the senses of smell and taste, either can be a mode of somatic experience by which concepts may be conveyed through presentational symbolism. The same may be said of other areas of human endeavor, including the ways in which men and women engage in ritual activity. To accept the notion that presentational symbolism can be "meaningful" expression is to imply the intellectual use of presentational symbolism to convey knowledge. The intellectual use toward which presentational symbols may convey knowledge, in turn, throws us into "the field of 'intuition,' 'deeper meaning,' 'artistic truth,' 'insight,' and so forth." (92) Unfortunately, those scholars who have ventured into this field often find they are having to defend themselves against accusations of mysticism and irrationalism. Langer has, however, an ally in one of her former professors, Alfred North Whitehead. It is Whitehead who once characterized the aims of philosophy as "mystical. For mysticism is direct insight into depths as yet unspoken. But the purpose of philosophy is to rationalize mysticism." (1968:174) Julius Seelye Bixler, discussing Whitehead's rejection of overly scientific approaches to truth, writes:

> The senses simplify, and it is well for us to seek simplicity; but we should distrust it when it is found. Reflective thought, which puts experiences into words, has also its danger of over-simplification. Language is a tricky instrument which does only partial justice to our deepest intuitions. The prominent facts of consciousness are the superficial facts; those that are important are on the fringe. Therefore we mistakenly criticize the mystic when he attaches importance to experiences he cannot explain. Some experiences are significant in the highest degree, even though it takes us a long time to tell what they are significant of. The present enthusiasm for the scientific method . . . is thus based on a misconception. Art and poetry . . . direct us to the inarticulate and incommunicable quality of the vivid flash of insight. (1951: 506–07)

Indeed, Langer believes she is able to rationalize her mysticism, if that be what it is, but a fuller discussion of how she does so will have to wait until we can explore Whitehead's concept of "experience." What this present discussion does help us to understand is that when Langer uses the term "virtual" she means by that the discursive and, more importantly, the presentational symbolic forms used by the various arts as modes by which aesthetic feeling and conceptual thoughts are meaningfully expressed.

When, in *Feeling and Form*, Langer comes to a discussion of poesis she argues that "the poet uses discourse to create an illusion, a pure appearance, which is a non-discursive symbolic form." (211) She goes on, in words close to Gardner's own to that University of Cincinnati audience, to state that "the poet's business is to create the appearance of 'experiences,' the semblance of events lived and felt, and to organize them so they constitute a purely and completely experienced reality, a piece of *virtual life*." (212) One might ask how poesis, using the discursive symbolism of language, can be described by Langer as "a non-discursive symbolic form." Her answer directs attention to the role of metaphor in language. It is by means of metaphor that non-literal abstractions can be made. If metaphor is, indeed, a bridge, then that bridge is the abstract form connecting the literal context for the metaphor to that to which the metaphor alludes. Further, it is by means of the metaphorical process that a symbol can take into itself many meanings, hence the polysemic character of a symbol, which is sometimes referred to as condensation. Victor Turner notes this aspect of symbols in ritual contexts when he writes:

> A single dominant symbol may stand for many things, and allows for the economic representation of key aspects of a whole system of culture and belief. Each dominant symbol has a fan, or spectrum, of referents, which are interlinked by a simple mode of association; the very simplicity of the outward form of a dominant symbol enables it to interconnect a wide variety of signata. (1978:246)

As an example, the words "bitter herbs" can, and usually do, act as a discursive symbol denoting certain forms of vegetation which have a particularly disagreeable taste. When a narrative describes the eating of bitter herbs during a Passover Seder meal, however, the words also have presentational symbolic value as a metaphor of the physical and spiritual pain the celebrant has experienced not only in his own life, but in that of his immediate family, in that of an earlier generation in the Nazi Holocaust, in that of much earlier generations seeking to maintain their faith in the face of threatened extermination, and even in that of those first Hebrews escaping the bondage of Egypt and the suffering they endured through 40 years of wandering in the wilderness. The effect of that ritual act can be deep emotional feelings on the part of the celebrant, and a narrative that is a "vivid and continuous" description of a Seder meal, in which the reader can participate in the "virtual life" of that narrative "dream," can also lead to deep emotional feelings on the part of a reader.

If the narrative is technically well written a reader can "lose himself" in the story, engaged in such a way that the presentational symbolism of the story can powerfully affect the emotions and feelings of the reader in ineffable yet potently meaningful ways. Gardner has even written a short story in which he describes a character who "loses himself" in the virtual life of fiction. Titled "The Library Horror," the story overtly takes note of the philosophical work of Langer as the protagonist, named Winfred, is described as having recently read a book on aesthetics. Though not able to remember the book's argument in detail, he does remember certain phrases from it, including "virtual time and space" and "organic forms." The book's title in the short story is *The Problems of Art*. Though there is no "The" in the actual title, Langer did publish a book on aesthetics under that same title in 1957. Winfred, while sitting in his library, restates the argument as best he can, recalling that the philosopher wrote about how one sees in paintings "virtual space," much as one does in a mirror. The philosopher meant by that a space that seems as real as any other physical space right up to the moment one tries to enter it. Similarly, Winfred recalls, the philosopher spoke of novels involving "virtual landscapes" and "virtual human beings" who come alive in the imagination of a reader, to speak and behave as do real men and women right up until that moment when they suddenly vanish back into the words on the page. The implications, Winston realizes, are staggering:

> These "apparitions" that come to us in music or, say, fiction are not all mere imitations, like the figures in a mirror. On the contrary, they are created expressions of life itself. They function in the same ways as do other living things; . . . I speak only, of course, of such works as we call successful, works that have "vitality" or "autonomous life." It was of course this idea—this *fact*, I should have said, for so it seems to me—that made my knees tremble. (1983:78)

The rest of the story involves Winfred reading in his library, and suddenly being accosted by the likes of Dostoevski's Raskolnikov,

Captain Ahab, Boswell's Dr. Johnson, Ebenezer Scrooge, Bunyan's Pilgrim, and Austin's Emma. Finally he is attacked by his boyhood hero, Achilles, who deals Winfred a cutting blow, leaving him bleeding from his chest. Immediately after the blow is struck his wife is calling down the stairs to the library asking what is wrong, and why he is screaming. The reason he had screamed, it is clear, is that he had become fully engaged in that vivid and continuous dream that is, when technically well done, narrative fiction.

In a debate with William Gass, perhaps with "The Library Horror" in mind, Gardner responds to Gass's position that one ought not "to be frightened by a character in a book or to cry at the death of a character" by arguing:

> I say it's not [wrong]. I say a book is nothing but a written symbol of a dream. If someone jumps at me with an ax in a nightmare, I scream, and I have every right to scream because I believe that person is real. In the same way, when the dream is transported to me by words and I see the character leap out at me with an ax, I have every right to believe that my head is going to be knocked in. I think it's very useful to talk about character in the traditional ways. Contemporary philosophy has reconstructed the world into its own words while distrusting the words that we've used over and over and over. Meaning exists in literature because of the way thousands of generations of people have used words. With just the slightest tap, you ring the whole gong of meaning. I'm more interested in the gong than the tap. I think Bill concentrates on the technique of the tap. (LeClair, 1983:29)

Perhaps another way of expressing the difference between their two views is to say Gass is more interested in a reader's aesthetic judgment to be made *after* undergoing an aesthetic experience, while Gardner has more of an interest in the dynamics of the reader *while in the midst* of an aesthetic experience. That may be unfair to Gass, but clearly Gardner's intent is to use narrative detail in such a way as to create a vivid and continuous dream so that the reader actually is experiencing a "virtual life" which will, in turn, have a powerful, pervasive, and long-lasting effect.

The allusion to Clifford Geertz's definition of religion,[4] in which he says religion is "a system of symbols which acts to establish powerful, pervasive, and long-lasting moods and motivations," is intended. Gardner's view of the role of literature in the lives of men and women appears to be quite similar to the way Geertz construes religion. It should also be noted that just as Geertz's definition of religion allows for no moral distinction between one religion and another, so, too, does Gardner's advocacy for literature to be a vivid and continuous dream make no distinction—at least not yet—between the moral worth of one narrative text over another.

Gardner admits that many writers with whom he disagrees morally are technically very skilled craftsmen. Sartre is a prime example of one Gardner feels "writes like an angel. . . . a wonderful writer," but one who is "a horror intellectually, figuratively, and morally." (Harvey, 1978:75) It is because he is such a technically gifted writer, and because he is able to engender in a reader a vivid and continuous dream, that Sartre is able to provide readers with powerful, pervasive, and long-lasting moods and motivations. Gardner simply believes the moods and motivations encouraged by Sartre's work are all wrong. Thus Gardner feels called upon to provide literary alternatives which bring to the foreground a view of life which, while acknowledging in an honest way the tragic in human life, presents what is, to his mind, a more comprehensive and adequate view of the world than that offered by Sartre and his heirs. It is, in part, in addressing the issue of the moral stature of the artist that Gardner speaks of three errors that may affect the quality of the vivid and continuous fictional dream toward which the writer should strive: sentimentality, frigidity, and mannered writing. Unlike the largely technical errors described earlier which could disrupt the vivid and continuous dream, Gardner argues in *The Art of Fiction* that these three mistakes are "faults of soul," flaws in the character of the writer. (115)

Sentimentality, in Gardner's view, is an attempt on the part of a writer to gain some effect without providing due cause. It is not the same as sentiment. Surely, a writer seeks to have a powerful effect on the sentiment of a reader. Sentimentality, however, is the mark of a writer seeking to elicit emotion on the part of a reader by means of cheap appeals to custom and prejudice. True art, Gardner insists, is when the writer realistically shows through characterization and plot what the fictional situation is and how the characters are being affected. True sentiment is generated as part of a vivid and continuous dream when several characters are placed in a situation which calls for each of them to make difficult choices, and it is because we have come to care for these characters that we can share the emotional import of the choices that are made. Sentimentality is when characters and situations are fictionalized in such a way as to generate little more than stock emotional responses. The typical television soap opera—or today, the television "trash talk" shows which set up audiences to boo and hiss "guests" before they appear—are cases in point.

A far more complex example of sentimentality, and the sort of example that tends to get Gardner into trouble with his peers, is Steinbeck's *Grapes of Wrath*, which Gardner views as a novel incapable of looking at a serious and complex issue in a manner fair to all points of view. Steinbeck's work should have been one of the great American novels, Gardner claims. However, the novel fails in Gardner's view because the moral vision of the novel is too one-sided. Steinbeck had a clear understanding of the sorrows endured by those "Okies" driven by circumstance from the midwest to California looking for jobs, Gardner argues, but he had no knowledge of those California ranchers who took advantage of the situation, leading to abusive employment practices and a series of injustices. "He had no clue to, or interest in, their reasons for behaving as they did," Gardner insists,

> and the result is that Steinbeck wrote not a great and firm novel but a disappointing melodrama in which complex good is pitted against unmitigated, unbelievable evil. . . . Truth is not so much valued where everybody agrees on what the truth is and no one is handy to speak up for the side that's been dismissed. (10–11)

It is characters and events which move the reader, Gardner maintains, not the sentimentalized opinions and emotions narratively expressed by the writer of a fiction.

Frigidity occurs when the author shows less concern for his characters than any normal person observing the situation would show. In other words, the writer lacks the ability, the passion, to enter fully and deeply into the emotional life of his fictional characters. If the writer, in his or her own life, has not delved deeply into the area of human feelings, how then can that writer produce a text which allows a reader, in the midst of that vivid and continuous dream, to feel deeply the emotions of the fictional characters? Cited by Gardner as a characteristic fault of contemporary literature and art, frigidity can also lead writers more and more to become dependent on form rather than content, as well as lead critics to literary approaches that take a diminished interest in "character, action, and the explicit ideas of the story." (118) He also suggests that frigidity may be the root cause of that faking of emotion that is sentimentality.

Gardner describes mannered writing as that writing which continually distracts the reader from the vivid and continuous dream by an intrusive style which serves to remind the reader of the writer's presence. Generally speaking, fiction writers have very healthy egos, and are often trying to distinguish themselves from other writers in their work. Gertrude Stein notwithstanding, Gardner believes it is wrong for an author to write in such a way that it is clear that his true interest is more for his own fictional style than for the characters of the story.

In looking at contemporary American fiction, particularly fiction that is valorized by literary professionals—e.g. writers, editors, university English professors—Gardner sees the literary landscape dominated by sentimentality, frigidity, and mannered writing. One of the reasons for this, in his view, has to do with the commercial aspects of publishing. The expense of publishing a writer can have a chilling effect as new writers with literary approaches deemed either new and untested, or old and no longer popular, are seen as not being worth the financial risk. This can lead to the continuing publication of a popular writer, even when that writer turns hack and begins producing little more than treacly melodrama once a year.

A second reason has to do with the way literature is treated in English Departments at many of our colleges and universities. It is Gardner's belief that standards of aesthetic judgment have been perverted by the institutional demands of the academy. If an English professor's role is, in part, to help students understand the latent significance and structure of narratives, then a text containing little symbolism, or few difficult and obscure allusions, becomes, in its own way, a difficult text to teach—even if that narrative be an aesthetically powerful one. All that can really be said about such a text is what is manifestly obvious to practically any reader. In such a case, the professor is left mouthing little more than platitudes. Give that same professor a less aesthetically powerful, yet recondite text and she will be able to dazzle her students endlessly—or at least until the end of the semester. Gardner feels every English Department graduate student is taught in turn to dazzle their peers with oh-so-trenchant talk of allusion and symbolism in works by clever, but nonetheless minor, writers. The unfortunate result, according to Gardner, is that the standards for what is aesthetically "good" comes to mean that which is tricky, academic and obscure. This, in his opinion, leads to a further problem: literature programs tend to waste young people's time by forcing them to read less than important books, rather than concentrate on those works of fiction which best exemplify the confluence of craft and artistic insight which allow in readers that "vivid and continuous dream" he argues is a part of all great fiction.

A third, more general reason for the abundant presence of sentimentality, frigidity, and mannered writing in contemporary literature has to do with the temper of the times. There is a sense in which twentieth-century men and women can be said to have boxed themselves into a philosophical corner. To understand the extent of this philosophical predicament we need to explore some of the philosophical assumptions that have been in place since the Enlightenment.

Rene Descartes is one of the great minds of the modern era. His methodology attempts to secure epistemological certainty by casting all assumed knowledge into doubt. The one fact that cannot be doubted, however, is his own existence. Starting from this absolute, he seeks to apply the rules of reason in order to attain an absolutely certain science of reality. Descartes seeks through rational means first to argue from his own existence to the certain existence of God, then from the certain existence of God to the certain existence of the physical world. Once he rationally proves the existence of the self, God, and the physical world to his own satisfaction, the question for Descartes becomes, as W. T. Jones puts it: "what *are* self, God, and matter?" (1952:675) For Descartes, reality is made up of either "substance" or the "qualities" of a substance. Since neither the self, nor God, nor matter are attributes, they clearly are substances. This, in turn, leads to the conundrum of the self being a "thinking substance" dependent on God, matter being "extensive substance" dependent on God, and God being "perfect substance" independent of all. The vexing problem, never resolved, is the mind/body problem of how mind, as a thinking substance, is able to interact with the body, as extensive substance.

Another aspect of Descartes's physical theory is that "the identification of material substance with extension and of extension with space was to make physics an absolutely certain science." (678) The laws of motion governing reality can then be simple, mathematically articulated absolutes, and events in the physical world can be fully explained by antecedent activity. Final causes, in the Aristotelian sense, are eliminated as an explanation of things, and efficient causes are valorized. When such an approach is applied to "thinking substance," it is at least theoretically possible in Descartes's philosophy to fully predict human behavior, if one could but know the full range of antecedent efficient causes. While substance is the "stuff" of reality, the "qualities" or "attributes" of substances are of secondary importance to Descartes, and play no role in the mechanistic world of substances posited in his philosophy. The perception of attributes is, for Descartes and his heirs, the arena of personal subjectivity and of error. The metaphor of man as "machine" is at its most powerful with a philosophy like that of Descartes.

A second major influence on modern philosophy is the epistemological work of David Hume. For his part, Hume takes the human perceptions very seriously and, as a good empiricist, comes to dismiss Descartes's felt certainty in the existence of a physical world. In confronting the Cartesian dualism of mind and body, Hume clearly resolves the issue on the side of mind, saying all an experiencing human being has are perceptions. In Hume's own words:

> [P]hilosophy . . . teaches us that nothing can ever be present to the mind but an image or perception, and that the senses are only the inlets through which these images are conveyed, without being able to produce any immediate intercourse between the mind and the object. . . .
> By what argument can it be proved that the perceptions of the mind must be caused by external objects, entirely different from them (if that be possible), and could not arise either from the energy of the mind itself or from the suggestion of some invisible and unknown spirit or from some other cause still more unknown to us? (1955:160–61)

Hume's argument against the existence of an external world is merely the pushing to its extreme the argument that all we can experience is our sense perceptions. It should be noted that Hume accepts that an external world would be a Cartesian world of distinct, independent, external, and extensive substances. He simply argues we cannot *rationally* prove such a world exists. All we have are sounds, tastes, and smells which, "though commonly regarded by the mind as continued independent qualities, appear not to have any existence in extension, and consequently cannot appear to the senses as situated externally to the

Some Intellectual Antecedents 47

body." (1962:222) While it can be argued Hume is nothing more than a corrective to the excesses of rationalism, in fact Hume is so persuasive that many feel compelled to accept a radical subjectivism.

Immanuel Kant sought to rectify the problems inherent to Hume's brand of empiricism, and in doing so he posits a third notion which has come to be assumed in the twentieth-century. Kant attempts to strike a compromise between the rationalists and the empiricists by arguing that the mind functions by correlating rational categories of the understanding, using time and space as modes of human perception, with a real external world physically felt by an experiencing subject. The rational categories of the understanding, or concepts, which are innate to the human mind, render sensory percepts derived by the physical senses from a spacio-temporal field into what he calls a "transcendental unity of apperception"—an experience. For Kant, concepts and percepts require each other. As he writes: "Gedanken ohne Inhalt sind leer, Anschauungen ohne Begriff sind blind."[5] Experience is a combining of the rational categories of the understanding with a real external world which we encounter through our senses. While Kant argues the necessity of an external physical world, he adopts enough of Hume's sensationalist argument to say we cannot know exactly what this external world is like in its particularity. This external world is a *noumenon*, unknown and unknowable as a thing-in-itself. What we experience of the external world is *phenomena*, which is the external world as it "appears" having been processed through the spacio-temporal manifold of our physical senses and the rational categories of the understanding. In short, whatever sense we derive of the external world is a by-product of our own subjectivity, our own mind.

Whitehead, in his penetrating review of the development of modern philosophy in *Science and the Modern World*, notes that the success of these ideas,

> yielding on the one hand *matter* with its *simple location* in space and time, and on the other hand *mind*, perceiving, suffering, reasoning, but not interfering, has foisted onto philosophy the task of accepting them as the most concrete rendering of fact. Thereby modern philosophy has been ruined. It has oscillated in a complex manner between three extremes: There are the dualists, who accept matter and mind as on an equal basis, and the two varieties of monists, those who put mind inside matter, and those who put matter inside mind. (55)

In the middle of the twentieth-century, when Gardner was coming of age, there appeared only two options for those wishing to pursue philosophy: the analytical school or existentialism. The analytical school consists of those philosophers who study the uses of language, taking critical notice of a language's ability to, in Wittgenstein's phrase, "bewitch" our intelligence. These philosophers have certainly helped in our understanding of the ways language, if not properly understood, can lead to various sorts of philosophical problems. When properly done, philosophical analysis can help show how some of our philosophical problems are actually not problems at all, but "pseudo-problems" that have to do with the ways we misconstrue language. Thus, if one were to understand and use language properly the philosophical "problem" would dissolve itself. Walter Kaufmann notes, however, that while analytical philosophers have resolved a number of philosophical disputes with "intellectual cleanliness and rigor," the tendency of these "analysts" is to exert their skills pursuing philosophical questions which are seen by most people as trivial and inconsequential. (1975:51)

The "big questions"—why is there evil in the world, what is the morally good life, what is the meaning of existence—tend not to be addressed by the analysts, and instead are left to those who came to be known as existentialists. Indeed, through essays, scholarly works, coffee house musings and the arts, those labeled existentialists certainly probe for answers to those questions deemed most important to men and women, regardless of their station in life. But, Kaufmann notes, the existentialists, too, have their weakness, for their philosophical approach is so evocative and vague, in contrast to the restrained and precise methods of the analysts, that existentialists tend to create more philosophical problems than they resolve. (51) Despite this perceived weakness, existentialism has been very influential among intellectuals, particularly readers and writers of fiction. Recognizing the philosophical box into which reasoned philosophies have forced them, existentialists critique the manner in which human rationality is valorized as the *sine qua non* of what it is to be human. Nevertheless, their acceptance of—or, perhaps more appropriately, their inability to reject—a Cartesian substance/quality doctrine of actuality, a Humean sensationalist doctrine of perception, and Kant's phenomenalism, force the honest existentialist to describe the human situation as that of a living individual, separate, distinct, and unrelated to his material environment, restricted to experiencing his own sensations only, living in a noumenal world he can know only as a phenomenal appearance. This is the existentialist view of "absurd" man. It is important to realize that the absurdity is not in the man or woman, nor in the world. According to Albert Camus, it is the disrelationship between an individual asking the question of meaning and significance of her life, and a universe which responds with mute silence that is the "absurd." One of the most influential existentialist depictions of a person's coming to recognize his absurd condition is from Jean-Paul Sartre's novel, *Nausea*.

The protagonist of *Nausea*, Antoine Roquentin, decides to keep a journal in which to write of his experiences. Near the beginning of the journal he describes an unpleasant experience while holding a pebble at the shore. Though he cannot explain it, he feels a sense of nausea, and is sure it has something to do with the pebble itself. Sometime later, while riding in a tram, his discomfort becomes stronger as he describes his experience of looking at a seat:

> I murmur: "It's a seat," a little like an exorcism. But the word stays on my lips: it refuses to go and put itself on the thing. It stays what it is, . . . Things are divorced from their names. They are there, grotesque, headstrong, gigantic and it seems ridiculous to call them seats or say anything at all about them: I am in the midst of things, nameless things. Alone, without words, defenseless, they surround me, are beneath me, behind me, above me. (125)

It is a felt sense of alienation that washes over Roquentin. After he leaves the tram he finds himself in a park amidst a group of chestnut trees:

> We are a heap of living creatures, irritated, embarrassed at ourselves, we hadn't the slightest reason to be there, none of us, each one, confused, vaguely alarmed, felt in the way in relation to the others. *In the way*: it was the only relationship I could establish between these trees, these gates, these stones....
> And I—soft, weak, obscene, digesting, juggling with dismal thoughts—I, too, was *In the way*. . . . I dreamed vaguely of killing myself to wipe out at least one of these superfluous lives. But even my death would have been *In the way*. *In the way*, my corpse, my blood on these stones, between these plants, at the back of this smiling garden. And the decomposed flesh would have been *In the way* in the earth which would receive my bones, at last, cleaned, stripped, peeled, proper and clean as teeth, it would have been *In the way*. I was *In the way* for eternity. (128–29)

The incident ends with Roquentin remarking on the absurdity of existence and of his discomfort once he realizes there is no ultimate purpose to the world, no ultimate answers in response to life's questions:

> And all these existents which bustled about this tree came from nowhere and were going nowhere. Suddenly they existed, then suddenly they existed no longer: existence is without memory; of the vanished it retains nothing—not even a memory. Existence everywhere, infinitely, in excess, for ever and everywhere; existence,—which is limited only by existence. I sank down on the bench, stupefied, stunned by this profusion of beings without origin: everywhere blossomings, hatchings out, my ears buzzed with existence, my very flesh throbbed and opened, abandoned itself to the universal burgeoning. It was repugnant.
> ... Tired and old, [the trees] kept on existing, against the grain, simply because they were too weak to die, because death could only come to them from the outside: ... Every existing thing is born without reason, prolongs itself out of weakness and dies by chance. (132–33)

Writers like Sartre and Camus, and existentialist philosophers like Husserl and Heidegger, are serious-minded thinkers. The existentialist movement to which they contributed, however, comes to be popularly accepted by many who, it can be said, enjoyed the social benefits of adopting an existentialist posture. Such individuals, according to Gardner, come to fulminate a "cynicism, despair, greed, sadism, and nihilism" that was to become increasingly more chic, with the result that fiction becomes more and more mean, more and more brutal and cynical. (1978:43) In part, Gardner places the blame for this on those writers who use an overly-intellectual approach to human experience. For such writers, it appears one's emotions and feelings are derived from conscious mental activity rather than consciousness being a response to one's emotions and feelings. Such an approach tends to valorize consciousness as foundational of all human experience. Fiction from such writers, while it can be intellectually exciting for a reader, does not convey what Gardner believes to be an adequate account of what it is to be human.

While Sartre is constantly cited by Gardner as an example of one whose overly-intellectual approach inappropriately valorizes conscious human experience, at least he grants Sartre the virtue of being a legitimately gifted writer and thinker. It is the purveyor of a cheap cynicism, playing the role of the metaphysically abandoned on the cocktail party circuit, that is most irksome to Gardner. He is also the most obvious to spot when he writes fiction, Gardner argues, for either he emphasizes texture—linguistic pyrotechnics and trendy stylistic tricks—or he relies on a simplistic structure, some trite melodrama trying to pass as profound metaphysical musings.

Clearly, Gardner is critical of what he considers inadequate renderings of human experience in the hands of contemporary writers. As we shall see in more detail later, many of his fictional characters, particularly those like the philosopher James Chandler, the protagonist of *The Resurrection*, have difficulty coming to terms with deeply felt human issues of guilt, ethical responsibility, and death, because they are too strongly dependent on only a conscious, intellectual, logocentric approach. Gardner typically attempts to indicate there are other, preconscious aspects of human experience which are integral to the lives of men and women. Indeed, it is these other aspects of experience which, in Gardner's view, more nearly constitute what it is to be human. It is, in part, in seeking to counter the inadequate renderings of human experience in contemporary fiction that Gardner displays a reliance on the thought of Alfred North Whitehead and his followers. It was Whitehead, Gardner recalls of his college years, who "said what I would say"; and it was Whitehead whose "world-view, incredibly, was like the world-view I had developed." (Harvey, 1978:74) Whitehead, together with Langer, are influential in helping Gardner to a broadened understanding of human experience—an understanding which seeks to break out from that "philosophical box" in which twentieth-century men and women have found themselves. In so doing, Gardner manages to create refreshingly full-bodied characters, both complex and interesting, in his fiction.

In Whitehead's preface to his major work, *Process and Reality*, he cites nine common habits of thought which he repudiates in his philosophy. Among them are: (1) a 20th century rejection of speculative philosophy, (2) an abiding trust in language as an adequate means to express propositions, (3) a Cartesian substance/quality doctrine of actuality, (4) a Humean sensationalist approach to perception, and (5) Kant's phenomenalism. Obviously, to repudiate the distrust of speculative philosophy implies a desire to *do* speculative philosophy, and Whitehead's "philosophy of organism," which has also come to be known as "process philosophy," is, in fact, a speculative attempt "to frame a coherent, logical, necessary system of general ideas in terms of which every element of our experience can be interpreted." (1978:3) Clearly, Whitehead is calling for more than a simple translation of Enlightenment philosophical positions into the popular idiom of the day. Rather, he is calling for a rigorous rethinking of basic philosophical concepts. It is forcefully argued by Whitehead that experience ought not to be restricted to "thinking" subjects. "The principle that I am adopting," he writes, "is that consciousness presupposes experience, and not experience consciousness." (53) Another "process" thinker, Bernard Meland, makes the same point with his famous remark, "we live more deeply than we think." There are vast, unexplored regions of experienced reality which are simply not available to consciousness, but which are, nevertheless, extremely important elements of our lives.

Whitehead cites several concepts central to his philosophy of organism which run contrary to previous philosophical thought. Two that are important in our current discussion are: an "actual entity," and "prehension." Actual entities, which he elsewhere refers to as "actual occasions," are the final ultimately real facts of which the world is made. There is nothing more real, no reality more basic, than an actual entity. They may differ among themselves, i.e. God in Whitehead's system is an actual entity as is the "most trivial puff of existence in far-off empty space." (18) As this example shows, while there may be actual entities of more or lesser importance, manifesting diverse functions, they all exemplify the same metaphysical principles. While reality is seen from a Cartesian view as consisting of independent substances, Whitehead's approach argues that reality is made up of complex and interdependent actual entities which are likened more to droplets of experience.

An actual entity is a momentary event which has emerged from a past actual world and, in a flash, will perish. The very existence of an actual entity is dependent on a past actual world, existing objectively, which the actual entity "prehends" or "feels" as it seeks to achieve its own "satisfaction." This experiencing of a past actual world, often referred to by process thinkers as an act of "concrescence," is part of the process whereby, in Whitehead's poetically pregnant line, "the many become one, and are increased by one." (21) Once an actual entity has integrated in itself those relevant factors of its past actual world in an act of concrescence it perishes, to then serve as a datum to be experienced by subsequent actual entities. With this scheme, Whitehead seeks to emphasize the dynamism of reality-in-process, to expand the notion of experience, and to demonstrate how the objects of reality are not independent, but exist interdependently as occasions of experience internally related to a past actual world. When Whitehead speaks of the differing levels of importance and diverse functions among actual entities, he is referring to the notion that there exists a range from low-grade actual occasions in which the past actual world is mirrored and continued with negligible novelty (e.g. stones, tables, etc.) to high-grade actual occasions that are able to prehend its past actual world and, in an act of concrescence, integrate the relevant aspects of that past actual world into a novel harmony of satisfaction (e.g. higher forms of life).

To "prehend" a past actual world is to take up elements from the past and carry them into the subjective immediacy of an actual entity in the present. Once an actual entity attains its telic goal of satisfaction in an act of concrescence, it then perishes. This is the sense behind Whitehead's remark, drawing on Locke, that reality is "perpetually perishing." However, it is important to note that in Whitehead's scheme an actual entity perishes only subjectively; once an actual entity perishes it becomes an objective datum to be prehended by subsequent percipient occasions, thus carrying it into the future.

Three important ideas emerge from Whitehead's discussion of actual entities and prehension. The first is that prehension is best characterized as a "vector." In physical theory, vectors are pulses of energy which have direction as well as magnitude, and Whitehead clearly wants prehension to be seen as a progression from the past, through the present, and into the future. Thus, prehension may be symbolized by an arrow. (Lowe, 1971:7) A second idea to emerge is the notion of "objective immortality." Victor Lowe states the matter concisely when he writes:

> Whitehead pictures reality as cumulative. When, upon the completion of an actual occasion, the creativity of the universe moves on to the next birth, it carries that occasion with it as an "object" which all future occasions are obliged to prehend. They will feel it as an efficient cause—as the immanence of the past in their immediacies of becoming. The end of an occasion's private life—its "perishing"—is the beginning of its public career. (8)

A third idea to emerge is that of "subjective form," also referred to as "subjective aim." An actual entity, seeking to attain satisfaction in its subjective immediacy, must be selective in prehending its past actual world. For Whitehead, this selectivity occurs at a pre-conscious level as an actual occasion prehends only those aspects of its past actual world which are relevant to its attainment of satisfaction. This subjective form of satisfaction can thus be characterized as involving "emotion and purpose, and valuation, and causation." (Whitehead, 1978:19) Clearly, this is an expansion of the notion of "experience" to include acts that are not necessarily a part of consciousness, though they may later rise to consciousness.

One can begin to see in this approach how "becoming" is a more central concept than "being," "interdependent" more central than "independent." One can also begin to see how the philosophy of organism acts to revert Kant's "second Copernican revolution," for Whitehead clearly rejects a Kantian phenomenalism which posits the objective world as a construct derived from subjective experience. Interestingly, Whitehead agrees with Kant's statement that "intuitions [percepts] without concepts are blind," but for an entirely different reason. Kant argues that there is nothing to know apart from rational concepts, and in this way Kant tries to argue that experience is a movement from subjectivity to objectivity. For his part, Whitehead wants to invert this and argue that experience emerges from an objectively real external world that is a datum, to the emergence of the subjectivity of individual experience. This notion is succinctly expressed in Whitehead's line: "For Kant, the world emerges from the subject; for the philosophy of organism, the subject emerges from the world." (88)

One of the strengths of Whitehead's speculative approach is its complementarity with contemporary science, particularly quantum physics. In seeking to give abstract expression to the smallest units of matter, quantum theory speaks of the basic building blocks of the universe as vectors of energy. Whereas Descartes and his heirs see the natural world as an extensive spatial plenum enduring through time, modern physics sees the natural world as energy transference in definite quanta, thus allowing for dynamism and change in the natural world. Susanne Langer owes much of her own intellectual development to Whitehead, and even dedicated her most popular book, *Philosophy in a New Key*, to "Alfred North Whitehead, my great teacher and friend." Like Whitehead, she attempts to bring together many strains of philosophical thought into a speculative system. Rather than draw on physics, however, Langer develops a process approach in complementarity with the science of biology.

In her broadly learned three-volume work, *Mind: An Essay on Human Feeling*, Langer seeks to describe what biologists know about life in its most simple forms, at the level of lowliest organic activity, and then proceeds to show by a meticulous step-by-step argument that human feeling, though different in quality from other biological organisms, shares with all living things the same *form*. Central to her argument is the concept of the "act," which she claims gives life its dynamism. Essentially, an act is a four-fold rhythmic sequence: (i) impulse, (ii) rise, (iii) consummation, and (iv) cadence. These rhythmic acts, she insists, are the *form of feeling* which pervades all of life. As she writes:

> It is with the concept of the act that I am approaching living form in nature, only to find it exemplified there at all levels of simplicity or complexity, in concatenations and in hierarchies, presenting many aspects and relationships that permit analysis and construction and special investigation....
>
> An act may subsume another act, or even many other acts. It may also span other acts which go on during its rise and consummation and cadence without becoming part of it. Two acts of separate inception may merge so that they jointly engender a subsequent act. These and many other relations among acts form the intricate dynamism of life which becomes more and more articulated, more and more concentrated and intense, until some of its elements attain the phase of being felt. [Ours is] the work of tracing and understanding that ever-progressive, self-weaving web of life in terms of acts and their interdependent functions. (1967:261–62)

What is clearly in the background of Langer's discussion of an "act" is Whitehead's discussion of actual entities. One may easily substitute Whitehead's language for Langer's above, thereby rendering the Whiteheadian notion:

> It is with the concept of the *actual entity* that I am approaching living form in nature, only to find it exemplified there at all levels of *low-grade actual occasions or high-grade actual occasions*, in concatenations and in hierarchies, presenting many aspects and relationships that permit analysis and construction and special investigation. . . .
>
> An *actual entity* may subsume another *actual entity*, or even many other *actual entities*. It may also span other *actual entities* which go on during its *act of concrescence* without becoming part of it. Two *actual entities* of separate inception may merge so that they jointly engender a subsequent *actual*

entity. These and many other relations among *actual entities* form the intricate dynamism of life which becomes more and more articulated, more and more concentrated and intense, until some of its elements attain the phase of being felt. [Ours is] the work of tracing and understanding that ever-progressive, self-weaving web of life in terms of *actual entities* and their interdependent functions.

Both Langer's "acts" and Whitehead's "actual entities" predominantly operate at a pre-conscious level. However, as the quote from Langer earlier in the chapter indicates,[6] a sentient creature, whether at the macro- or microorganismic level, must be selective in what it experiences so as not to find itself living in the midst of "a blooming, buzzing confusion." For Langer, that means the organism "must select certain predominant forms." (*Philosophy in a New Key*:89) This is an echo of Whitehead's notion that "in the philosophy of organism it is not 'substance' which is permanent, but 'form'." (1978:29) In process thought, the principle of selectivity is the "subjective aim" of each actual entity in an act of concrescence, seeking to select those relevant aspects of its past actual world that will lead to its own "satisfaction." Langer speaks of "entrainment" rather than subjective aim, but the meaning is the same. "The principle of entrainment," she writes, "simplifies the tangle of separately directed impulses by massing their expressions into a few organized acts. Entrainment is the fundamental process of individuation, as it is of nucleation and inward coherence." (1982:91) It is by means of entrainment, for example, that the "acts" of the muscles of the heart adopt the predominant form of previous "acts" of heart muscle in order to attain its own satisfaction. Thus is the rhythm of life.

This is why Langer, in *Philosophy in a New Key*, can speak of the "unconscious appreciation of forms" being "the primitive root of all abstraction, which in turn is the keynote of rationality; so it appears that the conditions for rationality lie deep in our pure animal experience." (89) Whitehead makes much the same point in *Adventures of Ideas* when he speaks of men and women being driven not just by physical factors in their bodies, but also by their thoughts and intelligence. Nonetheless, he warns, it would be mistaken to overintellectualize the myriad forms of human experience. As animal life forms we may be at the head of the primates, he grants, but what that should mean to us is that we are incapable of escaping certain habits of mind which are very closely tied to requisite habits of the body.

It should be noted that Whitehead and his philosophy of organism have severe critics as well as strong advocates. And while I would not want to argue that Gardner did a close analysis of Whiteheadian metaphysical thought, nor would I want to argue that he adopts an exclusively Whiteheadian view of the world, clearly it is the case that Gardner finds process thought a fruitful alternative to the alienated angst depicted in much of contemporary fiction. Throughout his own fictional work, as we shall see, Gardner draws upon the ideas—and sometimes the exact language—of Whitehead in attempting to give a more adequate rendering of human experience.

As will be shown in the final chapter, more influential on Gardner than the Whitehead of *Process and Reality* is the Whitehead of *Adventures of Ideas*, where the philosophy of organism is used by Whitehead in his fecund and erudite cultural history of human thought. It is in this provocative work that Whitehead gives extended discussions of the five elements he believes vital to any civilization: Truth, Beauty, Art, Adventure, and Peace. Whether it be a Whitehead seeking to understand the death of his son in World War I, or Gardner trying to come to grips with the death of his brother, the philosophy of organism is a formulation of human experience which acknowledges human suffering without giving way to cynicism and despair. It is a world of adventure and joy, Whitehead insists, as well as a world of tragedy; it is also a world in which the totality of our lives are "objectively immortalized" and taken up into the future. Adopted by Gardner, Whitehead's rendering of human experience is a far cry from Sartre's world where men and women are merely "in the way," and "existents . . . came from nowhere and were going nowhere." As we shall see, Gardner's fictional world is one in which communities of fallible, finite, sometimes fearful and sometimes courageous men and women, confronting the mysteries of life in all its joys and brutalities, share their dreams and tell their stories and keep each other warm around the hearth at night, sure in the knowledge that, despite the tragedies along the way, faith and love are active and make a difference.

CHAPTER III:
Of Pattern-Making and Art

While detailed explications of his fictional texts have already been written, the effort here is to highlight three aspects of Gardner's fiction: (1) how his fictional texts revolve around the issues and imagery of death and guilt, so central a part of Gardner's own life, (2) how they exemplify elements of Whiteheadian thought which, noted only in passing by some critics, have helped mold Gardner's intellectual approach, and (3) how his fiction represents ritual activity as characters seek both a sense of identity in the midst of chaos and change, as well as a sense of transcendent, often mystical, interconnectedness with nature and other people. It is hoped that some of the reasons why Gardner is a significant writer of themes broadly religious will become more explicit.

Stephen Wigler, in an interview conducted shortly before Gardner's death, comments that Gardner is old-fashioned in his values, in "his belief in family, in the redeeming power of love, and, ultimately, in faith in God—*or something very like Him.*" [emphasis mine] (1990:279) "Artistic choices are moral choices," a friend of Gardner's reports him as saying. "If one thing is better than another, then there's a hierarchy of values. He believes deeply in God as the end of the hierarchy of values." (280) What is clear is that Gardner addresses religious themes not in a narrowly sectarian sense, but in the more etymologically consistent sense of identifying that which helps bind and tie a community of men and women together.

It will be helpful here to take note of Wesley A. Kort's work on the religious implications of the four elements of fictional narratives, i.e. character, plot, atmosphere, and tone. Each element is present in all narratives, Kort argues, though a particular narrative will tend to emphasize one narrative element over all the others. The sorts of religious questions which arise in the course of a narrative is, in Kort's view, a function of which narrative element is dominant. (1975:18) Atmosphere, sometimes referred to as "setting," helps set physical limitations to characters and events. As such, atmosphere can lead to questions about that which is beyond our limits, and to contemplation of otherness, of that which "cannot be controlled or, even, understood." (109) Tone refers to the narrative presence of the teller of the tale, a presence which may be intimately involved in the story or reflexively distanced, an encouraging voice of admiration and praise or a cynical voice of derision and ridicule. Tone stands as a presence within a narrative which actively judges the actions, attitudes, and values expressed in the story.

For his part, Gardner is clear in his belief that character and plot, rather than tone and atmosphere, ought to be the dominant elements of literature. The central driving force of any Shakespearean play as well as any other great work of literature, he suggests in *The Art of Fiction*, is character. The writer's job, he insists, is to enable a reader to experience vividly what a story's characters see and feel. In other words, the skilled author will enable a reader to know and experience what a story's characters know and experience, albeit vicariously. Closely aligned with character in Gardner's work as a writer is the narrative element of plot, which he says ought to be of utmost concern to a writer. He contends that a recognizable and orderly flow of events is needed both to increase the reader's interest by moving characters toward situations of conflict and crisis, and to avoid silly or senseless situations that might act to disrupt the vivid and continuous dream of the reader.

A weakness of contemporary fiction, Gardner believes, is the tendency among today's writers to move away from the more traditional expectations of character and plot in their work. Traditional notions of character and plot would have a writer explain what is happening to a character, why it is happening, how the character either allowed it to happen or could not avoid it happening, and what the character intends to do in response to what has happened, for good or ill. As such, fiction can delve into some of the mysteries that are endemic to the human condition. Gardner argues many contemporary writers seem to believe the mysteries of life have been demystified by the natural and social sciences, and are no more than cultural relics of a more primitive age. For these writers, what can fiction explain to readers about suicide that psychology hasn't already told us? What can a novelist tell readers about the affairs of the heart that haven't already been publicly explored for mass consumption by Donahue or Dr. Ruth? The novelist appears left with no alternative but to smirk cynically at the absurd situation in which modern men and women today find themselves. Thus, in Gardner's view, too many contemporary novelists have abandoned character and plot as vehicles of explanation about life's inexorable processes, and have instead couched their work in the narrative element of tone.

The dominant presence of a narrator, usually a cynical presence mocking the actions and situations of the narrative's characters, is typical of much contemporary fiction. Often, the narrator's judgment on the values expressed in the narrative are indistinguishable from that of the author. This is particularly true of metafictionist writers. For them, characters are more akin to cartoon figures, often "strawmen" set up in order to take an intellectual pratfall. Plots tend to be of a more abstract sort, put together in order to satisfy an intellectual argument. A good example is provided by Gardner himself in his novel-within-a-novel, *Smugglers of Lost Soul's Rock*, contained in *October Light*. Clearly, literature through the ages has been written with a polemical intent, and to the extent literature is able to use character and plot effectively it may be an aesthetically powerful instrument. Gardner seems to be saying, however, that contemporary literature's continuing valorization of tone over character and plot has led to fiction which is less powerful aesthetically. Gardner is willing to grant that a story written by a metafictionist can fascinate, can even be brilliant, but he goes on to say such a story will never achieve its fullest fictive power. And the reason is because control of the fiction's action is entirely intellectual. "It does not rise out of the essence of things," Gardner insists, "it does not capture *process*." (166) When all is said and done, Gardner simply believes a purely intellectual structure will never have the same power and aesthetic impact as "a structure that appeals simultaneously to our intellect and to subtler faculties, our deepest emotions (sympathy and empathy) and our intuition of *reality's process*. (167) [emphasis mine]

In looking at Gardner's novels it is helpful to keep in mind the sorts of religious questions Kort identifies as related to the narrative elements of character and plot. Character in fiction is a paradigm of human possibilities, "a paradigm of what man is, can be, should be, or must be." (1975:56) Narratives in which character is dominant address questions having to do with the moral and spiritual condition of men and women, questions of what is the good life and how to live it, questions of the seeming intractability of evil. Plots, for their part, give coherence to time, and thus "are images of recognizable processes, particularly of growth or dissolution." (62) Plots, it can be said, take the seeming chaos of nature, that "buzzing, blooming confusion," and help transform it into a humanly recognizable and meaningful world. This is the sense behind Gardner's statement in *On Moral Fiction* that "life is all conjunctions, one damn thing after another, cows *and* wars *and* chewing gum *and* mountains; art—the best, most important art—is all subordination: guilt *because of* sin *because of* pain." (6) Kort goes on to argue that plot leads to considerations of the ways men and women seek symbolically to order their experience. Correctly, he further argues that plot has close associations with ritual, as both seek mimetically to represent life "processes which are not wholly invented and imposed, processes which are in themselves coherent, meaningful, and lifelike." (80) It is important to be sensitive to the ways Gardner's characters assess their moral or spiritual condition, especially in light of intractable evils like death and guilt. It will also be instructive to attend to the ways his characters use ritual activity in coming to an understanding of their social, as well as their ontological, reality.

Perhaps Gardner's most enduring novel is *Grendel*, which burst upon the literary scene in 1971. Whatever reservations critics may have had about *The Resurrection* and *The Wreckage of Agathon* were removed by the publication of this seriocomic retelling of the Beowulf epic from the point of view of the monster, Grendel. Much of its popularity at the time, as Begiebing points out, is because it was taken "to be one more timely issue of nihilistic black humor. The unreliable narrator is so convincing and such a likable monster that he was taken at his word." (1989:76) Critical consensus of those who have taken the time to give judicious consideration to Gardner's work has come around to the position of David Cowart:

> [Gardner] makes Grendel the narrator of his novel, and in that role the monster becomes in effect the Shaper's rival artist. Thus the battle between Grendel and Beowulf, a contrast of strength, takes second place in importance to the indirect competition between Grendel and the Shaper—a contest of art. The story ultimately concerns the triumph of good art over bad, for in it Grendel manages only self-indictment. He unwittingly produces a case history of the bad artist, as John Gardner would define such a monster. (1983:38)

It is important we look at *Grendel* before studying Gardner's other novels because it, more clearly than the others, manifests his ongoing search for patterns and explanations for how and why the world is as it is. Lifton cites a survivor's drive to develop a conceptual schema by which to explain and understand the tragedies that befall one, and *Grendel*, in particular, shows Gardner seeking patterns and systems by which to make sense of the world. Not only do the characters in *Grendel* impose system and order on the world around them, but the novel itself reflects an obvious patterning. The sensitive reader quickly recognizes a zodiacal scheme as a ram (i.e. Aries, March 21–April 19) is introduced in the first line of the first chapter and a bull (i.e. Taurus, April 20–May 20) is a part of the second chapter. Indeed, each of the twelve chapters uses, metaphorically, the zodiacal sign of that month.[1] Use of this organizational pattern clues the reader that central to the novel are the various patterns used in deriving a sense of orderliness.

We are introduced to Grendel in the twelfth year of his war against Hrothgar. He is in the midst of a monologue which continues throughout the text. The entire novel is from a first person point of view—a narrative voice which Gardner generally avoided in his novels. His use of first person narrative voice helps to magnify for the reader Grendel's isolation from others. Grendel is very much *alone*, without benefit of community, and his thoughts are the only thoughts to which the reader has access. And Grendel thinks unceasingly, advocating his own views of how the world really is. While using words and making patterns, he is under no illusion about the ontological status of these words and patterns: "Talking, talking. Spinning a web of words, pale walls of dreams, between myself and all I see." (8) The only communicant for his words are his "shadow," which he characterizes as his only friend. Pitching between the two meanings of shadow—that blockage of light which is always present and follows near us, and that dark side of our personalities which, metaphorically, is always present and wallows within us—it is seen by Grendel as the one true comfort that the world affords him.

Alone, excluded from a sense of community, Grendel develops a philosophy by which to justify his situation. His seeming courage in accepting his philosophical isolation is a false courage, however. It really is nothing more than a display to the world of his own anger at his seeming abandonment. Philosophically, Grendel understands that the world is a concatenation of brute existents, a mechanical chaos of blind forces upon which he, in his own stupid and ridiculous way, attempts to impose purpose and meaning. But it is all for naught. He knows that, too. The world is blind, and cares not at all for his hopes and fears.

Absolutely and finally, he is alone. To the extent this chaotic world of brute enmity is a *uni*verse, he creates it "blink by blink." (22)

These are his thoughts one day after his ankle is caught in a crack between two old tree trunks. Inescapably trapped, he fears for his life as a bull keeps ramming the tree. Though the bull eventually tires and walks away, being trapped is the occasion of Grendel's first encounter with humans. A hunting party comes upon Grendel and, not knowing who or what he is, they simply stop and begin talking with one another. Grendel realizes that he understands the language being used by these unusual creatures. And they are unusual-looking, with their vacant eyes and their ashen faces. Nevertheless, he recognizes a similarity between himself and these creatures. Though he considers them laughable, they are nonetheless interesting and mysterious little beasts, their mannerisms "stiff and regular, as if figured by logic." (24) There is an attempt at communication, but the humans are frightened when Grendel tries to speak, and then feel threatened when Grendel laughs. The leader, Hrothgar, throws an ax at Grendel, nicking the monster seriously enough that he bleeds. Hrothgar then orders his men to surround Grendel and protect the horses. At that moment Grendel knows he is dealing with something far more dangerous than a ramming bull. These are "thinking creatures, pattern makers, the most dangerous things I'd ever met." (27) Afterwards, saved from the situation by his mother, Grendel begins to watch these men and women to learn more about them, and is puzzled at how they would argue, fight, and occasionally murder one another. At times one who had murdered another would be banished to the woods where Grendel would try to befriend him. He comes to learn such men are treacherous, however, and he finds it necessary to eat them in the end.

He is particularly puzzled one night when he comes upon a meadhall destroyed by marauders. The cows all lay dead, bleeding from their nostrils and from the many holes punctured in them by the javelins of the attackers. What was oddest of all, however, was that none of them had been eaten. The now destroyed meadhall had been engulfed in flames, with a rancid smoke rising from the timbers, the people inside burned black and shriveling in the heat. What is so puzzling is the *amount* of destruction and killing. Why kill, Grendel wonders, if you do not then eat that which you have killed? And the way these creatures would fight is also an enigma to Grendel. They would stand in groups some distance apart, screaming at one another while swinging their swords and javelins menacingly. They would howl terrible threats to each other, and then curses about their counterpart's fathers and grandfathers. In the name of justice and honor they would promise to do the most unspeakable of things to each other. And then they would fight. Their outlandish brutality leaves Grendel sickened. Though safe in a tree watching, and though these men are nothing to him personally, Grendel finds himself confused and frightened in a way he cannot fathom. And, again incredibly, all that they kill, all the horses and all the cows and all the men and women, are left to rot or be devoured by fire. Grendel continues to watch them, year after year, and the one who threw the ax at him, King Hrothgar, becomes the leader of a powerful band of men who conquer many a meadhall, vanquishing their enemies, stealing their gold and other valuables, and making vassals of other groups of men and women who are forced to pay tribute in order not to be destroyed themselves. It is no secret how Hrothgar and his men accomplish these deeds: they are more merciless, brutal, and violently destructive than any other competing band of warriors. Wealth and power, clearly, belong to the ruthless.

Then an old blind man arrives at Hrothgar's meadhall. He is a poet who, harp in hand, would sing songs of the glory and honor of long-ago battles fought in the name of righteousness. He begins singing, and as he does so it becomes clear that a quantum change in the life of the people is about to occur. One of his songs begins:

> *Lo, we have heard the honor of the Speardanes,*
> *nation-kings, in days now gone,*
> *how those battle lords brought themselves glory.* (41)

We recognize the lines as from the epic poem *Beowulf*. In Gardner's novel, the lines hush Hrothgar's people to silence as they listen, rapt, to the poet's song of honor and daring deeds. "He knew his art," Grendel, listening to the old man through a window, cedes. "He was king of the Shapers." (42) Grendel realizes that men and women, inspired by the Shaper, would be unified in thought and deed and thus able to seize control of the rivers, the oceans, and the stars—and all in Hrothgar's name. So skilled is this poet in shaping the thoughts and actions of others that he "had changed the world, had torn up the past by its thick, gnarled roots and had transmuted it, and they, who knew the truth, remembered it his way—and so did I." (43) This, in Gardner's view, is the power of art when, in a religious sense, it "transcends the mundane and takes on the richness and universality of ritual," resulting in a virtual dream which is "at once the real and the real transmuted." (*The Art of Fiction*:116–17)

As he continues to listen to the songs of the Shaper over the years, Grendel and the people begin to act more peaceably. But, Grendel knows the Shaper's stories to be preposterous flattery, mere illusion. Despite the fact he knows the poetic claims to be untrue, he cannot deny their positive effect on the people—and on himself. The Shaper's songs tell of the mighty deeds of heroes and of Hrothgar's goodness, but also of those evil threats that seek to plunge the world of men back into barbarity. Grendel, more and more feeling grief at his own blood-thirsty acts, shrinks before the songs of the Shaper in hopes of escaping their accusatory verses. The images from the Shaper's songs would torment Grendel, though deep down he knows just how ludicrous it all is. As for the Thanes, they would fill the meadhall, spilling out into surrounding pastures and hills, silently absorbed as the Shaper spins his gossamer reality over them. The Shaper, through his songs and playing of the harp, acts, in Whitehead's phrase, as a "lure for feeling" on the part of the people and Grendel. He provides one image of what it is to be human: a creature capable of valor and acts of courage and love in a world evolving toward novel orders of creativity and peace. Grendel, during those moments he is not under sway of the Shaper, cannot fully accept the old man's vision in spite of its attractions, for Grendel is a self-proclaimed truth-teller who will not let go of what he knows to be a more accurate depiction of the human: a murderer capable of the most self-serving and vicious acts in a manifestly absurd world of ultimately meaningless actions.

The battle between Grendel and the Shaper is set when Grendel hears the poet's story about an ancient conflict that pits brother against brother, resulting in a split between darkness and light that has continued throughout time. Grendel, it is clear from the Shaper's song, is to be counted among those in league with the dark side, a terrible race that God has cursed. Under the spell of the Shaper's art Grendel believes him, and in a moment of abandon he enters the meadhall to unburden himself before all of Hrothgar's people, hoping to join them in that world envisioned by the Shaper. His attempt at reconciliation, however, is seen as an attack by the uncomprehending men and women gathered. Screaming, they rush at him in righteous indignation, their battle axes drawn, and hack away at his body. To protect himself Grendel strikes back, killing two. He flees the hall and races to the center of the forest where his mind roars with tumultuous emotions. It was not just his being rejected by Hrothgar's people, but his feelings of utter abandonment that lead to passionate fulminations against his condition. Then, he stops.

> My sudden awareness of my foolishness made me calm.
> I looked up through the treetops, ludicrously hopeful. I think I was half prepared, in my dark, demented state, to see God, bearded and gray as geometry, scowling down at me, shaking his bloodless finger.
> "Why can't I have someone to talk to?" I said. The stars said nothing, but I pretended to ignore the rudeness. (52–53)

Perhaps it would be that the Shaper would improve the minds of men and women, help them to attain that life of peace and harmony he describes in his songs, but Grendel knows better. He's seen them at their worst, generation after generation. Grendel is no longer to be seduced by such tales of sweetness. He knows what he knows, and what he knows is the terrible bruteness of things and the terrible emptiness of space. Grendel decides he will stand in stark contrast to the tales of the Shaper; by his actions he will expose the lie of what the Shaper posits the world to be. And it is a lie, "a cold-blooded lie that a god had lovingly made the world and set out the sun and moon as lights to landdwellers, that brothers had fought, that one of the races was saved, the other cursed. Yet he, the old Shaper, might make it true, by the sweetness of his harp, his cunning trickery." (55) Grendel would also be a "shaper," but the world he would present is an absurd world of thinking pattern-makers idiotically imposing their systems and narratives on a deaf and mute world.

Grendel has a mentor in the person of the Dragon, from whom the young Grendel gains his Sartrean view of the world. According to the Dragon, the world is a concatenation of simple facts in isolation. What humans do is supply other facts by which to connect them, even though there be no such facts. It is all a lie, the Dragon insists, and men and women occasionally begin to realize it is a lie. But this is where they are saved by the Shaper, for his songs provide for the people a new, fresher image of reality, a world of connectedness in which the actions of men and women are full of purpose and meaning. "Mere tripe," the Dragon concludes, for the Shaper knows no more about reality than do the people themselves. The reality the Shaper places before them is but an illusion, the Dragon insists, but a successful one in that it manages to keep the people going from generation to generation.

It is the negative side of the exact same argument Gardner makes in *On Moral Fiction*. Gardner insists art is a game played against chaos and death, which men and women who play it must, of necessity, eventually lose. But artists continue to play, nonetheless, because of art's ability to build "temporary walls against life's leveling force, the ruin of what is splendidly unnatural in us, consciousness, the state in which not all atoms are equal." (1978:6) But while Gardner believes such activity to be a heroic assertion of human values in the face of the forces of dissolution, the Dragon sees such activity on the part of the Shaper and the people as an illusory denial of the ultimate truth of the matter: death and entropy are the final facts. The Dragon shares his cosmology with Grendel, saying all that exists comes and goes, and that in the sheer expanse of time everything will have come and gone in many different forms. Even he, the Dragon, will one day be gone. "A certain man will absurdly kill me," he says. (70) It is all meaningless, the Dragon says, these constant comings and goings are meaningless. Grendel challenges the Dragon, saying it is not possible for the Dragon to *know* this. The Dragon just smiles at his pupil, and suddenly Grendel "knew he knew it." (70) The Dragon then makes the case for the universe being nothing more than a grand cosmic accident, where dustspecks manage to combine and evolve and, over time, take on many different forms: there is that dust which is sensitive, there is that dust which seeks a "good time," there is that dust which prays, etc. The Dragon lets out a hollow laugh before delivering his final judgment: as for the end of it all just "pick an apocalypse, any apocalypse." It is with manic glee that he expresses his stark vision, chilling in its lack of hopefulness.

Grendel is not entirely sure whether to believe the Dragon or not, for he can also hear, in the back of his mind, the Shaper's harp. Finally, the Dragon tells him to do what he will; if he prefers to become a part of the Shaper's world then he should do so. Be a monster in their world, the

Dragon tells Grendel, be that by which these human beings understand and define themselves. Improve them and stimulate them, if you will, drive them to the comfort of their poetry, spur them to the enlightenment of their science, scare them to seek the protection of their gods. By all means be a part of the Shaper's world, the Dragon concludes: "Scare him to glory! It's all the same in the end, matter and motion, simple or complex. No difference, finally. Death, transfiguration. Ashes to ashes and slime to slime, amen." (73)

One result of Grendel's visit with the Dragon is that a charm is placed on Grendel rendering him inviolate from the weapons of the Thanes. Physically invulnerable, he now finds himself even more isolated from Hrothgar and his men. Before, when he would fight with them, there was an equality of relationship that existed—the actions of either could result in injury to the other. The gift of inviolability changes that. Like an impassible god, Grendel can now affect the lives of the Thanes but they can have no physical affect on him. He misunderstands the gift at the beginning, thinking it to be an advantage. Instead, he comes to realize it made him even more solitary and lonely than he was before.

Taking the Dragon's words to heart, Grendel figures to "scare [them] to glory." The best way to make a mockery of the people's Shaper-inspired confidence, Grendel finally decides, is with an attack on their meadhall. Grabbing seven of Hrothgar's men as they sleep, the monster eviscerates them and devours them in front of the others. Curiously, the carnage he has wrought gives him a sense of joy; he is transformed. Where before he had hung in the balance, drifting between what he knew the world to be on the one hand, and the emotionally compelling conjurings of the Shaper on the other, he now sees himself as the center of his and Hrothgar's world. For now, reborn, he knows himself to be "Grendel, Ruiner of Meadhalls, Wrecker of Kings." (80) But he also knows himself to be very, very lonely. On one level, Grendel allows himself to be caught in the net of the Shaper's songs, and on that level the Shaper's vision of the world becomes the people's vision of the world. On another level, Grendel becomes his own storyteller giving his own commentary to the songs and actions of both the Shaper and the people of Hrothgar's community. Whether his vision of the world is to be accepted is not a question faced by the Shaper, by Hrothgar, or by Hrothgar's people, for they have no access to Grendel's thoughts. Rather, it is the *reader* of the novel *Grendel* who will decide which vision is to be accepted, for it is only the reader of the text who has available both renderings of the world.

Grendel doesn't have to wait long to demonstrate his contempt for the heroic ideal advocated by the Shaper, as a Thane named Unferth confronts Grendel in battle. It is clear Unferth is there to fulfill what he believes to be a noble quest: he would marshall all of the virtues espoused by the Shaper and slay the monster that had brought death and destruction to Hrothgar's meadhall. Whether he survives the battle or not, Unferth would be a hero. A mocking Grendel chooses to taunt him, saying that heroes only exist in poetry. While polishing an apple, Grendel teases Unferth by noting how difficult it must be to be a hero, with everyone watching him, measuring him, seeing if he is still heroic. Must be difficult, Grendel says, though the rewards of gaining the respect of men—not to mention easy success with admiring women—may make the burden worthwhile. Unferth is not amused. Angered, he lifts his sword and prepares to attack the monster. Grendel laughs, then throws an apple at him. In fact, Grendel throws a barrage of apples, so many that Unferth is unable to get near the monster. Instead, Unferth's nose is bloodied, and our would-be hero is left screaming and thrashing and crying the tears of a young boy. "Such is life, . . . Such is dignity," is Grendel's summary of the battle. (85–86)

To his surprise, however, Unferth does not give up, but trails Grendel to his lair. There, Unferth tells Grendel what it is to be a hero, saying no one will know, here in Grendel's cave, whether he died at the hands of the monster or fled the scene like a coward. Only the two of them and God would know the truth of what happens, Unferth tells him, and that is part of what it is to be a hero. Grendel is growing tired of the whole affair, particularly the boy's use of the word "hero." But true to his heroic vision, Unferth is unfazed. "Except in the life of a hero," he says, "the whole world's meaningless. The hero sees values beyond what's possible. That's the nature of a hero. It kills him, of course, ultimately. But it makes the whole struggle of humanity worthwhile." (89) Grendel's final act of ridicule comes when Unferth says one of them will die that night. Not true, Grendel says. Instead, the monster tells Unferth he will be carried back to the meadhall unharmed. There could be no worse torment for Unferth. When he is returned, the monster makes sure to kill the two guards so no one would mistake that Unferth is being purposely spared. Instead of being a hero, he becomes the man who is carried back to the meadhall by Grendel. Instead of a hero, Unferth becomes the object of resentment on the part of those who have lost loved ones to Grendel. Henceforth, whenever Grendel would attack the meadhall he would see Unferth charge at him sword in hand, and Grendel would always spare him. Unferth is shamed because he is the one who is always spared; his life becomes one of frustration and anger. "So much for heroism," Grendel concludes. (90)

Despite Unferth's bitter destiny, what he has to say to Grendel about heroism bears notice. It is Gardner's position that Unferth's naive heroism can be criticized as being too sentimental and too romantic, that it neglects the basic truth that "life's potential for turning tragic is a fact of our existence." (1978:45) Nonetheless, he would also affirm the basic intuition of Unferth's statements about heroism and the artistic vision that led him to want to emulate the heroic ideal: namely, as he argues in *On Moral Fiction*, that art "designs visions worth trying to make fact." (100) What Gardner attempts to do in his fiction is provide models to be emulated, but in such a way that life's tragedies are also enumerated in the overall accounting of human life. In doing so, he approaches that notion of "peace" that Whitehead sees as a culminating insight, a culminating wisdom, into the nature of things.

Grendel continues his attacks on Hrothgar and the Thanes, and does his best to make a mockery of their poetically informed world view. He even embarrasses the King's new wife, Wealtheow, in the crudest of ways—by exposing her nakedness—after seeing how beloved she is and hearing the Shaper's songs of love and virtue inspired by her. Grendel intends to kill her, then thinks not to, that it would be as meaningless to kill her as it would be to let her live. But Wealtheow does have a curious affect on him, and he is somewhat changed by her presence. As he thinks about Wealtheow he is of two minds, hung in the balance (note this is in chapter seven, with the seventh sign of the zodiac being Libra, the Balance). On one hand, unreasonable as it sounds, he truly believes her to be not only physically beautiful, but a truly good and caring woman. This leads him to resolve to kill himself, for the sake of the person he used to be before completely coming under the influence of the Dragon. In his posthumously published *Stillness and Shadows* Gardner has a character give a theory of human behavior that is germane here:

> "We have an idea of ourselves, when we're kids: noble-hearted, honourable, unselfish. It's a beautiful image, and in fact it's true—it's the truth about us—but we betray it, or the nature of the world betrays it. We betray it again and again, one way or another. We can't do what's decent. Our commitments prevent it, or it's beyond our means. There are only so many causes you can die for, only so many good women you can love with all your heart, and even the best twist you downward, limit possibilities, limit your potential. So we lose touch with ourselves, turn our backs on the image, believe ourselves to be the ugly thing we've by now half-proved we are. The image is still there, the shadow we cast into the future when we were young. It's still there haunting us, beckoning us toward it; only now there's that second shadow, the shadow, behind us, of all those acts unworthy of us." (268–69)

A part of Grendel recognizes that shadow of failed possibilities of "the Baby Grendel that used to be," (110) and indeed that may be the very shadow that earlier he identified as his only friend, but in the next instant, dismissing these thoughts about Wealtheow and his more innocent self, he changes his mind for no particular reason.

Watching Hrothgar and the Thanes, Grendel begins to see that religion is becoming empty ceremony for most of the people. One night, sitting among the stone gods of the community while the rest of the people are asleep, Grendel hears someone approaching him. It is an old priest named Ork who, like the Shaper, is blind—but also like the Shaper, full of vision. Grendel confronts the blind priest, claiming to be "the Destroyer." Ork falls to his knees whimpering his worshipfulness, then proclaims that he is the only person still living who has bothered to think through all of the mysteries. Intrigued, Grendel orders him to speak what he knows of the King of the Gods. In language that is taken directly from Whitehead, Ork delivers an impassioned treatise which describes God as the actual entity by which the varied eternal objects obtain their graded relevance to each stage of concrescence, and that apart from God there can be no relevant novelty. The words used are philosophically technical, but Grendel sees that Ork is moved to tears by his blind vision. God's purpose, the awed priest says, is to evoke novel intensities of feeling in the creative advance of the world, and thus God is a lure for our feeling. Grendel doesn't know what to think as the priest raises his hands and begins to weep openly. God is the ongoing urge of desire, Ork continues, which establishes purposes for all creatures, but also an infinite patience, a tender care that nothing in the universe be vain.

These statements are pure Whitehead, taken from his book, *Process and Reality*. What is interesting in the scene is the contrast between the language and the emotion being displayed. The language, as anyone familiar with the neologisms used by Whitehead knows, is quite technical and seemingly sterile. Yet, as those same Whiteheadians also know, Whitehead is at times poetic in expressing his philosophical views. A good example is Chapter Two of Part Five, "God and the World," in *Process and Reality*. What stands behind the technical philosophy is an idealized and romantic, indeed Wordsworthian, vision of the world that, for its adherents, is a truly satisfying harmony of emotion and intellect, of mind and spirit. Indeed, many theologians have turned to Whitehead as an inspiration in their theological work, resulting in a movement known as Process Theology. While Ork's language, like many a "process theologian's," is couched in the technical jargon of "process" thought, what is clear is that the basic intuition of life's process is central to his theological vision, as evidenced by his actions.

It is a cardinal principle of Whitehead's thought that language is a simplification of the full bodily flow of feeling that is our experience. The danger, of course, is when the language of a particular philosophical perspective is engaged by rote rather than being the best expression possible of genuine intensities of feeling. This is one of the problems, as Kierkegaard notes, of the "disciple at second-hand." Gardner gives his own expression to the problem as he has other priests, awakened by Ork's tearful explication, gather around him. Grendel hides when the others approach, but he hears their disbelief and their mocking as they dismiss, for a variety of personal and doctrinal reasons, Ork's account of talking with "the Great Destroyer." Religion, like the Shaper and Grendel, seeks to give people an understandable and believable picture of the world, and as such, religion may be life-enhancing or life-denying. These priests, representing a variety of theological views, are a corollary in Gardner's mind of the literary critics who do criticism by rote, without genuine intensities of feeling. For Gardner, the debasement of art and religion, of literary criticism and theology, are all of a piece.

The novel ends with the coming of Beowulf to the shores of the Thanes. After seeing Beowulf and his friends being greeted, Grendel realizes that this stranger is somehow different from other men. In the final chapter of the novel, representing the twelfth sign of the zodiac, Pisces, or the Fish, Grendel and Beowulf finally confront one another. The Christian symbolism of the Fish as Christ, a symbol of rebirth at the end of the zodiacal cycle as the seasons turn toward renascent life, is not lost on Gardner. As Grendel kills several men in the meadhall Beowulf waits his opportunity. When it comes, Beowulf grips Grendel and pulls the monster's arm from its socket, causing Grendel to scream from the searing pain. What is worse, Beowulf is at Grendel's ear mocking his approaching death with the words of the Dragon. Grendel knows now that his life is coming to an end, and that the man killing him represents a new age inspired by art to noble acts. This art will be like fish, on which people might be nourished until the spring of their rebirth. The world, instead of being a dark plain of mechanical and meaningless human action, will become green with new life, with sperm building up new generations of men and women, each adventurously seeking to make her way in the world. These new generations will manifest in their own lives those poetic virtues that allow men and women to live together profitably in community, sharing in the joys of harvest as well as the pain of suffering and defeat. Their lives will have meaning. Even in death they will be remembered by family and friends for their good deeds, for the love and compassion they showed others, for their acts of valor and their many acts of kindness that helped bind them together as a community.

Grendel has lost. It is the Shaper's vision which wins out in the novel. Whether the Shaper's vision wins out for the reader is for the reader to decide. For those critics who believe *Grendel* to be a nihilistic black-humor satire of contemporary life, Grendel is the truth-teller of the story and the Shaper but an illusionist. It is Grendel's world view they take at face value, and the Shaper's they ridicule as naively idealistic, or, more cynically, as a self-serving manipulation of art as a social control over the ignorant and easily manipulated masses. For those familiar with Gardner's work, Grendel, though in some ways worthy of our sympathy, is, nonetheless, a monster, a destroyer of human accomplishments and a mocker of human endeavors. *Grendel*, a wonderful entertainment full of wit and wisdom, is, in the end, a statement of the worth of human life, as envisioned and projected in the art of a culture, and emulated in the lives of men and women in a community. What we are as humans, in other words, has much to do with those patterns we come to see in the world around us, with the stories we tell ourselves about ourselves.

CHAPTER IV:
Pilgrimages Toward Death

One cannot help but note how a number of characters in Gardner's fiction undergo a pilgrimage of some kind, almost always initiated by that character's expectation of death, fear of death, or guilt because of a death. Sometimes the pilgrimage is a personal return to one's roots and one's past, characteristically marked by a painful period of self-examination, while at other times it is a movement toward a dimly perceived future of novel possibilities. Two of Gardner's characters typify what may be called a pilgrimage toward death: James Chandler from *The Resurrection* and Agathon from *The Wreckage of Agathon*.

The Resurrection opens with a brief prologue set in a cemetery. There, the reader is informed that among the tombstones is one, newer than the rest, engraved with the name James Chandler. Years of time pass in the few pages of the narrative prologue; those visitors to the grave who were once old are now dead, and those who were once children are now adults. The reader is not told who they are. We are simply, and provocatively, informed that they are among the "few who are not fully reconciled." (1)

The chronological beginning of the story describes a 41-year-old James Chandler, secure in his position as an Associate Professor of Philosophy with numerous books and articles to his credit. He is happily married with three small children, all daughters. Recently, he had published a monograph with the ironic title, "Am I Now Dreaming?" which he considers perhaps his finest work to date, a perfect combination of both form and substance. Aside from his professional career, his personal life is also deeply satisfying. His home, with wife Marie and daughters Karen, Susie and Annie, is a comfortable refuge where he could enter his study, light up his old pipe, take hold of his pen, and continue his intellectual adventures. James is especially happy with his wife, a practical woman he met when she was one of his students. It is she who organizes not only the house but their social lives, the children, and the bills. She is the one who really decided that James would make the move from Oberlin College to Stanford. At the height of his personal and professional powers, however, James Chandler's world comes crashing in on him. He is informed by his doctor that he has leukemia, and has but a month, perhaps two or three, to live. Reifying modern philosophy's "mind/body problem" in a brutal way, Chandler's world of rationally balanced systematization, characterized by a life of the mind, disintegrates when his body engages in the chaotically uncontrolled production of white blood cells. Rather than spend his remaining days in a San Francisco hospital, it is decided that he and his family will travel back to Batavia, NY, the home of his youth.

The motif of returning to one's home, or returning to the place of one's youth, is a common one in American literature, and usually signals a return to one's roots, to one's community, to one's innocence, or, more broadly, a return to Nature. As a return to one's beginnings, revisiting one's home can be seen as a return to a place of testing and self-realization, which is then followed by either renewal or personal demise. To the extent a return can be seen as an approach toward some historically and/or socially-based reality that will act as a criterion by which to assess and judge one's life, the return is a pilgrimage. Victor and Edith Turner have given helpful insights into the significance of pilgrimage in the social life of a community. In their text, *Image and Pilgrimage in Christian Culture*, they describe pilgrimage as "exteriorized mysticism," with mysticism being an "interior pilgrimage." (7) James Chandler experiences both in his return to Batavia. The Turners also point to the centrality of the concept of "liminality" in understanding the dynamics of pilgrimage. The term is borrowed from Arnold van Gennep, who demonstrates a three-fold succession of phases in traditional "rites of passage": 1) *separation* of an individual or group from the dominant structures of the community, 2) a *liminal* period in which the individual or group is in an ambiguous state, "betwixt and between all familiar lines of classification," no longer what they were and not yet what they are about to become, and 3) the *aggregation* of the individual or group back into the recognizable structures of the community. (Turner, 1978:2) Liminality, in the hands of Victor Turner in particular, has become a fruitful concept by which to analyze social change:

> Liminality is now seen to apply to all phases of decisive cultural change, in which previous orderings of thought and behavior are subject to revision and criticism, when hitherto unprecedented modes of ordering relations between ideas and people become possible and desirable. . . . [I]n the limina throughout actual history, when sharp divisions begin to appear between the root paradigms which have guided social action over long tracts of time and the

antiparadigmatic behavior of multitudes responding to totally new pressures and incentives, we tend to find the prolific generation of new experimental models. (2–3)

Anthropologically, Turner refers to the liminal stage of ritual as a time when, in a traditional rite of passage, the initiand is "a *tabula rasa*, a blank slate, on which is inscribed the knowledge and wisdom of the group." This knowledge, he points out, "is not just an aggregation of words and sentences; it has ontological value, it refashions the very being of the neophyte." (1977:103) Clearly liminality, especially as Turner uses it as an analytical tool in understanding social change, is a mark not only of transition but of potentiality. Liminality is a time of new possibilities, a time of new perspectives. To use Whitehead's term, it is a time of *novelty*. James Chandler is in a liminal state, betwixt and between life and death. It is a time of transition as he prepares for his own death, but it is also a time full of potentiality as he seeks a perspective from which to understand, holistically, the purpose and meaning of his life, and of life in general. He is not a neophyte undergoing a traditional rite of passage, however, and is thus not a *tabula rasa*, a blank slate. His own intellectualism will not allow him to accept an authority outside of himself. Knowledge and wisdom is for Chandler the academic discipline of philosophy and the intellectual venture of human thought as recorded through the centuries by great thinkers and scholars. It remains for him to learn the knowledge and wisdom of the community-at-large, a knowledge and wisdom that is grounded more in the rhythms of nature than in the quality of one's library.

Once back in Batavia, Chandler recognizes that the town of his youth is considerably run down, and is, in fact, undergoing a kind of death of its own. Riding in a cab after his cross-country train trip he sees deteriorating buildings and unkempt grounds at once great houses. He is somewhat frightened by the decay, as the orderly town of his youth appears to be regressing back "into a buzzing, blooming confusion." (18) Taking a roundabout route from the train station, James sees street after street being ripped up for sewage repairs, and stores in old Polish and Italian neighborhoods that are run down and neglected. It is hard for James "to square what he saw with what he remembered." (19) The huge Massey-Harris manufacturing plant stands empty, a monument to an earlier time of prosperity. Even the cemetery across the street from the factory looks unfamiliar to James, though the lawns and the hedges are maintained as they had always been. At some level, though, in a mysteriously profound way, James knows that things are not what they were.

James returns to his boyhood home, where his mother welcomes him and his family. Soon, in conversation, his mother tells him of the deaths of friends from his youth, as well as of the deaths of some of the old and familiar names of the town. This, in turn, evokes in him memories of the deaths of his own father and grandfather. Though surrounded by semes of death, there is one glimmering idea in his mind: destruction is also a sign of progress. Paradoxically, there is also that part of him which rebels at this intellectual panacea. Yes, there is omnipresent change; and yes, nature is never spent. Yet, in the midst of his own hurtling toward death, something more needs to be said, something about that which is more permanent. "Something must be certain," Chandler says out loud to himself, else to what end do we live our lives?

Encouraged by his mother he visits the home of the Staley sisters, where he was taught to play the piano as a child. There, hung on a wall in its usual place, is a painting titled "The Old Mill," done by a younger Emma Staley and enjoyed by James when he visited as a child. He remembers how the painting would cause in him a dark mood of apprehension as he looked at the disintegrating remains of that painted mill. Now, looking at the painting, he mocks himself for having been so easily impressed as a youth. In his "intellectual expertness" all he sees now is that amateurish layering of paint and varnish to attain a certain sentimental effect. His own analytical intellectualism, it would seem, allows him to see only the surface texture of the painting, the technique of the brushstrokes. Then, unexpectedly, he undergoes an epiphany of sorts: the old mood he used to experience as a child rises in him again, and with it an ardent yearning for his childhood past, for that youthful freedom filled with possibilities which, because of his illness, is no longer possible. James stands a long time in front of that painting, squinting his eyes, trying to explore all the dimensions of his ambivalence. Perfectly still, he is at one and the same time intensely dissatisfied and exuberantly joyful, both extremes of passion which, in his search for Aristotelian moderation, he thought he had left behind many years before. His exploration of what he feels takes a characteristically intellectual bent, however, and he ultimately decides what he is feeling is not an emotion at all, "but its shadow, a violent waking of memory." (52) In other words, it is the memory of his reaction to the painting that he is experiencing rather than the painting itself. At least, that is what he tells himself. After all, how could such an amateurish painting engender real emotion in a sophisticated thinker like himself? The incident is a prolepsis of later incidents in the novel.

At the Staley's he meets Viola, a fanciful niece of the Staley's enamored of Romantic notions of death draped with sentimentality. She would just as soon take her leave of this chaotic world of human foibles and emotions and give herself over to the cool certainties of death. As a six-year-old she saw her father in a casket, and recalls feelings more of envy than of grief. Then, spurred by memories of the nuns telling her that her father was now happy she, too, wished to be dead, or at least to be a nun, remote from life. It is Viola who comes to James's rescue when, weakened by his disease, he collapses on a street. From this intercession she becomes a part of the Chandler's lives, watching over the three children while Marie cares for James in the hospital. It is in her interaction with the Chandlers that the reader sees Viola's constant attempts to transform life into dramaturgy. Viola's constant evocations of death[1] and her attempts to "dramatize" life are taken to extremes, all in an effort to control her interactions with people and thereby avoid the risks associated with true human contact. It is her inability to get beyond her role-playing, her inability to get beyond "a melancholy Romantic vision" of death (Butts, 1988:7), her inability to make herself truly vulnerable to another person that makes it impossible for her to reach out to another in an act of real love. There is a sense in which James and Viola are mirror images of each other: James being raw intelligence unable to integrate his own feelings, and Viola being reliant on feelings and maudlin sentimentality without the acuity of reason. It is in their interaction that each will learn important lessons about life and love.

Marie, James's wife, emerges as perhaps the strongest character in the novel. Whereas James is living the life of intellectual knight-errant, Marie is the one paying the bills, feeding the family, watching over the children, and organizing the household. It is Marie who has her feet planted squarely on the ground. Her mind was of a more practical bent than James's, and she could never compete with her husband verbally. At one point, in the midst of a marital spat, James rebukes her by calling her a "damned pragmatist." (99) In fact, she is more of a muse. While James has his words and his wit, she has intuition into the nature of things. James is often quoting R.G. Collingwood: "Man's world is infested by *Sphinxes*, demonic beings of mixed and monstrous nature which ask him riddles and eat him if he cannot answer them, compelling him to play a game of wits where the stake is life and his only weapon is his tongue." (101) Death, to some extent, is always present, threatening to come into James's and Marie's lives at the most inopportune time and "eat them." Their respective approaches to the ongoing presence of death as the inexorable end toward which all life moves differs, however. James feels he can, by his wits, keep death at bay. For her part, Marie is one who hopes the day can be won "not by wits but by intuition, which is to say, one of those beautiful and good artistic people who fight courageously on the side of mankind and always get eaten in the end." (101)

This less articulate, but intuitively perceptive and experientially powerful approach is evidenced in a passage where James recalls a memory—or perhaps a dream, the author of "Am I Now Dreaming?" isn't quite sure—of him and Marie on a hillside with their two oldest daughters and another married couple. Marie is eight months pregnant with their third daughter at the time, and the other children are gamboling about the hillside while James and the married couple are debating the "truthfulness" of a collection of grotesqueries seen at an art exhibit they had recently visited. Marie hadn't said anything all afternoon:

> . . . but all at once she said, with enormous conviction: "This is much truer—whatever that may mean." All three of them looked at the same time, as if perfectly understanding her, at the miles of gray-green, dwarfish trees, the cliffs to the right, the ocean falling away to Japan, the wide storm of birds. What Chandler, at least, had seen that instant was Death, wheeling and howling, and two little girls in red coats running down the path toward them, laughing. Marie sat like a Buddha, her legs out like sticks, her red hands resting tranquilly on her enormous belly. Her face was full of light. (155)

In an inarticulate act of intuition Marie has a profound vision of life, taking note of the ongoing presence of grotesqueries like death, but also recognizing the strength of men and women to create an orderly and meaningful space in which friends can share, children can grow, and love can be expressive of our best hopes. There may be grotesqueries in the world, but so long as we love and have faith in one another the grotesqueries are not *here*, and they are not *now*.

James, facing death, is having his own visions, mostly of a mysterious old woman in his dreams. Vaguely associated with death, this brooding presence is forcing the writer of "Am I Now Dreaming?" to question his own heretofore unquestioned abilities to distinguish appearance from reality. Confronted with forces he does not fully understand, and without the emotional and intuitive tools to address the questions now impending on his life, he retreats to that which he knows best: he decides to write a philosophical essay. The essay is never finished. At a time when he is asking questions about ultimate things, he is realizing there is no stable center which can act as a criterion of ultimacy. The one tool that had served him well all his adult life was intellectual reason, and in spite of the fact that his disease is sapping his strength, and perhaps distorting his reasoning, logic and philosophical method are the only tools open to him that he trusts. He still works to consider every possibility, hanging on to objectivity and scrutinizing arguments and evidence in order to identify bias. It is an important matter, for if the search for philosophical truth is a game, a "search for the center of a labyrinth that for all he knew might have no center," (161) then it certainly is the case that the stakes are far higher this time around.

In the midst of his writing James recalls a time from his childhood when he stayed at his grandfather's house. The room in which he stayed was perfectly ordered and distinct, and, though separated by a pane of glass, the world outside his bedroom window was also ordered and distinct. Echoing Whitehead, his was the experience of the unity of all the objects he saw about him. It was not until later that he developed a vocabulary to explain his joyful feeling of the interpenetrability of everything within the universe. Though distinct from the universe, there was a mystical sense in which he also felt himself the sum of it. At the same time, however, he also felt a threatening presence, both in those regions of country he could not see beyond the horizon, and even in his room at night when the clear distinctions of daytime would break down. Thus one morning he walked beyond his grandfather's orchard fence to get a glimpse of what was over the horizon. After walking a ways he looked back. The house was gone, and all of a sudden that comfortable and stable world of his experience crumbled. He starts to run, desperately seeking his mother, his father, some protection from this world gone strange. He then falls between two fence posts, tangled in barbed-wire. The next memory is of tractor lights bearing down on him, and the voice of his father calling his name. Though scolded for leaving his grandfather's house, James recalls the moment as a happy one, for "the world was in order again. Even though he didn't yet know where he was. The center had reestablished itself." (134) As an adult, James has centered his life on his ability to reason, his ability to exercise his intellect, and his ability to mesmerize the *sphinxes* with his wisdom and wit. Now, being pressed by time and with his life in the balance, he is beginning to feel the anchorless drift of his own intellectualism. There is no father to give him a sense of "centeredness" this time around. But why is that? What has happened in those intervening years that has left him adrift when he is most in need of assurance?

There is a sense in which Chandler and Viola are able to come to an insightful understanding of the human condition by watching and thinking about children's games. Early after his return to Batavia, while walking with his daughters, James stops to watch children from the blind school play baseball. The children would follow strings leading them to the bases while the fielders would react to the jingle made by the ball as it moved through the field. Sometimes they would run into each other, but the game would continue. At one point, however, the ball comes to rest in the outfield before a player can reach it. Suddenly, with no noise being made, the game comes to an abrupt halt. The players then moved toward the outfield, toward where they last heard the jingle, on their hands and knees, seeking the ball so their game could continue. Later, Viola watches the Chandler children play a game in which Karen would roll an imaginary pair of dice, then inform her two sisters what the dice show and how many steps they may then take. Viola is mystified at the fact that there appear to be no rules for the game, at least no obvious rules. And it isn't as if Karen has all the power, for all one of the other children would have to do is walk away and that would be the end of the game. But they continue to play, and be happy when they win and out of sorts when they lose.

The children's games are actually a kind of analogy. To the extent that modern life has no intellectual or spiritual center giving men and women a sense of direction and meaning, they are like the blind children who have lost the ball because it no longer "jingles" and gives them a sense of direction and purpose, a sense of what one must do from one moment to the next. Significantly, the children do not throw up their hands in despair, cynically telling each other of the sheer folly and meaninglessness of it all. Rather, as a community they face the challenge by getting on their hands and knees to work toward reestablishing the game (i.e. life) they are in the midst of playing (i.e. living). As for the game Viola witnesses, she is puzzled by the lack of rules, but mostly because of her inability to understand human affairs. She simply cannot perceive the reality that is playing itself out right before her eyes, which is the reality of love that the Chandler sisters display for each other. What connects them together in the game is not the rules, or Karen's power to compel them, but their experiences as a family, their lifetimes of depending on one another.

By the end of the novel James comes to realize the truth of his daughters's game: it's not the rules, the "empty celebrations" that are the reality to be celebrated. When earlier he visited the Staley sisters, politely shaking their hands and recalling with them the past, he is struck by how much he enjoys "this game of empty forms, communion as pure gesture." (56) But he comes to see that such rules and gestures, like the philosophical notion of "beauty" about which he tries to write an essay in his remaining days, are important only to the extent they can organize our thoughts and emotions and dispositions toward that which was truly real and important: "It was not the beauty of the world one must affirm but *the world*, the buzzing blooming confusion itself. He had slipped from celebrating what was to the celebration of empty celebration." (229)

The novel comes to a climax as Viola, who has dramatized in her mind a tragic relationship with James, expresses her love to the professor. She runs a risk in doing so; for one, she has left her senile Aunt Emma alone in order to speak with James, and for another she risks being spurned. In fact, James does reject her declaration of love, telling her she is far too young to know what real love is. She is stunned. Through unbridled sentiment and her tendency toward dramaturgy, she had observed subtle signals she believed he had made toward her and built it into a love affair. She cannot believe he is not enveloping her with his arms. Nonetheless, it is an important moment for Viola for she risks making real contact with another, regardless of the awkwardness of her misguided attempt. When she recovers from the blow, she realizes the potential danger from her Aunt Emma being left alone and immediately excuses herself to race home.

It is an important moment for James as well. Suddenly feeling he has insulted Viola with his immediate—almost scoffing—rebuff, he intuitively realizes he must find her and affirm that within her that sought to reach out to another human being. At the risk of his own life, terribly weakened from his leukemia, he goes out after her. When he reaches the Staley home he realizes the worst has happened. In Viola's absence the senile Emma Staley has wandered away. Viola is completely distraught, with the double blow of being rejected by James and feeling the impending guilt of Emma's probable death. For Viola, it appears an apt, though brutal, confirmation that reaching out in love to another person just isn't worth the risk. But here James intercedes. Barely able to crawl himself, he takes hold of Viola's ankle and, with his final breath, says simply: "No harm. It's done us no harm." (232)

For Gregory Morris these final words are tragically pathetic. He believes Chandler's final moments a "virtual act of suicide" which has hurtful repercussions on his wife and family. (1984:36–37) A more satisfying interpretation is that of Leonard Butts, who sees Chandler's final act as a new acceptance of "what it is to be human, to exist as a part of the whole." (1988:12) As such, Chandler's pilgrimage toward death, and more importantly his pilgrimage toward an understanding of what is truly important and real in his life, is completed. It isn't the incisive philosophical argument, but the reaching out with charity toward another that allows that other the opportunity to live fruitfully, passing on that legacy of charity to future generations. Chandler's sacrificial act of reaching Viola with the message, "No harm. It's done us no harm," is an act of love helping to free Viola from the crippling guilt that might otherwise have resulted at being the cause of Emma's death. Viola recognizes her debt to James, and it is she who, as described in the prologue, continues to visit his grave.

Gardner provides two other possible interpretations of Chandler's final act: the one negative, and the other positive. In the novel's last two sections, which occur immediately after Chandler's death scene, we read of the philosophical musings of a hospital patient who had met James earlier, and we also read of a piano recital given by Elizabeth

Staley which is attended by Marie and her daughter, Karen, as well as many other members of the Batavia community. The hospital patient, John Horne, mouths the overblown verbiage of existentialism to the effect that the one unalterable law of the universe is blind force. Sounding much like a latter-day Grendel, he tells James of how he broods on the world, with the result of his broodings being that men and women should either rush to their graves or, if willing to maintain the absurdity, provide illusions by which they and others can be distracted for a time. Horne's is an interpretation of human life that Gardner believes is given full voice in contemporary fiction. If accepted as a true vision of life, then Chandler's final act is, indeed, a pathetic act of no meaningful consequence.

An image Gardner prefers to bring forward, however, is contained in the last section of the novel, where a community of men and women are gathered together for a piano recital. On one level, there are the conventions and ordinary rituals of human behavior that are observed before and during the recital. They are but the form by which those gathered might interact and meaningfully express themselves. The recital is an annual event, attended by former music students of Elizabeth Staley, former vocal students of Maud Staley (though Maud no longer teaches voice), and former painting students of Emma Staley (though she, too, no longer gives lessons). At the conclusion of the regular program by her current students Elizabeth announces it will be the last recital and that she would now play a piece to end her piano teaching career. Those gathered know they are witnessing an important event, the sad yet splendid culmination of an age. As she begins to play it is obvious that, though her notes are precise, she has no inkling of the force of her strokes. Karen whispers to her mother that Miss Staley is deaf, to which her mother orders her to be still. All of those gathered "sat listening, perfectly silent, as if deeply impressed, staring at their knees. And whether or not they knew what it was they were witnessing, no stranger could have said." (244) Certainly Karen could not have said. Just as Viola could not see the love that bound the Chandler children together in their manifestly absurd game of dice, just as Horne could not see the love that bound people together in their manifestly absurd game of life, so Karen in her youth cannot yet see the love for Elizabeth Staley that binds the community gathered around her as she announces, in effect, the beginning of her absence from the community—her death.

It is love that endures and sustains a community, and in the case of Marie and Karen and the other children it is the love within a family that allows them to continue from moment to moment when one loses a loved one. It is a love that feels pain at the time of death. It is the real pain of loss rather than theatrical sentimentality, as Viola needs to learn. But it is also felt very deeply at the level of intuition and emotion rather than just intellectually, as James comes to learn in his pilgrimage. It is a love which allows men and women to continue to live meaningful lives in the midst of tragedy, and continue the process of vibrant rebirth and growth in the midst of death and decay.

The Wreckage of Agathon presents a situation somewhat similar to *The Resurrection* as the protagonist, an ancient Greek philosopher named Agathon, awaits his death in a prison cell. A contemporary of Solon of Athens and Lykourgos of Sparta, he has been jailed in Sparta presumably because he is a corruptor of youth and a friend to the rebelling Helots. It is also the case that he is generally offensive in his bodily appearance (he is unwashed and slovenly), in his physical actions (he often scratches inappropriate places in public and has an unending tendency toward flatulence), and in his verbal comments (he makes untoward suggestions to cleaning ladies). Agathon, in short, is a disgusting dirty old man awaiting his execution accompanied by his one pupil, a young man named Peeker. Agathon is, for Gardner, a most obvious caricature of what becomes of a person who gives his life over to pure intellect. He is divorced from his own emotions and intuitions, and has abdicated any sense of social obligation to the wider community. It is the world of ideas to which Agathon owes allegiance, and his physical decay and social ineptitude are merely outward signs of an inward insensitivity and lost sense of personal meaningfulness. He was not always so hideous, as a series of flashbacks make clear.

While in his cell Agathon is given ample time to reflect on how he came to be jailed. Narratively, 19 of the 34 chapters are recounted by Agathon, allowing the reader to participate in Agathon's inner dialogue, the story he tells himself about himself. The remaining chapters are from the perspective of Peeker, allowing for a more critically distanced assessment of Agathon's actions and thoughts. In the process the reader is given a vivid picture of the philosophical training undergone by Agathon under the tutelage of Klinias, a skeptic who taught, among other lessons, that ethics is nothing but a set of general rules, and that the first rule is to not let specific cases be decided by these general rules. When a young Agathon objects to such a view he is admonished by his teacher that "ethics is like medicine, to be taken only when needed." (68) This sort of sophistry tends to view truth as perspectival and loyalty as a myth imposed by means of social skulduggery. Echoing Heisenberg's "uncertainty principle," Agathon relates a story to Peeker of an encounter with a jailer, to whom he expresses his more mature philosophy. He tells the jailer that everything is modified by our studying it: things that are poked by sticks behave as if poked by sticks, and light that is bounced off stones or bent in water or squeezed through holes act as if bounced and bent and squeezed. In short, we create by our own actions what we later come to call knowledge. He goes on to ask the jailer if he has considered that sundials are not instruments to measure time, but the means by which to create time. The world of Agathon is a postmodernist one. Indeed, echoing contemporary post-modernist literary critics, Agathon maintains that "what matters in the world . . . is not so much what is true as what is entertaining, at least so long as the truth itself is unknowable." (33) In another passage, sounding as if it could have come straight from Paul de Man, Agathon claims, "what matters in natural philosophy is not so much what is true as what is interesting." (111) While many literary scholars will hear in Agathon's words echoes of de Man and other postmodernist critics, that would only be a part of the picture. Actually, it is Whitehead who is being woven into the text, for it is he who, in *Process and Reality*, argues that the emphasis on a proposition's truth value in logic, and the moral valorization of truthful propositions, have disguised the actual role that propositions play in the real world. As a result, the important role that false propositions play in our lives has been obscured. The fact is, Whitehead suggests, "in the real world it is more important that a proposition be interesting than that it be true." (259) For Whitehead, propositions act as lures for feeling. Even false propositions are efficacious in that they act as a lure for one to think of new possibilities, and thus open up novel ways of experiencing. As stated, Agathon can hardly be faulted for interpreting this approach as allowing only for a thoroughgoing relativism. Perhaps this is as far as his teacher, Klinias, could go on the subject. What is not taken into account is Whitehead's next line: "The importance of truth is, that it adds to interest." (259) Agathon discards notions of there being real truth, whereas Whitehead's philosophy of organism places immense cultural value on the concept of truth.

The fact that Whitehead is being woven into the text is further evidenced by the several references to Agathon's love of "adventures and ideas," which reflects the title of a Whitehead book, *Adventures of Ideas*. Peeker imagines Agathon eventually being dragged out of his cell and killed, which will mark the end of Agathon's "adventures and ideas." (32) At one point Agathon tells Peeker that he loves his wife second only to "adventures and ideas." (58) Nearing death, Agathon considers his life to have been one of sickness as well as discovery, which he realizes is that same old tension that he believes has plagued him all his life: "brute adventure, the brutality of idea." (221) The most prolonged discussion of "adventures and ideas" occurs when Agathon tries to seduce Iona, a revolutionary whose husband, Dorkis, is planning to assassinate the tyrant Lykourgos. While a dissatisfied Agathon sits beside her, desirous of new experiences—whether it be Iona's body or some other adventure—she asks him if he is aware of what Dorkis is planning to do. He is, and he tells her he thinks it is a very bad idea, though when pressed by her he cannot explain why. Iona has her own theory to explain his opposition. She accuses Agathon of wanting Lykourgos to remain alive despite his ongoing oppression of the Helots: "He interests you," Iona chides, and goes on to say that Agathon cares more for interesting ideas—even ones as monstrous as Lykourgos—than for the sufferings of people. (99) Agathon thoughtfully asks: "An adventure or an idea?" (100)

Agathon then proceeds to explain to Iona the difference between "adventures" and "ideas." He tells her it reflects a cliché he has used since his first youthful attempts at metaphysics. Adventures and ideas, it turns out, is his answer to the question of ultimate reality. An adventure he likens to someone punching you in the face, while an idea is the nominal concept of "punchness." Iona challenges him again, saying that can't possibly be the full content of his view of life. Her smiling, scoffing indignation fuels Agathon's desire for her, but he answers that he does indeed believe it, and that Dorkis does as well. It's what Dorkis means "when he talks about riding reality like a bird," Agathon tells her. (100) Iona, quite serious now, says only a part of Dorkis believes that: "What's best in him makes adventures *out* of ideas. Such as killing Lykourgos." (100) Agathon thought that very clever, but quite wrong.

Cynically, he ridicules her: "So people can *change* reality." She snaps back: "Of course they can." (100)

One reason Agathon is driven to accept a thoroughgoing moral relativism is that to reject it would lead to an unbearable guilt on his part. One of his fellow students was Konon, who argued that the world is one large mechanism devoid of inherent value. Even religion, he argued, was a machine, a mechanized linquistic system of words and gestures that are used to comfort the weak, to be abandoned as soon as the weak are comforted. For Konon, everything that exists physically is substance, while all the rest is "drunkenness and illusion." (141) It is a position Agathon himself comes to adopt over time, but with an existentialist twist. Konon's actions in the world, however, belie his stated philosophy, for he decides he will attempt to kill Solon, a friend of Agathon's and the leader of Athens. He did not succeed, and was himself executed. His mistake, Agathon tells Iona, was that he confided his plans to a friend. Iona guessed correctly that the "friend" was Agathon. "But what made him tell you?" she asks. "Didn't he know how you felt about Solon?" "Oh, he knew," Agathon tells her, "but we were friends." (142) Agathon tells her more about their friendship, about how they grew up together, learned at the knee of Klinias together, would lay in bed together sharing their thoughts, had arguments, would sometimes fight. But through it all they would always see each other as brothers. Once, when Agathon stole something, Konon lied to protect him. It's what a brother would do. When Konon shared with Agathon his plan to assassinate Solon, Agathon tried to talk him out of it. Instead, Konon elicited from him a promise not to tell anyone. "I gave him my word," Agathon tells Iona. "He knew what that meant to me, in those days. He felt safe." (143) Instead, he told the authorities, and Konon was arrested and executed.

There are a number of possible explanations as to why he informed on Konon, but the one most understandable to him was simply that he did it by impulse. When, some days after his betrayal, guards came to make an arrest, Konon gave him an uncomprehending look, his face twisted and, despite it all, trying to manage a smile. After being told of his betrayal, Iona also gave Agathon an uncomprehending look which he was not able to understand. He tried to understand what his true feelings were about his betrayal of Konon, and found that he really hadn't any feelings about it at all. In an act of self-preservation, it seems, Agathon needs now to maintain a personal philosophy that rejects the relevant moral imperatives, and hence meaningfulness, of such incidents. To accept a world of real love, of real obligation, of real commitment, of real ethical imperatives, and of real truth, would mean he would have to bear responsibility for his actions, as well as the subsequent guilt. Agathon's is the easy way out. Iona, as a revolutionary able to justify ideologically a number of brutal acts under the guise of "justice," "equality," and other political slogans, also manages to avoid any sense of guilt for her actions. Her's, too, is the easy way out. Gardner, having to deal with his own sense of guilt at the death of his brother, is well aware of the allure of various escapes from responsibility and guilt. More importantly, he recognizes the moral abyss such escapes represent. Rather, he seeks to show through his fiction how guilt can be a part of a meaningful world of human action. Iona's husband, Dorkis, embodies a model of human behavior that acknowledges evil, recognizes responsibility, and is able, nonetheless, to integrate guilt into the meaningful living of a life.

Leonard Butts has an insightful discussion of Dorkis in his work, *The Novels of John Gardner*, but even his excellent presentation does not fully appreciate how Whitehead is being weaved into the text. Butts has a particularly arresting and appropriate line when he writes: "If Agathon were more receptive to the rituals and verities in life, he could learn to recapture the innocence and genuine feeling of his youth by emulating Iona's husband Dorkis. . . . Dorkis always presents a case not for the revolution . . . but for the 'buzzing blooming confusion' of life itself." (69) Agathon takes an immediate liking to Iona and Dorkis, the former because of her beauty and sexual allure and the latter because he was more interested in playing with ideas than in eating. Agathon concedes later, however, that this first impression of Dorkis was wrong. While imprisoned and awaiting his own execution, Dorkis lovingly chides Agathon for being what Agathon previously had believed Dorkis to be: "You care more for knowledge than for people." (167) Dorkis is described as being from the East and of mixed Ionian and Asian blood. He worked among and was deeply respected by the Helots, those who had become virtual slaves of the Spartans. For their part, the Spartans trusted Dorkis, having put him in charge of selecting and preparing food at the Spartan communal eating halls. He is described by Agathon as having a kind of religiosity hanging about him which made him seem incorruptible in the eyes of others. But his is not a completely otherworldly or ascetic religiosity, for among Dorkis's fervent interests are sex, wine, and the other pleasures of life. On one level, Dorkis "sounds" a lot like Agathon, which is probably why Agathon misinterprets Dorkis's love of ideas as the same as his own. At the party where the two first meet, Dorkis, slightly drunk, begins to extemporize on our understanding of coherence, essentially saying that the world is not some metaphysical One, but rather a bundle of truths competing with each other but each, nonetheless, true. A priest nearby scolded him, saying that as mere mortals we ought not to presume knowledge of such divine things. Dorkis had little patience for such people, for they would have men and women dampen their curiosity and abdicate their human responsibility to think and to know. Continuing his own thoughts on the matter, he counsels the others at the party to avoid pursuing any one, solitary, single truth, looking neither to the left or right, for that's when life will suddenly come crashing in on you. Then, contrary to what he had said just a moment earlier, he claims that it is fair to say that nothing is true, that life, and life's experiences, are forever changing shape. "There's a sense in which as soon as you learn its laws it's become something else," Dorkis says. "It wreaks havoc on ethical theories." (46) Life is but air, he claims, and one must be able to make their way in life much as a bird makes its way in the air, riding it and going where it takes you.

What Dorkis says does sound similar to what Agathon believes, but of course Agathon eventually comes to corrupt and vulgarize Dorkis's statements. At first, Agathon believes they are in full philosophical agreement, which is why he insists that his love of adventures and ideas is what Dorkis means by riding reality like a bird. But Dorkis clearly means so much more than Agathon realizes. Only in his cell, reflecting on the events leading to his own arrest, does Agathon come to realize how different he is from Dorkis, though he still cannot fully grasp what the difference is. In fact, the major difference between them is that while both accept the Whiteheadian notion that truth is perspectival, Agathon concludes there is no truth while Dorkis concludes truth exists nonetheless. It's a bit like Gardner's insistence on moral realities amidst the hoots and hollers of his critics. Agathon goes the way of many moderns today, and finds himself living in a world he believes devoid of meaningful values. Dorkis opts for a world view which recognizes and accepts human limitations to knowledge, yet nevertheless experiences the world as a dynamic process of ongoing life where values are worth defending and one's ethical actions have meaningful consequences.

In his cell, Agathon recollects a conversation with Dorkis, and in the process comes to see they are, indeed, quite different in their approaches to the world. Speaking of the tensions and political changes that were occurring around them, Agathon quotes Solon as saying it is all a great adventure. Even so, he wonders how human nature could have allowed the kind of political life that exists in militaristic Sparta. Dorkis merely responds that human nature is very much overestimated, and that there is little *reason* behind it all. "All you can do is act," he says, "and pray." (152) This leads to a discussion, with Iona joining in, of the role of the gods. Agathon wants to know if the gods hear his prayers, to which Dorkis smiles and replies that somebody must be listening to them. Iona then challenges him: what if the gods are not listening. Dorkis answers his wife, but intends it for everyone present: Are we ready to look at life and accept its challenges without the gods? His question is met with silence, until Agathon wonders out loud just what it is that the gods do. After getting Agathon to admit that he does nothing except on impulse, Dorkis asks if he knows from whence these impulses come. Agathon, in his own way, is impressed:

> His absolute and simple faith filled the room like autumn light, like a sea breeze. Even when his ideas were crazy, the man had sophrosyne, as they used to call it in the old days. There are men in this world—wizards, witches, people like Lykourgos—who spread anger, or doubt, or self-pity, or the cold stink of cynicism, wherever they walk: the sky darkens over their heads, the grass withers under their feet, and, downwind of them, ships perish at sea. And then there are men, here and there, like Dorkis. God only knows what to make of them. Their ideas are ludicrous, when you look at them. Peasant ideas. Childlike. But what tranquility! (152–53)

Agathon, being a good philosopher, then queries Dorkis as to whether the gods are the source of all the bad impulses as well, or just the good ones.

> He wasn't put off. Benevolent. "There's a sense in which there are many gods," he said, "and they're not all in agreement. But what we call good, with our little minds . . ." His eyes snapped away. "There's a sense in which nothing is evil," he said, calm as spring. "To certain people, everything that happens in the world is holy." (153)

Agathon is partly responsible for the death of Dorkis, as well. When Iona goes to Agathon, knowing he has a secret hiding place for a book of philosophy written by his teacher, Klinias, he tells her of the place—a crypt with a secret entrance. Informed of the place, she directs many of the Helot revolutionaries to hide there, but they are discovered by the Spartans. After pouring oil into the crypt and lighting it, the Spartan soldiers allow the Helots to be burned to death, striking down any who manage to make their way out of the crypt. After the soldiers have left and loved ones have come to reclaim the Helot dead, Agathon is busy trying to rescue what remains of the scrolls on which his master's philosophy was written. In his rush to save the book, he would stumble over and step on the remains of those Helots who had died, much to the increasing anger of those relatives who had come to claim the dead. Agathon would bring some of the parchment out, see under torchlight that they are completely destroyed, then turn and push his way through the mourners seeking to find more remains of his "dead knowledge." Once the Helots realize that Agathon's crazed actions are because of the loss of a book instead of the loss of a relative, they turn on him. Seizing him, they drag him to the ground and, in a frenzy, beat and kick him. It is Dorkis who keeps the crowd from killing him, telling them that they have no idea how much Agathon is anguished at the loss of his book. He tells them all to go home and mourn their own dead. It is this act of saving Agathon, witnessed by some Spartans, that eventually leads to his unmasking as a Helot revolutionary leader. Ultimately, it leads to his arrest and execution.

Agathon visits a shackled and badly beaten Dorkis just before Dorkis is to be executed. There, Agathon comes to see that there is something that makes Dorkis seem more dignified and more powerful than any of his jailers. The Spartans confront Agathon, thinking he may have instructed Dorkis in the writing of a political tract that has helped fuel the rebellion, a tract actually written by Iona. Both Dorkis and Agathon work to keep Iona's role secret and thus save her life, but for different reasons. Dorkis wants to save her from painful suffering while in jail; Agathon self-servingly wants to remain free so that he might become her lover. Dorkis, a man willing to suffer for the sake of another, is executed in the public square. In language suggestive of the crucifixion, Dorkis is described as wearing only a loincloth, and full of a patience and grace that was humbling to see. Agathon believed at that moment that Dorkis was the embodiment of tenderness, and that Dorkis had somehow undergone a transformation in the process. Suddenly, Agathon realizes what it is that makes Dorkis different from all the others—certainly from himself: "He had accepted evil. Not any specific evil, such as hatred, or suffering, or death, but evil as a necessary principle of the world—time as a perpetual perishing, space as creation and wreckage." (198)

The acceptance that Dorkis manifests in his final moments is the attainment of that "peace" which is described in Whitehead's work. It is a recognition that for life to have adventure and creativity it must, as a necessary principle of the world, also have failures of adventure and creativity that may, in its broadest terms, be called evil. Nevertheless, human creativity as part of an overall process of creativity can bring great joy and meaningfulness to people, though that joy and meaningfulness be in a constant flux of "perpetual perishing"—perhaps to be positively prehended by subsequent generations of occasions (i.e. creation) and thereby kept alive, or perhaps to be forever lost (i.e. wreckage). The "wreckage" of Agathon is that, though having available to him many of the same ideas as Dorkis, he cannot forge a creative advance of those ideas that would lead to increased creativity and satisfaction. Dorkis, by contrast, recognizes the perspectival nature of truth, but is nonetheless able to forge a creative advance with those ideas to bring about a renewed sense of joy and meaning to human life.

In an important section near the end of the book, after Peeker and Agathon have been set free by the revolutionaries, Peeker overhears some of the talk among the Helots. One of them asks to hear the story about the "Snake," which is the revolutionary moniker for Dorkis. Then a huge man, like the Shaper and the priest Ork in *Grendel*, blind, begins to tell those gathered that "Snake" was the only truly religious person he had ever known. Echoing the *shema* of Judaism, he tells them that "Snake" loved God with all of his heart and with all of his soul, and that he also turned that love to man. The blind man repeated to them the prayer "Snake" would always say before meals, a prayer with many recognizable elements of the Lord's prayer in Christianity. Whether or not Dorkis actually did use this prayer before meals is not the point, and will be left for Form Critics to decide. Dorkis's life and death becomes a model by which other's lives are enriched. It should be noted, however, that many gathered and listening to the blind man immediately point out that Dorkis did not show any love for the Spartans, and that Dorkis is for them an exemplar of one who uses violence as a tool of Justice to resist oppression. No one can completely predict exactly the influence one actual occasion may have on a subsequent high-grade actual occasion. Truth, after all, remains perspectival. Regardless, it is Dorkis, as a past actual occasion, who provides a datum to be prehended by subsequent generations. In the scene where the blind man describes "Snake" we have, as Gregory Morris perceptively notes, Dorkis being "transmogrified into art." (1984:48) The fact that Dorkis's prayer, as passed down by the blind man, is suggestive of the Jewish *shema*, the Great Commandment of Hillel/Jesus, and the Lord's prayer—all advanced by impractical thinkers who did not fare well in their Spartanesque worlds—is an indication that the ideas creatively advanced by Dorkis will take root and thrive.

CHAPTER V:
Isolation by Guilt

The last of Gardner's novels to be published while he was still alive is *Mickelsson's Ghosts*, which appeared in 1982. Read by a literary critical audience still smarting from Gardner's broadsides in *On Moral Fiction*, it was not well received. Indeed, many armed themselves with what they took to be his moral argument and used it as a bludgeon by which to judge the work, thus attempting to label Gardner's novel as "immoral." Aside from the fact such reviews usually made use of "straw man" versions of his position, it is clear many literary critics were lying in wait to pounce on Gardner.

For his part, Gardner was also smarting from the angry denunciations he had received after publication of *On Moral Fiction*, as well as from accusations of plagiarism in his books about Chaucer and *The Sunlight Dialogues*. This is unmistakably on his mind in the writing of *Mickelsson's Ghosts* as he provides a quite unusual "acknowledgment" section at the beginning of the novel. In it, he indicates a wide variety of sources, some important and some picayune, and also includes a catchall: "The diligent will perhaps discover that I have additional literary sources, more than I know myself." (vii) When Mickelsson, the protagonist, complains in the novel of the reception a book he had written—a "short, quite brilliant book (in Mickelsson's opinion)"—he remarks that "[h]e had not guessed how 'controversial'—that is, how deeply hated in some quarters—his book would be." (75–76) Without doubt, this is Gardner's voice as well, with his reaction to the controversy surrounding *On Moral Fiction*. At one point, Mickelsson characterizes the chairman of the Philosophy Department in which he teaches as a member "of the enemy camp" who sees Mickelsson's success as fraudulent, "a shrill pitch to the philosophical right." (191) This is almost the exact language John Barth uses in criticizing *On Moral Fiction*.[1] It is arguable whether this "personalizing" of his literary feuds detracts from the novel itself. The general consensus is, however, that *Mickelsson's Ghosts* is not one his better novels. Nonetheless, certain themes we have come to associate with Gardner are still present in the work.

In *Mickelsson's Ghosts* he returns to the use of an overly intellectual philosopher as the protagonist. The fact that Gardner writes the entire text using the limited third-person point of view may explain his use of a philosopher as the main character. The "common man" as protagonist, which will be examined more closely in the next few chapters, simply cannot maintain an inner dialogue of the depth and intellectual sophistication he requires in fictionalizing the issues he wants to address. To make the points and explore the issues Gardner chooses to fictionalize, and maintain that vivid and continuous dream toward which he strives, he must have a character who believably might have the sorts of thoughts capable of addressing these philosophical issues. In a limited third-person text, a point of view he avoided and has advised in *The Art of Fiction* was too limiting for a long piece of fiction, the reader has access only to one character's thoughts. Thus Peter Mickelsson becomes the epistemic center of the novel.

Unlike James Chandler and Agathon, Peter Mickelsson is not facing his own immediate death. He (much like Gardner about this time) is in the throes of a deep despair as he begins to realize his life has been one of unfulfilled promise. As a Brown University tenured professor he was once a rising star in philosophical circles. As the novel opens, however, his philosophical outlook is little attended to, and he now finds himself teaching at what is, to his mind, a backwater university (i.e. S.U.N.Y. Binghamton). Where once he had a wife and two children and, for all intents, was the model of family life, he is now divorced with no ongoing relationship with anyone. Once trusted and respected as one who fulfilled his commitments, he is now hounded by the Internal Revenue Service for unpaid taxes and regularly bounces checks in the town in which he lives. In short, Peter Mickelsson's life is disintegrating.

His disintegration is manifest in his attitudes and actions. Once the strict moralist, he now finds himself fabricating information for a loan application to buy a farmhouse. Those who had known him to be a strict moralist in the past would, no doubt, be shocked at the change in his character. Where once he publicly played the role of moral jeremiad against an age losing its moral direction, striking out at any—from the political left or right—who would advocate the "frivolous and false," now he finds himself filling out a loan application that is, in fact, "a pack of lies." (31) Another measure of Mickelsson's disintegration is his killing of a dog while walking one night. Encountering the growling canine, he swings his cane expecting it to back off. To his surprise the dog does not move at all, and the cane crushes its skull. Back in his apartment he wonders what he ought to do next. Were he the ethicist he always had imagined himself to be he would simply call the police and explain what had happened. Indeed, back when he lived in Providence there would have been no question—he would have gone to the police at once. But then again, were he in Providence he would never have killed the dog. Before realizing it, he is developing justifications for himself, at one moment saying it was an accident, at another buoying himself with the fact that the city's leash law was on his side. But he is not entirely comfortable, for he begins to realize that his self-justifications are starting to sound a little like the explanations used to defend Heidegger's actions during the Nazi regime in Germany. His feelings of guilt are but a prelude to his thorough sense of debasement when, as a result of his actions, a man dies when Mickelsson robs him.

The early portion of the narrative, in addition to introducing the reader to Mickelsson and his plight, tells the reader of Mickelsson's search for a house in the country. Partly, he needs the house as an escape from the turmoil of the university and the city, but also an escape from the I.R.S. and the lawyers for his ex-wife. In time, he finds a farmhouse in the Endless Mountains of Pennsylvania. When first seeing the house he is struck by the "strange, charged light" of the place, "a luminous, strained, Scandinavian unearthliness." (21) Indeed, stories are told that the house is haunted by ghosts of the Sprague family, who were earlier owners. The mother and father were rumored to have had a child who was murdered, which then led to their own deaths in a double-suicide, or, to hear some tell it, a murder-suicide. There were also stories of incest. Another legend held that the house was once owned by Joseph Smith, the founder of the Church of Jesus Christ of Latter-Day Saints—the Mormons. In any case, Mickelsson likes the place, deciding to buy and renovate it.

Beginning to feel his own mortality, Mickelsson finds that he is thinking more and more about that favorite old problem faced by philosophers since the time of Heraclitus: "the perishability of time," (60). It is the intractability of time, this perpetually perishing, that troubles him, recognizing as he does that no matter how vital a life he lives he could vanish at any moment from the earth. Unsettled by some unnamable grief he feels is edging toward him, he sees life as a dark space in front of him into which he cannot peer. Despite this ineffable feeling of dread, tears well up in his eyes as he stands for the first time in his newly purchased home, with the hills of the Endless Mountains surrounding him. A train sounds in the distance as Mickelsson reflects on his current understanding of the world: Life is a constant giving and taking until the day of one's death. "That was Nature's process." (61)

Indeed, after a lifetime of seeing even the most magnificent of Ozymandian structures—like those grand hotels he used to visit in the Adirondack mountains—give way to the brute unconscious forces of Nature, he finally, grudgingly, is learning to accept it. "That was the real death, Mickelsson thought." (61) Nonetheless, renovating the house would become, for Mickelsson, a denial of that death that is "Nature's process." To bring about the renewed life of that old farmhouse was to give Mickelsson a renewed sense of control over time and circumstance. Simply, the renovation of the house is a metaphor for Mickelsson's own life as he struggles to regain control. When all seems to be crashing down around him he thinks that the house may yet save him. If he can bring the house back, then there is hope that, despite his circumstances, he might be saved as well. There is a lesson about the house it takes a long time for Mickelsson to learn, however. It has to do with the ghosts Mickelsson dimly feels are present in the house. Until he comes to understand this ghostly presence he continues to find himself more and more isolated, more and more out of control.

One of Mickelsson's new students is an intense young man named Michael Nugent. A former engineering student, Nugent had recently suffered a number of personal setbacks leading to an attempted suicide. Recovered, he decides to major in philosophy. At their first meeting Nugent is the eager student, saying that while the rest of the department did "analytical" philosophy Mickelsson was the only one doing "real" philosophy. The philosophically more sophisticated—and cynical—Mickelsson advises the young man not to pin all his hopes on philosophy. In fact, he invokes the name of perhaps the most revered analytic philosopher to make his point, citing Wittgenstein's insistence that it is in getting the questions just right, rather than in finding answers, that philosophy manages to do its best work. Nugent has difficulty fighting through his emotions as he tells Mickelsson that philosophy is the only discipline that even remotely cares about real knowledge. The other disciplines, he says, for the most part just "tinker" around. Becoming even more emotional, he acknowledges that some philosophers may not have lived up to their promise, which leaves Mickelsson wondering if the young man is referring to him. Nugent immediately follows up by saying that philosophy, in and of itself, is the "highest activity known to man." Then, somewhat disconcertingly to Mickelsson, the young man concludes: "I don't mean to fawn or anything, but I know how you live, I know how much—." (15) With the dawning recognition that what he is being confronted with is a disciple, Mickelsson snaps at the young man: "It sounds to me like what you're looking for is religion." (15) Though reluctant, Mickelsson allows Nugent to sign up for his course on Plato and Aristotle.

A second student, Alan Blassenheim, is bright and popular, and usually at the center of classroom discussions. Early in the semester Mickelsson is lecturing on transcendent ideals, arguing that they have been put to less than democratic uses in the past. Maybe, he concludes, Plato—the father of transcendent ideals—needs to go. Pursuing the matter, Mickelsson asks his class if ideals exist in physical reality or only in one's fleeting emotions. In other words, do ideals exist "out there" or "in here." This leads Blassenheim to comment that to argue that the ideal is "in here," as Darwin might, would mean that there is nothing that is intrinsically good about those creatures which survive except the mere fact of their survival. Mickelsson quickly recognizes the argument because it is one he developed in one of his own books. Blassenheim continues by asking whether reality doesn't have innate standards, and that perhaps a creature increases its ability to survive as it approaches those standards. Mickelsson, seeing the argument drifting toward the vitalism of Henri Bergson, cuts it off, saying it amounts to an argument that Nature is trying by "random evolutionary groping" (91) to find those standards, much like a roomful of monkeys trying to stumble onto *War and Peace* while sitting at some typewriters. Mickelsson concludes the session with a statement to the effect that anything constant must both transcend experience as well as be immanent in experience, and under those circumstances we might at least have a chance of finding out the truth of the matter. This last comment is Whitehead's view of Plato, where he argues in *Adventures of Ideas* that "Plato's cosmology tends to a fusion of the doctrines of imposition [Whitehead's term for transcendence] and immanence." (122)

The same general subject crops up again in a later class session when Blassenheim tries to make the case that both Plato and Aristotle are fascists, imposing their own class values on others. His particular point is against Aristotle's notion that "reason" ought to be the guarantor of philosophically correct and appropriate argument. As counterexamples, Blassenheim cites a number of cases in which it is appropriate for people not to be reasonable. Pressed by Mickelsson, Blassenheim finally asserts that while logic has its proper uses, it can also be used by the unscrupulous to trick people. Mickelsson then asks how normative statements may ever be justified if not by reason. Blassenheim answers with an incisive comment that goes to the heart of the moral vision of the novel, and indeed in much of Gardner's fiction: "I don't know," the young man says, "maybe the wisdom of the whole community, like, tested over time." (185)

Blassenheim then launches into a discussion of Kierkegaard's rendering, in *Fear and Trembling*, of the Biblical story of Abraham's sacrifice of Isaac. Insisting Kierkegaard got it wrong, he argues the purpose of the story is not about a person going against prevailing custom and tradition when he hears the voice of God. Rather, the young man says, what is important is that it reconfirms the community's stance against human sacrifice. What makes the story important, in other words, is not God's whisper in Abraham's ear, but the fact that the story is told generation after generation of Abraham's *not* sacrificing his son. Blassenheim's answer emphasizing the role of the community, rather than the usual existentialist twist to the Abraham story, impresses Mickelsson, an easy mark for notions like "common sense" or "community." His eyes would grow sentimentally moist at such times, though, in fact, he despised most every community of which he had ever been a part. Like James Chandler, Mickelsson has so intellectualized his experiences that he is out of touch with his own, more vague, feelings and emotions. Thus, concepts like "common sense" and "community" are just that: mere intellectual concepts. The rest of the novel shows Mickelsson's discovery, at a more primal and intuitive level, of what community actually means.

After mumbling a few words at the blackboard about Whitehead and Aristotle, all quite confusing and irrelevant, he acknowledges the risen hand of Nugent, who proceeds to take over the class. He opens with a verbal backhand at Blassenheim by saying it is wrong to dismiss Plato and Aristotle out of hand, suggesting that those who do so dismiss the idea of perceptible truth simply because they would rather not have to think. The argument Nugent then gives is actually the Aristotelian "virtue ethics" argument made by Alasdair MacIntyre in his book, *After Virtue*. Essentially, it states we are at a terrible disadvantage in coming to terms with notions like "virtue" because we have, over time, lost knowledge of essential concepts and practices which inform our use of the term. MacIntyre uses a "thought experiment" to ask what would happen if there were a technologically-driven world catastrophe. And what if, seeing the end toward which technology had been used, survivors came to blame the scientists and technicians for the holocaust, thus leading to riots, the destruction of scientific laboratories and libraries, and the executions of physicists, chemists, and engineers? MacIntyre suggests that what would remain is the scientific equivalent of the "Know-Nothing Party." Basic underlying principles of science would be lost. While those remaining alive would still use the language of science, they would nevertheless lack knowledge of the essential concepts and practices which stand behind the language. When they then attempted to *do* science, what they would be doing would no longer *be* science. He claims that philosophical "analysis," as well as "existentialism" and "phenomenology," would be of no help. Each of these methods of philosophical investigation is ineluctably tied to the present, he argues, and thus unable to discern that there is anything wrong. "The hypothesis which I wish to advance," MacIntyre writes,

> is that in the actual world which we inhabit the language of morality is in the same state of grave disorder as the language of natural science in the imaginary world which I described. What we possess, if this view is true, are the fragments of a conceptual scheme, parts which now lack those contexts from which their significance derived. We possess indeed simulacra of morality, we continue to use many of the key expressions. But we have—very largely, if not entirely—lost our comprehension, both theoretical and practical, [of] morality. (2)

MacIntyre then proceeds with what he believes to be the only effective approach—an historical analysis—to re-contextualize the language of morality. One of the points of emphasis in his explication is the return to the Aristotelian notion of a teleological dimension to human character, a notion fairly ignored today. There is, MacIntyre insists, in the original language of virtue a telos, or goal, toward which men and women move and strive

In Nugent's hands the argument is used to advocate the belief that truth is discernible. In fact, he argues that it is the belief that truth is discernible that allows men and women to keep going, that makes life possible. Each person, he asserts, needs a sense of dignity, a sense that she is on the side of the angels. However, between Aristotle's time and ours the use to which we put words like "morality" and "virtue" has shifted, such that today we really don't know how they used to be used. As a result, moderns sometimes appear as if concepts like "virtue" have simply ceased to exist. "That's why Kierkegaard's so strange," he says,

> "he tells you right out that he doesn't know what virtue is, maybe it's God's whisper in Abraham's ear, maybe it's just insanity. I think he"—Nugent nodded toward Blassenheim—"might be right: maybe Aristotle really didn't *know* what he was talking about, he was just saying how we do things in Athens or wherever. . . . But if he really *did* know what he was talking about, it seems like it must be lost knowledge, like how to fuse brick." (187–88)

The arguments presented by Nugent and Blassenheim are worth noting because they reverberate throughout the text as Mickelsson seeks to find his way in an ever more confusing set of circumstances. Indeed, one reason he finds himself in a set of philosophical contradictions, and unable to see his way clear, is because there are "missing pieces" to his world view (e.g. a telic dimension to life, understanding that he is internally related to a past actual world). Further, it becomes clear that one of his difficulties is his attempt to ground his own ethical actions on strictly intellectual reasoning, thereby denying any connection between ethics and "the wisdom of the whole community, . . . tested over time." (185)

Much of the novel's plot has to do with Mickelsson's burgeoning relationships with two women: Donnie Matthews, a 17-year-old prostitute, and recently widowed Jessica Stark, a faculty colleague who teaches in the Sociology Department. Donnie's appeal is strictly—and strongly—to Mickelsson's erotic desires. She is to become for him an indispensable presence symbolizing all things "lubricious and lewd, meretricious, debauched, profligate and goatish." (338) She is Mother Earth in which he wants to plant his seed. Jessica is for him more of a Platonic ideal, "the point at which the finite and infinite touch." (338)

As such, she provides a more mature attraction, and acts as a sort of "lure" trying to bring him back into the society of other men and women. The fact that he sees each of these women more as filling an intellectual category rather than as living embodiments of many complex characteristics merely demonstrates part of his difficulty.

It is the relationship with Donnie that ultimately leads to the death of a man Mickelsson robs. He notices one day, quite by accident as he is trying to enter Donnie's apartment from the fire escape, a huge fat man in another apartment counting stacks of money. Later, visiting Donnie, she tells him she is pregnant and wants an abortion. His first reaction is to question whether he is the father. Despite his belief that she is a prostitute with many customers—a perception she helped foster because, she says, he seemed to like it—she insists he is the only man with whom she is having sexual relations. Convinced he is the father, he then invokes his long-standing intellectual opposition to abortion. A third objection has to do with money: he simply doesn't have the funds to pay for an abortion. None of his objections sway Donnie. In a moment of abandon he decides to rob the fat man downstairs. Believing him gone from his apartment, Mickelsson breaks down the man's door only to find the chain lock is in place from the inside, meaning the fat man must be home. Roused from his stupor, the fat man lurches toward his dresser to get a gun. Suddenly, the fat man's mouth opens, he cringes, slams his fist to his chest and begins clutching at himself. He is having a heart attack. Seeing the man is dying, Mickelsson's first instinct is to run. But then he remembers the money. After a brief search he finds it, and only then leaves the apartment. As for getting help for the fat man—perhaps he would have if he were still living in Providence. Now, Mickelsson is no more likely to get help or call the police than he was for the dog whose skull he crushed some weeks before. Instead, he rushes to Donnie's apartment and heaves all the money on her bed, taking nothing for himself. It is the last time he would see her.

His sense of guilt over the death of the fat man—and an unborn child—paralyzes Mickelsson and leads him to feel utterly cut off from others. He comes to believe there is no longer anything for which to personally hope. There is a sense, however, that having nothing to look forward to allows him to experience a vaulting sense of freedom, and of being unafraid of the future. It must be said, though, that the facade of freedom Mickelsson tries to project hides, like a latter-day Raskolnikov, a crippling guilt. If he believes himself to be completely cut off from his community—and Mickelsson certainly does—it implies for a certainty the existence of moral standards, as well as criteria of appropriate behavior that judges Mickelsson's actions as ethically wrong. His difficulty is he cannot articulate in a purely rational way just what those standards are and how they might be justified. This is the dilemma in which he finds himself. Another implication: once he accepts the notion that there are standards, the real question for Mickelsson becomes whether, once a violation of a community's standards occurs, he might be reintegrated into that community. It is obvious Mickelsson believes he cannot. Blinded by his own intellectualism, he cannot see his way to an understanding of what it truly means to live in community with other men and women. What he does understand is companionship, and that his relationship with Donnie had only partly to do with sex. He understands that for life to be full and meaningful there must be "company, security, trust," (213–14) and not just sex. Having one's physical desires met, Mickelsson realizes, is not the same as being an integral part of that social give-and-take and felt obligation for the welfare of others that is a part of life-in-community.

Mickelsson's working on his house gives him the opportunity to reflect back to a time when, as a part of his parent's world, he was a member of a community. Of particular importance are memories of his father. He recalls, for example, how much time his father and uncle had spent doing various odd jobs on the farm. And in thinking of all the building and unbuilding they had done, he only now is coming to realize that it wasn't work for them at all, but play. It is a revelation to discover after all these years that the two of them had been playing all the while, whether it be working a field or making a wooden chest. It was play. In their own way, Mickelsson thought, they were artists. In comparing their lives to his own he begins to yield to self pity. How foolish his life seems to him now when compared to theirs. If there are "supermen," Mickelsson would think later while pondering Nietzsche, they are people like his father "who had given up thought long ago: men who simply acted—not out of pity but with infallible faith and love." (476) It was his father's sense of who he was, as well as his family and communal obligations, which grounded his father solidly in the real world. Speaking with Jessica one night, Mickelsson recalls his family, and his father, fondly. Though he thought his family somewhat queer, as many children do, he came to realize that his father was a truly good man who, when he was dying, was constantly surrounded by ever-changing numbers of friends and neighbors who admired him. Unsaid, but no doubt hovering over Mickelsson's words, is his loneliness and expectation of dying without anyone to mourn for him. He also tells Jessica about a psychiatrist he used to visit in Providence who tried to say his father was wrong to show only his best side. But Mickelsson comes to disagree with the psychiatrist. His father didn't merely show his noble side but was, in fact, a noble man, universally beloved. "It's good having a model of perfection," he concludes. "If you don't measure up, then you don't; but at least it's there, it exists." (322) Near the end, Mickelsson comes to realize another difference between him and his father: Though both had grieved during their lives, his father's grief had arisen from love over events he could not possibly have prevented, while his had arisen from guilt. In this, as in all things, Mickelsson knows his father to have been a better man. An example of the difference has to do with Jessica. Throughout his struggles in attempting to rebuild his life Mickelsson has the support of Jessica Stark. Yet, despite her concern and love, even she is spurned by Mickelsson at a time when she desperately needs his help. As one of the few non-Marxists in the Sociology Department, a move is on to have her removed from her position. Mickelsson could have helped stave off the "barbarians," but he does not. In the midst of his own troubles with Donnie, and with the death of the fat man, he simply abandons Jessica. In time, it becomes for him a further source of guilt.

There is another subplot. With all of these problems crashing down on him, Mickelsson believes his mind is beginning to slip toward insanity. There are these ghosts he keeps seeing in his house. At first they seemed just gossamer shadows moving at the fringes of his sight. Over time, however, the ghosts become more and more clear to him. While unsettling, they are giving his house a sense of history, a sense of a past, a sense that there were real people who lived there and left an imprint which has an effect even in the present. There is a sense in which these ghosts represent the ongoing life, the immortality, of earlier generations of people. This intuitive sense of the "objective immortality" of former residents begins to lead Mickelsson along new paths of thought, and ultimately toward a spiritual crisis, the catalyst of which is Nugent.

There comes a time when Mickelsson is shocked to learn Nugent has committed suicide. Much of his shock stems from the fact Nugent had seemed quite happy the last time they were together. In fact, Nugent even told him of an evening when he was sitting alone in his dormitory room reading a book by Wittgenstein. While Wittgenstein's words may have contributed to the mood, Nugent's vision is more nearly Whiteheadian. Nugent comes to tell Mickelsson of his vision "of a universe of infinitely precious glowing particles, every one of them necessarily *against* every other, that was the tragic law of individuation in space and time, but each and every one lit up by the ruby, emerald, sapphire, and diamond shine of God's consciousness." (422) Nugent's image is similar to a vision of Mickelsson's, written as a philosophical argument many years before while staying in the Adirondack mountains. It is an argument he eventually threw out as over-wrought nonsense, but it points to Bergson and Whitehead as metaphysical guides. Of course, metaphysics *is* nonsense in twentieth-century analytic philosophy. Mickelsson's argument, as he recalls it, was essentially that the "primal nut" of the origins of the universe was in some way Mind, but Mind unable to know itself. Not subject to time, space or matter, Mind simply had no way of knowing anything. Evolution, then, according to Mickelsson's vision, is the history of this Mind seeking to understand itself, or "God's rise into self-awareness." (482) It is Whitehead's "primordial nature" of God that is being described here, whereas God's "self-awareness" is, in Whitehead's terminology, God's "consequent nature." Thinking about it, Mickelsson tells himself it was the mood set by the mountainous surroundings that created the theory. He was an atheist, after all, and there he was writing like some apologist for God, though he knew his reflections could not be made to fit with classical theistic thought. Nonetheless, there was a kind of pleasure in writing with seeming confidence about God. Later, back in Providence, he was unable to well up that religious-like feeling again, so he simply abandoned it. It was a theory, though, that he felt he ought to have mentioned to Blassenheim as a comfort to his religious idealism. He also thought he ought to have mentioned it to Nugent. It would have provided a sense of meaningfulness to each of his students, he thought, even if he had come to think it all a bit silly.

Nugent's philosophical vision, in which he sees the world as individual entities competing with one another, each heading toward an irreversible entropic end, and Mickelsson's, in which he envisions this process of competition within an overarching orderliness in the Mind of God, are, when taken together, an intuition of that "wisdom" Whitehead speaks of as "peace." Thinking about his current problems, Mickelsson begins to grasp that despite his earlier rejection of the theory, it gives him a sense of peace and serenity to think that his despair—an emotional state which is often described, particularly by existentialists, as the most intense and terrible of human experiences—is really nothing more than a perfectly natural process. Seeing life from this perspective helps to lift him from his doldrums; recognizing that life is "perpetually perishing" provides a kind of balm that, in an unusual way, soothes him. Some succumb to despair, but it is possible, he is just now beginning to realize, to come through despair and be a stronger person because of the experience. He imagines himself now to be like a grandfather unable to help when his grandchildren begin to cry over what, to them, is some immense grief in their lives. Mickelsson "felt not anger at the bitterness of life or dismay at his inability to help, but only cool sympathy, a guarded Boethian amusement." (523) Incredibly, only a few moments later he is holding a shotgun and giving serious thought to suicide. He stops cold when he thinks of his father, guilt washing through him once again. It is the moment at which he hits emotional and spiritual bottom. Having put the gun down, he finds he is sick to death of his unhappiness, the ugliness of his life, and his feeling of being trapped. He is left pondering how it is that he could be at one moment almost serene in his despair and at the very next moment drowning in guilt and dread.

 The reason why Mickelsson can at one moment stoically accept hurt and loneliness as a normal aspect of life and then suddenly be prepared to kill himself in despair is because his life is not grounded in a larger community. His notion of community is only intellectual. While a recognition that tragedy and feelings of despair are, indeed, a part of that encompassing view of life Whitehead speaks of as "peace," Mickelsson cannot attain this Whiteheadian ideal until he is able—emotionally and spiritually—to become a part of a community. It is the felt obligations of a community that help rein in those thoughtless, impetuous acts like suicide, and give an individual personal and societal goals to be attained beyond those inevitable moments of grief and despair. Mickelsson is, in many respects, like the characterization of human beings given by the Abbot in Gardner's story, *In The Suicide Mountains*:

> "We human beings glimpse lofty ideals, catch ourselves betraying them, and sink to suicidal despair—despair from which only the love of our friends can save us, since friends see in us those nobler qualities we ourselves, out of a long familiarity, have forgotten we possess. That, of course, is why the suicidal person is so difficult around his friends. . . . 'Get rid of all friends,' thinks the poor mad suicidal, 'and the end becomes a possibility.' So he insults his friends, teaches himself to hate them; yet even then secretly he hopes they will save him; even then he reaches out, bawls for new friends! . . . [T]o be human is, inevitably, to hate oneself sometimes, to hunger for the perfect stability and in a way the perfect justice—or at least perfect punishment for our numerous imperfections—called death." (103)

It is Mickelsson's lack of friends and lack of community that allow him seriously to entertain notions of self-destruction. But there is also the memory—the ideal—of his father, an ambivalent ideal which both rebukes Mickelsson for who he has become and invites him to change. If only he could get back to who he once was, a child in a loving family in a supportive community. Famous philosopher that he is, his life no longer seems much worth living.

At this, his weakest and most aggrieved moment, he receives a fortuitous telephone call from Donnie. Now living in California with her family, she calls to tell Mickelsson that she had the abortion, but also to tell him she had thrown the money—which she called blood-money—into the ocean. She mostly called to tell Mickelsson what a wonderful person he was, and to thank him for all he had done for her. Recalling the night he robbed the fat man, she told him that his face was absolutely ashen when he came to her apartment with the money, as if he had died. Seeing him, she knew how horrifying the whole experience had been for him. The fact that he did not keep any of the money made even more of an impression on her, realizing the risk he had taken just for her, as if he had given up his life just for her. So she is thankful. She recognizes his sacrificial act in trying to help her, but also recognizes her feelings of guilt at being the indirect cause of another man's death. Ultimately it has led her to make important changes in her life. She tells Mickelsson that she is an entirely different person now, that she is "born again" and attends church regularly, and no longer works as a prostitute. Movingly, she tells him that she misses him, and tears well up in his eyes. It is what he most needs to hear. At the most serendipitous time, here is someone who cares enough to reach out to him. And the message she brings is particularly pertinent. Not only does she express her thanks, indicating that he has done something positive for another, but she also is someone who has managed to turn her life around. Perhaps there is hope for him yet.

The novel reaches a climax when, after Donnie's call, Mickelsson receives an unexpected visitor. A philosophy colleague of his, Edward Lawler, comes by to see if Mickelsson, who has missed many days of classes while in the midst of his depression, is all right. After being assured everything is fine, Lawler begins speaking about the terrible murders and fires and suicides that have been happening. This leads to a discussion of the Mormons. Lawler, a Mormon himself, tells Mickelsson that one of the murder victims, a chemistry professor who also happened to be a friend of Nugent's, was a Mormon apostate. Mickelsson, trying to be sociable, tells Lawler that, according to legend, his house was once owned by Joseph Smith, the original leader of the Mormons. Mickelsson recalled Nugent telling him that the chemistry professor, just before he was murdered, had done some investigating around Mickelsson's house looking for toxic pollution. Lawler, however, suggests that what the Chemistry professor was actually looking for were documents that would forever discredit the Mormon religion. In fact, Lawler begins to press Mickelsson for information about what he might have discovered as he was remodeling the house.

In a twinkling, Mickelsson realizes who murdered the chemistry professor—and Nugent! Nugent's death was not a suicide, he now knows. He was murdered because of his friendship with the chemistry professor. Lawler, now confronted with a knowing Mickelsson, admits to committing the murders and setting the arson fires. As a "Son of Dan" committed to protecting the Mormon faith against outside threats, he was doing his religious duty as he saw it. In a lengthy diatribe Lawler explains that people are basically stupid and lazy, willing to turn over their autonomy to anyone capable of providing them sufficient security and creature comforts. And this is what the Mormon Church provides them, he contends. The Church neither encourages nor allows men and women to think; rather, the church tells them what to think. And the people are happy, Lawler says. "Make no mistake," he tells Mickelsson, "we don't make people weaker than they are. We make them *profoundly* what they are." (543)

Lawler, not to put too fine a point on it, is nuts. While he accurately notes the human need for being part of a larger community of people, his image of community is one of ideological oppression rather than of loving support. His image is of a knowledgeable and powerful elite lording over an ignorant and submissive mass, rather than the free give and take of members of a community sharing a wisdom attained through experience, "the wisdom of the whole community, tested over time." Lawler is, in a sense, like John Horne in *The Resurrection*, the *reductio ad absurdum* of a person whose notion of community is purely intellectual. Lawler is quite alone, as Mickelsson sees, and has told himself a fable about doing great works for the sake of his church. As one of a cadre of brilliant and imaginative believers, Lawler sees his action as worthy of a hero, worthy of legends to be told of him in the future by admiring Mormons. Mickelsson sees the truth of the matter: Lawler is a lone-wolf religious fanatic who has succumbed to a demented story he tells himself about himself. Though Lawler is clearly deranged, Mickelsson, nonetheless, is confronted with a man pointing a gun at him with every intention of killing him when he is ready. Before killing him, however, Lawler wants to find the documents for which he believes the chemistry professor was searching—documents which do not exist. Mickelsson is told he must tear down the house he has worked at refurbishing, piece by piece, until the documents are found. He has little choice but to begin the dismantling of his house; he has little hope but to pray. Then disgusted by the hypocrisy of praying to a God he rejects when he isn't in need, he stops praying. There are his silent screams, however, heard by the ghosts in his house.

Throughout the novel there are intimations and arguments for the ability of the body to have knowledge that is denied consciousness. For example, at a faculty gathering Mickelsson is told of an experiment in which a young woman has wires attached to her body to measure respiration, heartbeat, blood pressure, brain wave patterns and other physiological data. Placed in a room, she is told to write down when a student in another room is being given random electric shocks. What they find is that her guesses are all wrong. But what is significant about the experiment is that while her guesses are wrong, her body as measured by the various instruments does know when the other student is being zapped. It is believed the experiment shows there is a gap between the higher cerebral activity of the human brain and that more primitive portion of the brain that poet Robert Bly refers to as the "reptile brain." Over evolutionary time there remains little connection

Isolation by Guilt 115

between the two. "Point is," says one of the experimenters, "simpler brains may possibly know a lot of things we can't." (371) What might escape conscious notice, in other words, may well be known by the body. What seems to have happened is that our advanced brains have locked the body out.

Indeed, the narrative indicates Mickelsson has on occasion experienced similar sorts of "body knowledge." At some intuitive level, for example, he senses that Nugent is in trouble just after the last time he spoke with him on the telephone—the very moment he was being murdered by Lawler. A similar sort of "knowledge" is demonstrated while Mickelsson is tearing apart the house under Lawler's threatening gaze. While screaming his silent screams there is a sudden knock at the door. Mickelsson takes advantage of Lawler's turning away at the sound of the knocking to hurl his pick-ax, hitting Lawler squarely in the head. Mickelsson is then able to grab the gun Lawler has dropped, and the reign of terror is over. The person knocking at the door is a Mr. Lepatofsky who, we are informed, has a young daughter who has never spoken a word to anyone. As Lepatofsky explains: "It was the strangest thing, . . . My little Lily never talked before. We was driving by the howse and all at once she yells out, *'Stahp! Stahp!'* . . . Lucky thing we *did* stahp." (555) A few moments later he remarks that they have driven by the house more than fifty times before, but for some reason this time his daughter yells for them to stop.

Mickelsson has been saved emotionally by Donnie, saved intellectually by seeing how ridiculous, absurd and dangerous a purely intellectual approach like Lawler's is, and saved physically by the little Lepatofsky girl. It still remains for him to assuage his guilt for the killing of the fat man and for his abandoning of Jessica Stark when she needed him most. He tries to rectify the former by confessing to the police his robbery, and subsequent "killing" of the fat man. Detective Tinklepaugh's reaction is to cite the fact they receive a number of crank confessions. Mickelsson persists, but Tinklepaugh says he isn't even sure there was a murder. Mickelsson is completely perplexed. Why, after he's confessed to what happened, isn't he being arrested? The detective, for no apparent reason, begins to muse about the town, saying how beautiful it once was. And while there are those who think the town will bounce back one day, the detective doubts it. Such towns are fragile things, Tinklepaugh submits, with each person playing a role in that town's life. If one should run up bills and then suddenly skip town, one or more businesses could find themselves in trouble. That's why it is important in small towns for everyone to be honest with each other and to pull their own weight. It's when somebody stops pulling his weight that a small town, especially if living near the edge to begin with, is in trouble. "We just all gotta be careful," Tinklepaugh concludes, "and watch out for each other." (569) Mickelsson, somewhat puzzled, asks incredulously if that is why he is being allowed to go free. The detective makes clear to him that he is free because it is not apparent that he has committed any crime.

After his ordeal with Lawler and confession to Tinklepaugh an exhausted Mickelsson collapses in his bed for a long rest. To his amazement, neighbors and others in the community enter his house to make meals for him while he is bedridden. Even more amazing, they work at cleaning up the living room that was nearly destroyed in Lawler's attempt to find the "documents." It is the community's way of lending support to one of its own, and also a message to Mickelsson that he is accepted, despite his faults and occasional failings. Perhaps there is nothing on earth, as he had earlier told Dr. Rifkin, that even remotely approached that level of perfection that he had all his life demanded. But then, maybe the reality of an accepting community, willing to lovingly reach out to its members, guided by a wisdom tested over time, is as close to perfection as one might achieve in a world of constant change and process. Just as quickly as they arrived, the neighbors quit coming. His strength had returned, and his house is now cleaned and ready for repairs. Now that the community has demonstrated its acceptance of him, it is up to him to demonstrate that he is willing to carry on his obligations to himself and to the community.

A last task Mickelsson must perform is to make amends with Jessica Stark. He arrives at her house uninvited to find a party in progress with many of Mickelsson's colleagues in attendance. Ghosts, symbolic of the presence of earlier generations, are more visibly real to Mickelsson now that he recognizes the need for human companionship in community. Outside of Jessica's house he encounters another ghost, Jessica's former husband, who encourages him to go in. Jessica answers the door. After an uncomfortable exchange, during which she allows him entry, Mickelsson manages to get the two of them alone in her bedroom. She thinks he is quite rude at best, perhaps quite insane. He insists he loves her, and—improbably—begins disrobing her. Eventually she succumbs. Described as smiling wildly, she remarks on there being so many people just outside her bedroom door as they make love. Narratively, the reader is told of more than just the people on the other side of the door: "Now the bedroom was packed tight with ghosts, not just people but also animals . . . more than Mickelsson or Jessie could name, . . . pitiful empty-headed nothings complaining to be born." (590)

It is a return to Jessica, a return to the city, a return to humanity for Mickelsson. His and Jessica's making love—as Gregory Morris has emphasized, "literally, in true Gardner fashion, make, create love" (1984:225)—is a spiritual rebirth. It is important to note that it is a rebirth into a community of men and women and animals and all of life interconnected with one another, as signaled by the presence of the ghosts. To put it in Whiteheadian language, the ghosts represent those objectively immortal past actual occasions of which we are all a part. If we but positively prehend them they, through their influence on actual occasions in the present, may yet be born anew. To prehend them, though, has more to do with the bodily flow of feeling than it does conscious experience. By the end of the novel Mickelsson becomes another of Gardner's valiant heroes who takes responsibility for his own actions, recognizing that he has made many mistakes in his life. It's okay for fictional heroes to make mistakes, Gardner seems to be saying, so long as they don't give in to despair and instead try to do something about it. In that way the hero affirms that life is good, despite the many tragedies along the way.

There are many, including some of Gardner's strongest admirers, who believe *Mickelsson's Ghosts* to be one of his lesser novels—an opinion that does seem justified. However, what is also plain is that the themes that concern Gardner at the beginning of his writing career are still being explored by him at the end. Death, guilt, responsibility, freedom, cynicism, hope, and community continue to be touchstones in Gardner's fictional attempts to understand a world full of both suffering and joy. Gardner contributes powerfully to our understanding of these issues in his philosopher-protagonist novels. It can be argued, however, that there are times when the philosophical depth demanded of the reader, and the seeming artificiality of some of the dialogue—especially the philosophical dialogue—disrupts in the reader's mind that "vivid and continuous dream" toward which Gardner insists the writer should strive. This is particularly true of *Mickelsson's Ghosts*, which has the further hindrance of some very strange and awkward plot twists as he attempts to weave together a story of private angst, a love story, a murder mystery, and a ghost story. Far more satisfying are Gardner's novels using characters of ordinary backgrounds, including a morbidly obese owner of a diner in upstate New York, a flint-edged Vermont farmer, and a nondescript Chief of Police in run-down Batavia. It is in these novels that the "vivid and continuous dream" Gardner seeks to construct appears almost seamless.

CHAPTER VI:
Pilgrimage Toward Life

In addition to Gardner's philosopher-protagonists, he also uses characters who lead common, ordinary and, for the most part, anonymous lives. These characters represent Gardner's fictional ideal as they work their way through many of the basic dilemmas and challenges of life. Being less articulate than James Chandler, Agathon, or Peter Mickelsson, these characters must show through their muddled emotions and their unreflective actions how they will approach questions of death and guilt, freedom and responsibility. Ultimately, having non-philosophers as protagonists challenges Gardner as an artist to use the tools of a writer to set moods and communicate human feelings. The result is that *Nickel Mountain*, and especially *The Sunlight Dialogues* and *October Light* are his most satisfying novels. Released from what at times seems the artificial dialogue of a character's philosophical analysis, these novels of day-to-day people more nearly satisfy Gardner's demand for fiction that is a "vivid and continuous dream."

Morbidly obese Henry Soames, the protagonist of *Nickel Mountain*, is like James Chandler and Agathon in that there is little standing between him and death. Having already suffered from one heart attack, and having to stay up at night in the midst of winter in order to service the few customers in his diner, he is ripe for another, probably fatal attack. He tells one of his patrons, an old man named Kuzitsky, that the doctors have given him only one more year to live. As he talks about the dizzy spells he sometimes suffers it is obvious that he is a frightened man. He explains to Kuzitsky how the doctor has said he could live another 20 years if he would lose 90 pounds. Incongruously, he shares this while stuffing apple pie into his mouth. A further frustration for him is that, unlike the more articulate James Chandler and Agathon, Henry almost always finds himself incapable of finding the right words to express his thoughts, even to himself. This linguistic handicap would often take the form of a streak of confused violence in his diner as he pounds the counter or a table top, or lifts and squeezes the sugar dispensers as if preparing to throw them. "Henry must have seen the hopelessness," the narrator says, "of trying to put what he meant into words, whatever it was, if anything, that he meant. He would check himself, straining to face death bravely, gallantly. But he was a weak man and childish." (5–6)

It is not a flattering picture we have of Henry Soames at the beginning of the text. His obesity is but a metaphor of how out of control his whole life has become—emotionally, spiritually and physically. On those ever more frequent occasions when his chest would lock in pain he would lean on his sink and wait for his breath to come back, waiting to see *if* it would come back. It's what he spent most of his time doing these days—waiting. As we are introduced to Henry there is little for him to look forward to in life but his own death, alone, at an isolated and usually empty diner. The mood shifts when a sixteen-year-old girl, Callie Wells, comes to work for him. She didn't want to earn money so much as gain experience before moving to New York City. The reader is informed that when she comes it is the beginning of Spring, the season of fertility and new birth.

Nonetheless, intimations of death surround Henry, including the accidental death early on of one of his few regular customers: old man Kuzitsky. George Loomis, a local collector who is also a regular at the diner, tells Henry of the automobile accident, and then jokes about Kuzitsky's passing. Henry takes to his bedroom, resisting an urge to break some things. After a few moments, remembering his work, he lumbers back into the diner. He wants to share with Callie something of what he is feeling, but his inarticulateness again frustrates him. He can feel a lifetime of words surging inside of him, but they remain jumbled confusions. With tears in his eyes, the most he can manage is to say that Kuzitsky lived alone, and that it would be a pretense for anyone to act as if they are sorry he is dead. When Callie follows with a remark that it is all probably for the best, Henry inexplicably explodes: "Shit," he bellows, slamming the counter top and knocking over napkin dispensers and a mustard pot. Henry's anger is not simply that he has difficulty expressing the multitude of jumbled feelings within him having to do with the death of Kuzitsky. His anger also has to do with how Kuzitsky's death is being treated. George Loomis cracks jokes about it, while Callie comments the old man's death is "all for the best." We can easily imagine Henry saying to himself: "Is this all I have to look forward to at my death? Is this what they will say about me?" What does one live for if all he has to expect in life is his own death, a death to be joked about and dismissed as "for the best"? Life holds little comfort, little by way of hope for Henry. Rather, life for Henry is little more than a dark and foreboding grave waiting for him.

Having Callie in the diner does make a difference, though. The place is becoming a little neater and a little cleaner, and customers are even beginning to remark on the changes. Henry is ambivalent, not sure if the changes are something of which he wants to be a part. But he does like having Callie in the diner and appreciates the little tasks she performs, freeing him up to relax more and, for the first time in a long while, get a reasonable amount of sleep at night. For her part, Callie is preparing for a life away from this upstate New York area. It is New York City where she hopes to move one day, at least temporarily. In the meantime, she is happy working in the diner and spending free hours with her boyfriend, Willard. The son of a successful farmer, Willard is planning to attend university and, though he talks of love, has no intention of maintaining any sort of permanent relationship with Callie. In fact, he doesn't even tell her he is leaving. He simply leaves. Her spirits pick up when she gets her first letter from him, but it is becoming obvious that she was little more than an object of sexual conquest. This is confirmed when she realizes she is pregnant with Willard's child. Though he does experience some guilt, the fact is he chooses to stay away, refusing any further correspondence with her.

Seeing her alone with no prospects, Henry comes to feel a great distress at her plight, even to the point of trying to pay George Loomis to marry her. George rejects the offer. Though he has his shortcomings, George proves insightful in the matter. "Why don't *you* marry her," he asks Henry. (52) At first Henry rejects the thought out of hand, deriding George for rejecting someone like Callie. But George continues to press the matter: "Why not you, Henry?" "Because I'm twenty-five years older than she is," Henry retorts, "and fat and ugly to boot." (52) George, a cat-like grin on his face, simply notes that Henry loves her. Henry continues to reject the idea, saying he will be dead in a year. "But you love her," George says, suddenly serious. Henry realizes it is true, that Callie is far more important to him than he had yet realized. As much as he had tried to convince himself of the folly of it all, the fact is he loves Callie Wells. In his own sentimental and undisciplined way he loves each of the few men and women, lonely hearts all, who visit his diner, but Callie has come to be a very special person in his life. Her plight of being pregnant and abandoned greatly moves him.

Henry has a physical relapse later that same night, and is ordered to bed by Doc Cathey after being examined. It is decided that Callie would move into Henry's residence in order to take care of both the diner and Henry. For the next two weeks, as a result of Callie's work and insistent care for Henry, he begins to regain his former strength, in part by eating more responsibly. When he is finally able to care for himself again Callie folds up her cot and returns to the nearby home of her parents. Henry, having become used to having her close, feels more lonely than ever after she leaves. Alone in his despair, he decides one night to close the diner's door, turn off all of the lights, and quietly lay in his bed. He is awakened some time later by an urgent pounding at his door. Henry shouts for the person to enter, thinking it is probably a customer. But the voice returning his call is that of Callie: "Don't get up." She is wet and breathing hard, indicating she had run from her home to the diner. "I'm sorry to bother you," she says. "I saw your lights were all off, and I thought—" (54) After a few awkward moments, with Henry thinking her tears had to do with losing Willard, she proceeds to tell him how thankful she is for his kindness, how like a father he has been to her, and how afraid she was that something had happened to him, what with the lights of the diner never being turned on. Caught up in the moment, he tells her he loves her and proposes.

Callie agrees to marry Henry, and in a serio-comical scene the two go to get the permission of her parents, the mother being a woman Henry used to date while in high school. Informed for the first time of Callie's pregnancy, her parents see, if not the wisdom, at least the utility of the decision. Responding to her mother's disappointment, Callie assures her that she loves Henry and that she is very happy. But her statement is belied just a few moments later when she thinks to herself that it is all a mistake, that she doesn't love him, and that he is ugly. Nevertheless, the wedding does take place—at her mother's insistence a church wedding with many relatives in attendance.

What we have in Gardner's description of the wedding is a wonderfully evocative account of a social ritual giving its participants both a sense of identity as well as a sense of transcendence. On her wedding day Callie finds herself in a room filled with presents from relatives, some of whom she was not particularly close to, and wondering why they had bothered. Her initial explanation to herself is to repeat a singsong about brides being beautiful and marriage being holy. She has seen many marriages herself, watching the brides slowly making their way down the aisle amidst family and friends, "transfigured, . . . lifted out of mere humanness into their perfect eternal instant." (68) As a virginal youth she envied them their knowledge of the mystery behind the wedding ceremony. She knows it isn't what happens in the marriage bed that is the mystery, though it might symbolize it. Rather, it is closer to the idea that when they move up the aisle they transcend the moment and are, for an instant, perfectly balanced in a moment of freedom between childhood and adulthood, between being someone's daughter and being someone's wife. To borrow Victor Turner's phrase, the bride is "betwixt and between," no longer what she was and not yet what she is about to be. Somehow, in the midst of the ceremony, the young bride is transformed from expectant youth with certain obligations and role expectations, to a married woman with quite different obligations and role expectations. "It was that that the relatives lifted up their offerings to," the narrator explains, "the common holy ground in all their lives." (69)

Bitterly, Callie believes such a transformation is not in store for her. The reason is because she sees her marrying of Henry as but a vicious act of selfishness on her part: here she is pregnant and alone while Henry—sweet fat Henry—was merely available and willing to help her. She imagines herself running away, even to the point of composing possible letters she would write Henry once she establishes herself someplace else. She also finds herself thinking that there must surely be a young and handsome man for her, someone as good-hearted as Henry without his obvious physical drawbacks. Surely, she thought, somewhere there is a young man who could make her heart race as Willard once did if only she waited. Then, thinking of the child developing inside her, she doubts she can ever love it because of the direction it has forced her life to take in marrying Henry. But then, at an intuitive level, there is a more positive message being expressed at the edge of consciousness: "the maples on the lawn said, *Be calm*." (71) Despite her personal misgivings about the wedding, there is a more solid and stately wisdom being presented. "Be calm" are the same words told her by her Uncle John when, as a little girl, she flew into a rage at not being able to use a hammer properly. His advice then was to be calm and to be patient—wisdom for the ages. Indeed, several memories of earlier family incidents flood her thoughts as she prepares to leave for the church. All are lessons on life which she is only now, at the moment of burgeoning adulthood, beginning to understand. These recollections, and the wisdom being conveyed to her, are a proleptic vision of that sense of "peace" toward which Gardner directs many of his fictional characters.

The wedding takes place and, despite her fears of being unworthy, she too experiences that mystery of transformation as she slowly walks down the aisle. She suddenly knows herself to be truly beautiful while at the same time feeling an inexplicable sense of freedom.

> Their faces surrounded her, . . . shining as if reflecting the secret radiance thinly veiled, her total and untouchable, virginal freedom. In a moment, she would feel her weight again, her mere humanness, the child inside, but not yet. The church window said, *All will be well*. The white of the cloth on the pulpit said, *Go slow*. She watched Henry, more solemn and splendid even than her Uncle Earle when he won the election for Mayor, more beautiful than Duncan, looking up, tossing a child in his arms, or Bill with his hand poised over the chessboard, or Aunt Anna paring apples with speckled, swift fingers. (81)

Callie knows that in a twinkling reality will come crashing back in on her, yet this brief time of transcendent possibilities is the most luminously liberating moment of her young life. After another breath or two the world will again gain weightiness, and entropy will again make its unyielding presence known. But for this pristine moment she is weightless as she makes that last stride toward adulthood, marriage, and motherhood. Yes, she knows that "in a moment she too would be real again. *Go slow*, said the room. *Be patient*, said the trees. She could feel weight coming, a murderous solidity, hunting her." (81) Though there is no escaping entropy, that weightiness inexorably grounding down every living creature, there are those moments in life, often entered by means of ritual performance, whereby one participates in, if only for a moment, a mode of being whereby one is fused with a more permanent, transcendent reality. Such moments of ritual transition can be moments of personal transformation as well. Freed from the more mundane and utilitarian expectations of daily life, one is opened to a period of liminality in which differing, perhaps novel, ways of explaining and understanding one's personal and social life is possible. From such ritual experiences a strong sense of personal meaningfulness may emerge: an understanding of why the world is as it is as well as an insight into one's place in the world. To the extent a community is able to bring to bear its own wisdom and insights upon an individual in the midst of a liminal period, that person can, in a very personal way, come to embody the wisdom of that community.

Callie, in remembering her uncles and aunts and cousins as she moves through her wedding, comes to embody the wisdom gained and passed on through generations of relatives who have lived, learned and, in innumerable acts of love, shared their hard-earned insights and wisdom. This is why Callie emerges from the novel as such a strong character. It is also why Henry seems so weak at the beginning of the novel. With no family, and only fleeting recollections of his parents, he has lived isolated from the shared wisdom of a loving community. Now married to Callie, the possibility of his transformation comes to the fore. Before his marriage Henry is much impressed with old man Kuzitsky's notion that a person needs "something to die for." (11) And in his own sentimental way Henry tries to justify his life in the diner as something worth dying for. Indeed, he imagines his death as the sacrificing of his life for the sake of those other lonely people who regularly gather at the diner. It certainly does his heart no good to stay up all hours of the night. But he does it. In his own eyes "he was a fat, blubbering Holy Jesus." (41) Once married, Henry takes on the responsibilities of a husband, and within a few months the responsibilities of a father as well. These family obligations help focus that chaos of inarticulate feeling and indiscriminate action toward a more disciplined display of concrete affection. For one, he begins to eat more responsibly. For another, he allows Callie—and even Callie's mother—to take over many of the tasks in the diner. Life is now calling him not to die for something, but to live for something: his wife and child.

As Gardner is wont to do, other characters act as alternative approaches to Henry's. Two of the most prominent are George Loomis and Simon Bale. George, a disabled veteran of the Korean War, lives alone in a house filled with fine furniture, detailed plate and glassware, and other exquisite and delicate items. The fact that he is living alone with rooms filled with "things" is a metaphor of his emotional hollowness. He is not mean, just deadened to human feeling. To a large extent his isolation is self-imposed, a result of his belief that his war injuries have left him ugly. His fear of rejection leaves him unable—or at least unwilling—to reach out to another. That he would want it to be different is evidenced by his admiration of what Henry and Callie have done for each other. The chapter titled "The Things," narrated from George's point of view, describes him leaving the Soames's home, Callie holding the baby, Henry beside her, their dog at their side. Standing in front of their well-lit house, surrounded by trees under a sky dotted with stars, they wave to him. It strikes George that Henry, Callie and the baby could be the "wholesome family" from some advertisement. Heading to his own house he fearfully begins to think again about the recent robbery and murder on Nickel Mountain, where a person who lived alone was beaten to death. He wonders whether he could be a victim, knowing he certainly has enough valuables in his house to make it worth a robber's while. Some of the items are family heirlooms over 200 years old, while others had been collected only recently. He was once asked by someone who saw his collection what he uses them for. Puzzled at the notion they are to be used at all, he finally manages to say that he sometimes just goes and touches them. Indeed, it is one of the highest pleasures of his life, "just picking them up, knowing they were his." (128) Much of his pleasure has to do with the craftsmanship worked into his pieces, all lovingly created by artists whose entire focus was on a woodcut for an edition of Goethe, or on some hand-crafted handles on a pistol, or on the intricate designs engraved into the wood of harmonica boxes. They are all reminders of a time of wholeness, a time before his body had become gnarled and, to his mind, useless. And what is perhaps most important: what is nice about "things" is they don't reject you.

Once home and out of his pickup truck he suddenly is aware "with a certainty that made him go as cold as ice" (135) that he is being watched by someone in his house. It is the same feeling he had on patrol in Korea just before he was shot. It was in Korea that he learned he is mortal. Now on Nickel Mountain he is distressed to realize that not only is he mortal but, injured as he had been in Korea and injured again in a recent farm accident, he would be an easy victim if someone wanted to kill him. It is nature's way—all that exists on earth is destructible. He makes it to his woodshed, gets his rifle, and then crawls through the weeds toward his house, occasionally glimpsing a trace of someone at a window. For a moment he thinks it is just nerves, and secretly realizes the truth of the matter: there is no one in the house. He still crawls, however, muddying his clothes, even clogging the ankle brace he has to wear. Finally, he jerks open the back door, the rifle leveled for action.

There is no one there. Through every room of his house, on every level, he searches. No one. No one is in his house but himself, and his collection of things. With bitter clarity he realizes the emptiness of his life, and thinks again of that image of Henry, Callie and the baby grouped together on their porch with their dog. If Henry had crawled through mud to protect his belongings, George thinks, at least his effort would have meant something. Even if it were all a delusion on Henry's part, "it would have counted." (139)

Simon Bale, a religious zealot, is one of those distasteful, intolerant characters Gardner often uses in his fiction, a character who attempts to explain all of the variety and complexity of life by means of a single abstract idea. John Horne in *The Resurrection* and Edward Lawler in *Mickelsson's Ghosts* are similar characters. These ideologues, surrendering themselves to abstract notions of perfection, often do unwitting violence to themselves and others in the name of an ideology that brooks no opposition. Simon Bale, left alone after his family is killed in a house fire, is a fundamentalist Jehovah's Witness who displays little reaction to the loss of his wife and children. For him, it is all a part of God's greater plan. Just as George has dulled himself to human feeling because of his attachment to "things," so, too, has Simon dulled himself to human feeling because of his attachment to his religious beliefs.

Henry, still indiscriminate in the care he shows others, invites Simon to stay with him and his family. Callie opposes this, and for good reason as the reader later learns. Little Jimmy, their son, begins having nightmares after Simon comes to live with them, and it is suspected Simon is part of the reason, though Callie cannot prove it. What becomes clear over time is that Simon is proselytizing Jimmy, telling him the world is a battlefield between the devil and God. Simon's renderings of the devil are what is leading to Jimmy's fear and nightmares. An indication of Simon's absolutism occurs when Henry asks him about his church. Simon has several tracts with him, one of them quoting Romans 14:10 as an answer to the question of who will be saved. Ironically, the passage actually criticizes the kind of judgmental attitude in which Simon engages, but in his zealotry Simon doesn't realize it. Henry asks if this is what Jehovah's Witnesses "believe." Simon angrily retorts that it is the *truth*, not merely something that they believe. He then unloads his theological ire at Henry, asking whether he is denying the Lord's judgment. After an awkward silence Simon relents, saying Henry has been kind to him despite the limitations of his understanding. Simon then manages to thank Henry for his help, emphasizing how grateful he is. His gratefulness is mitigated, however, by the fact he cannot recall Henry's name, and is left saying, "May the Lord keep you, Mr.____." (174)

The episode with Simon Bale reaches a climax when Henry hears Jimmy screaming in his bedroom one night, yelling "It's the devil." Henry finds his son crouching on the floor and staring into the room's shadows. In a moment, Simon is there in the hallway. With Jimmy now in his arms, Henry comes to a full realization of what Simon has done to his son. In a rage, Henry moves toward Simon, who wheels suddenly and bounds toward the stairs. Fairly leaping over the landing, Simon hits halfway down the stairs in a terrible fall and ends crumpled at the bottom, where he dies. Henry, still trying to protect his son, turns his body so Jimmy cannot see what has happened. Once his rage has passed, Henry stays in the bedroom with his son, groaning, wishing Callie would hurry home to comfort him and tell him what to do.

What follows is a chapter in which Henry, believing himself responsible for the death of Simon, tries to come to terms with his guilt. Thus, Henry is forced to deal with those issues facing other survivors of such incidents, as explicated earlier by Lifton and lived through by Gardner in his own life. Henry keeps remarking about how he keeps seeing the incident replayed in his mind's eye over and over. "I see it clearer even than it was, slowed down, like a movie," Henry says. (233) In words echoing Gardner's own memories of the accident with Gilbert, Henry remarks that remembering the accident is "like a wound in your soul." (234) Eventually, that wound becomes a prod toward artistic expression in Gardner. Henry, however, begins to lose control of his life, much as other Gardner characters lose control when saddled with guilt over another's death (e.g. James Page in *October Light* and Peter Mickelsson in *Mickelsson's Ghosts*). Henry returns to his old eating habits. The weight he had lost since his marriage is regained, and Callie becomes distressed thinking she and Jimmy may soon be left alone. Dust begins to settle in the diner as Henry becomes lax in his duties, and he more and more turns to the little white pills he takes for his heart. One day Callie explodes, telling Henry that he is acting as if he were crazy. But it wasn't the ax-waving, foaming at the mouth, waiting in the dark to attack innocent children kind of craziness that she sees in him, but the kind of craziness that forgets that a son needs his father, and a wife needs her husband, and a community needs each of its members supporting each other. The community knows that when a person decides to kill himself, he ought to be stopped. Callie, grounded more firmly in a community than Henry has ever been, knows that she must intercede to help save Henry. But she doesn't know how.

Callie hopes George Loomis might be able to get through to Henry, but unknown to her and the others, George is crippled by his own secret guilt after a recent automobile accident in which he ran over and killed an itinerant old woman known as the "Goat Lady," a name given her because she cared little about her appearance or about what others thought of her. George does his best to reason with Henry, reassuring him that his feelings of guilt come from a false sense of human dignity. Cynically, he adds that Henry needs to feel guilt because he needs to believe that the world is ordered and that actions have a meaningful purpose. To admit that Simon Bale's death was an act of pure chance would be, according to this view, an admission of the meaninglessness of human action. George may, for his own reasons, want that to be true, but later events would show even he cannot fully accept such a prospect. Callie keeps the conversation going by asking why people insist on having dignity. George's reply is that "dignity" is just a word, an empty word. Henry chimes in wondering why everyone can't be a little more like the "Goat Lady." George blanches. Narratively, it is the first indication that George may have had something to do with the "Goat Lady's" disappearance. It is made explicit a few pages later that, quite by accident, the woman was hit by George while he was driving his car over the top of a ridge. The argument he gives trying to unburden Henry of his guilt, it turns out, is an argument George would fervently like to believe himself.

It all comes to a head when George is debating whether to tell Henry and Callie of the accident, knowing that to do so would, in his eyes, diminish his own sense of dignity. After the three of them, together with some neighbors, have spent the entire evening making undignified fools of themselves trying to make rain come to their parched land, George shares some of his feelings: "I'll tell you something, I'm beginning to believe in the Goat Lady." (255) He feels uneasy after having said it. Indeed, Callie follows up by asking: "You saw her, didn't you? . . . What happened?" (255) George has an important decision to make.

They all wait, expectantly, "precariously balanced over a chasm." (255) What would happen next depended entirely on George, who sat staring at his lit cigarette. Henry, too, knows this to be a pivotal moment as he silently pulls at the fat beneath his chin, an uneaten cookie in his hand. If George would simply tell them, his closest friends, he could experience that liberating moment of confession which grounds one's private guilt in the shared love and concern of a community. But then, someone would know of his guilt, his shame, his embarrassment, and what dignity would be left to him then. Then again, maybe it is the abandoning of such notions of dignity that truly allows one to be free. Back and forth George's mind would race until finally, with no turning back, George stands up and says, "No. I never saw her." (256)

Henry looks at George with pity, and in looking at him he sees a man trapped by his own limited view of the world. Without realizing it, the cookie in Henry's hand breaks and crumbles to the floor. Callie sees the irony of it all, for she knows that George managed to save them after all:

> She felt herself going weightless, as though she were fainting. And something said in her mind, . . . *Nevertheless, all shall be saved.* She thought: *What?* And again: *All. Everything. Even the sticks and stones. Nothing is lost.* She thought: *How? Why should sticks and stones be saved?* But the waking dream was passing quickly, a thing so fragile that she would not even remember tomorrow that she'd had it. The room was suddenly filled with ghosts. (256)

This passage evokes the Whiteheadian portrayal of "objective immortality," a metaphysical notion of the world as a place of "tender care that nothing be lost." (Whitehead, 1978:346) This notion, much as in the wedding sequence, is also expressed in the text by the felt ghostly presence of earlier generations, a permanence immanent in the flux of things. It is Callie, primarily, who experiences this presence. But the clear implication is that Henry, under the influence of Callie and their son, is himself now influenced by these earlier generations. Henry is able to see how guilt imprisons George in a suffocating vault of silence, unable to express his feelings—indeed his humanity—to another. Henry's breaking of the cookie symbolizes that moment when he frees himself from his uncontrolled eating. His freeing of himself is coextensive with his realization that he has the love and support of others—his family and those in the wider community. Through an act of love, one can be accepted despite one's physical appearance and despite one's actions. It is a lesson Henry needs to be able to accept personally, so that he can continue living a meaningful life. The same may be said for Gardner.

The novel ends with Henry hunting rabbits with his son. After shooting a rabbit on the grounds of a cemetery Henry realizes that this is probably the first dead animal Jimmy has ever seen. And he attempts, in his own inarticulate way, to teach his son about life and death. Not very patient for Henry's muddled thoughts on such topics, Jimmy quickly loses interest in the dead rabbit. What Jimmy does notice are some grave diggers in the distance along with an elderly couple, and he is curious about what they are all doing. When Henry and Jimmy get nearer they see the couple are having someone exhumed. It is their only child, a son who died 50 years earlier at the age of 14, struck by lightning. It is just another one of those inexplicable tragedies that are a part of life. The woman believes her son to be "in Glory" while the father, an atheist, believes his son to be "dead and rotten." It is a sad couple, with no heirs to carry their name, and perhaps no one else to carry their memories into the future. But their's is a limited view. Henry, with an insight gained during the time of the novel, knows that life will go on. He derives some measure of satisfaction at the thought, a "pleasant sense of grief." (304) He knows that he probably will not live many years more, and knows that Callie and Jimmy will be deeply saddened by his death, as he was at the time of his father's early death. But more importantly, in time they will turn from their grief and yield to the prosaic day-to-day activities of their lives, as is right and proper.

For Henry, his is a pilgrimage toward a new life of commitment and meaning. Where once he marked time, cookie by cookie, waiting for the cold earth to suck him back into oblivion, now he sees the world more as communion. Now he has a child and a wife. Though it is not easy being a good father and husband, and though it often seems there is little by way of reward for being a good father and husband, Henry has come to know that life demands a commitment to see one's familial and communal obligations to their natural end. As father and son walk home from the cemetery the reader is told in the novel's final words that Henry is tired, and would like "to lie down, only for a little while, and rest." (309) The allusion is to Robert Frost and those last few lines from his poem "Stopping by Woods on a Snowy Evening." There are times when each of us may wish to just stop and rest a long, long time, but then there are those commitments we have made as a parent, as a loving spouse, as a contributing member of our community, those promises which we need to keep for the sake of all. And though they may at times seem burdensome, it would seem they are also that which saves us from a tedious anomie.

CHAPTER VII:
Freedom and Responsibility

The Sunlight Dialogues is Gardner's most complex novel with respect to plot and number of interconnecting characters. Though somewhat difficult reading and ambitious in scope, the novel, again set in Batavia, NY, this time during the social upheaval of the late 1960s and early 1970s, is quite successful in bringing forward a number of themes common to Gardner's fiction. In particular, the role of the individual in a community is highlighted, especially as it reflects on the question of individual freedom versus individual responsibility for the welfare of the community.

Other scholars have commented on the complex structuring and sources for the novel, particularly Gardner's reliance on A. Leo Oppenheim's *Ancient Mesopotamia: Portrait of a Dead Civilization* for much of the material in those segments of the novel where the Sunlight Man discourses on ancient ways of conceiving the universe. (Morris, 1984:72–73; Maier, 1977:33–48) This was to cause Gardner some grief in later years after accusations of plagiarism arose with the publication of his two works on Chaucer. Just as scholars accused him of lifting whole sections of scholarly works on Chaucer, word for word, from various sources and using them in his own volumes without acknowledgment, so too was he accused of lifting whole passages from Oppenheim's work and placing them in the mouth of the Sunlight Man. Gardner never answered these charges very convincingly,[1] no doubt leading to the petulance of his "preface" to *Mickelsson's Ghosts*.

The Sunlight Dialogues essentially revolves around the conflict between two characters: Batavia's Chief of Police Fred Clumly, and a mysterious visitor given the name the "Sunlight Man." It is later revealed that the Sunlight Man is actually Taggart Hodge, a son of one of the leading families in the city. The Sunlight Man is arrested for painting "love" on a street, and while in jail his antics and tricks confound his jailers and fellow prisoners so much that an appointment is made for a psychiatric examination. Descriptions lead the reader to think of the Sunlight Man as a member of the "love generation," a "hippie," but it quickly becomes clear that his purposes are not so benign as they might at first appear. Indeed, the malevolence of the

Sunlight Man seems to grow throughout the time of the novel. Police Chief Clumly is the first to realize that the Sunlight Man presents a threat, though he is unable to articulate just what sort of threat he believes him to be.

The entire novel is couched in the imagery of death and decay. Funerals abound, though it is not simply men and women who are dying, but a way of life, a set of values, a meaningful universe. Gardner captures the sense of frustration many felt during the late 1960s and early 1970s as they wondered what was happening to their communities and their nation, caught in the grip of inflamed passions on the one hand and paralyzed thought on the other. Much as the lines from that poem of William Butler Yeats, "The Second Coming," the cultural center seemed not to be holding as society appeared on the brink of anarchy. In the name of this or that ideology blood was being spilled in the streets, and while many good citizens stood by, perplexed by what was happening all around them, other less-than-noble zealots exhorted their idealistic followers to dangerous levels of passionate intensity. It was a very difficult time, and Gardner manages to capture it well.

The novel details the breakdown and loss of influence of the Hodge family, from the patriarchal Senator Arthur Hodge, Sr., to his embezzling offspring. It is a metaphor for the social and moral breakdown that is taking place throughout society. The senator can see what is coming, and while he is still alive he openly worries about what will become of the country. He wonders, for example, what will happen if people simply stop being reasonable, so sure of their own rightness that they no longer even bother trying to hear and understand other points of view. In the subsequent confusion he worries that all points of view will become muddled and confused, "and the *pluribus* becomes so complicated and, more important, so *dense* that no human mind or even group of minds can fathom the *unum*." (151) If such were to happen, the senator believes, religion and politics will be in full decline, and the younger generation will grow more "dangerous and irrational, shameless, selfish, anarchistic." (151) Indeed, one of the senator's sons, contemplating his father's words, believes that the world has already changed along the lines the senator fears. Where once one could count on the world as a place of rock-solid verities, those same verities now appear to have "decayed to ambiguity." (154) To the extent it could be said anyone is clearly right or wrong, it is on a private and subjective scale. Even God seems to have dropped out of sight. Instead of being the embodiment of purposeful direction allowing for social confidence and sureness of step, God instead has become a mere observer of human foibles, a wise yet far less awesome entity impotently "watching the world with half-averted eyes, chewing his ancient lip thoughtfully, mildly, venturing an occasional rueful smile." (154) Though individuals still follow societal rules, send their children to school, attend the church of their choice, and obey the traffic laws so long as it doesn't inconvenience them, the underlying commitment to a set of values which justifies their following of these rules is decaying. In the language of existentialism, people are living "inauthentic" lives, not knowing why they are making the choices they are making and, more importantly, not accepting responsibility for the consequences of their choices.

The Sunlight Man is, in many ways, the quintessential existentialist who, in the name of a freedom which refuses constraint, flouts the generally accepted codes of behavior. He reaches this moment of self-affirming freedom having journeyed a torturous road of personal tragedy, which had mostly to do with the mental problems of his wife, the interference of his father-in-law, the ruining of his career in law, and the severe scarring of his face in a fire set by his deranged wife. It is this scarring that made it impossible for people—even his family—to realize it was Taggart Hodge when he returned to Batavia after many years of absence. In his youth he followed the rules, but he lacked his father's good fortune in establishing himself as an important member of his community. Instead, with his father the Senator setting an impossibly high standard, Taggart Hodge found himself tormented and frustrated at every turn. In time he was finally forced to the conclusion that the rules do not really exist in any metaphysical sort of way; they are only utilitarian in value—and even then only for certain people. Which is to say, the rules are to be accepted or rejected as one pleases. As he demonstrates in his later dialogues with Chief Clumly, he manifests the truth of the senator's and his brother's words as his discourses on "law and justice become abstruse questions of metaphysics" and the rightness or wrongness of acts are measured on "private scales."

Fred Clumly is the more complex character playing off of the Sunlight Man's "trickster" persona, and the story really revolves around Clumly's transformation. His name sounds distasteful and unattractive.

Indeed, he is described as being hairless as a result of a previous illness, and as having unnaturally white skin. At 64, he has lived his entire life in Batavia but for his time in the Navy. Clumly's unquestioning adherence to rules and regulations is emphasized. Though he now finds his wife in many ways repulsive, his public commitment to their marriage makes the idea of divorce unacceptable. He makes several comments about his job being the maintaining of law and order, saying at one point to a deputy that as long as there is a law on the books it is his responsibility to see to it that the law is enforced. He realizes there may be differing opinions on the laws that are on the books, but when it comes right down to it "a cop hasn't got opinions." (23) Though he personally doesn't like church, he would take his wife there each week and would tolerate the visits of the minister. It was all a part of a felt sense of obligation to his wife and his job—indeed, to society as a whole.

There are hints he yearns to be free from these obligations, however. For example, at home with his wife one night he suddenly recalls being at sea when he was still a young man, remembering a night when he looked down on the prow of a ship as it cut through the dark swells of the ocean. Conjuring in his memory both the mysterious unknown depths that undulated beneath him and the clear and unambiguous night sky that hung over him, Clumly remembers both the portent of dread the ocean embodied as well as the night sky's heralding a life of unlimited possibilities. Standing as he is in his bathroom, calling to his wife, seeing his future as little more that a constant repetition of bathroom calls to his wife, he welcomes the fleeting thought of liberation, a pleasant temptation to embrace an open future. As pleasant as it is, though, he recognizes it for what it is—temptation. A moment later he refers to his reverie as a never ending "struggle with the devil." (12) Clearly, he has made a commitment. He has given up personal freedoms in order to play his part in maintaining what he elsewhere calls "the fabric of society." (30) He is deeply troubled by the lack of respect citizens in the community show him and other public servants, seeing it as a tearing at that fabric that holds the society together in mutual obligation for the public good.

Into his well-ordered world comes the Sunlight Man, flouting authority and violating the rules. The police chief sees him as a threat, to be sure, but is not clear exactly what sort of threat. What does, at some intuitive level, seem apparent with the coming of the Sunlight Man is that the times are portentous of change. Clumly is fearful, though inarticulately so, of mysterious forces that are converging in Batavia. He could "feel" the change coming, sense it in the trees and in the activity of birds, a change that would wreak havoc on the citizens and forever alter their world. At an intuitive level Clumly senses the "perpetual perishing" of things, and "feels" that something new is coming, if he could but articulate his feelings. The articulation will come at a later time, as Whitehead suggests, for conscious experience is a later phase of the broader notion of what he—and Gardner—indicate experience to be.

One reason Clumly sees the Sunlight Man as a threat is because he cannot put him in any sort of recognizable category. The Sunlight Man is uncanny. At the end of his interview with the prisoner Clumly is amazed to have the Sunlight Man hand him, in turn, his wallet, his brass whistle, the bullets from the rifle of one of the deputies, his keys, his pistol, and the handcuffs that were worn by the Sunlight Man during the interview. When the Sunlight Man turns to leave Clumly points his pistol at him and tells him not to try escaping. The Sunlight Man continues on. When Clumly fires his pistol into the air as a warning there is only the click of an empty chamber, whereupon the Sunlight Man "recalls" he also took Clumly's bullets. Clumly then tries to grab the Sunlight Man to keep him from escaping, and in the ensuing struggle he comes to realize that, instead of the Sunlight Man, he is holding on to an old man who was also in the room. The Sunlight Man makes good his escape.

Later in his bedroom, replaying the incident in his mind, all Clumly can do is keep asking, "How?" His is the "tortured cry as old as mankind, the awed and outraged howl of sanity's indignation." (126) As an anomaly to all that Clumly recognizes as normal, the Sunlight Man is a source of danger. Mary Douglas notes in her anthropological work that among the options when facing a social anomaly are, first, to physically control it (e.g. the penal system) and, second, to label it dangerous and taboo, thereby putting the subject above dispute. (1980: 39–40) Though these are his first reactions, Clumly eventually allows himself to glean from the Sunlight Man that which is worth integrating into his own life. In other words, Clumly is the one figure in the novel who, when faced with a novel approach challenging traditional ways of thinking and demanding a subsequent change in attitude and behavior, is able to grow from the experience.

One of the characteristics of Clumly that makes him unique in the novel, and perhaps the trait that most allows him to grow from his experience with the Sunlight Man, is his willingness to accept responsibility. The novel's characters are forever, and for a variety of reasons, rejecting their own culpability in bringing about events, and further deny responsibility for the consequences of these events. The most blatant example is the thief who leads a double-life: as Walter Boyle he is a professional burglar, while as Walter Benson he is a respected citizen living with his wife in suburban Buffalo, NY. A man of cheap sentiment, Benson/Boyle is often quoting memorized poetry from Edgar Guest. But, to use a Kierkegaardian term, he does not "reduplicate" in his own actions the values described either in the poetry of Guest or in his own moral statements. At one point we are told that he and his wife are childless because, in his view, it is wrong to bring children into a world full of poor people, sick people, and crazy people, not to mention cruel people, dishonest people, and thieving people. He simply does not acknowledge that he is part of the reason why the world is as it is. Rather, he blames his wife, his tenant, and the Sunlight Man among others. He blames everyone but himself.

But Benson/Boyle is merely the most egregious example. All of the characters deny responsibility. A phrase repeated throughout the text, in the mouths of a variety of characters, is "It's not my fault" or, from the authorial omniscient point of view, "It is not his fault." By contrast, Clumly accepts his responsibility from the beginning. He tells one of his deputies over and over that as Sheriff he is responsible, thus conveying his sense of obligation to maintain law and order. Later, he explains to that same deputy what it means to be responsible, comparing his position to that of a king who must rise to the occasion and save his people when the laws or his knights fail him. He even compares himself to God, saying that it is God's responsibility to fix the world when the world becomes confused and is in need of fixing. Thus, when it is learned that the Sunlight Man has played a role in three murders since his escape from jail, Clumly's first reaction is to lay the blame entirely on himself for allowing the escape to have happened at all. Later, in a confrontation with the town's mayor and three councilmen, Clumly defends his unorthodox investigation into the crime spree centering around the Sunlight Man by simply stating, "Times are changing." (651) Then, influenced by earlier conversations with the Sunlight Man, he tries to explain that the four of them have no real understanding of the effect of their laws, and of their responsibility in bringing about the sort of community that exists in Batavia:

> You're responsible for it, if you want the truth: it's because of your kind I have to deal with the other kind, but you don't know it, you don't know they exist. That's your advantage. You're responsible, but you're not *responsible*. It's your laws they hang by, and if one of you slips over from your side to their side, it's your laws *he* hangs by. (651)

There may be virtue in order, Clumly is saying, but order can also be a sort of anesthetic, deadening one's recognition to the part played by one in making the world as it is. When a person does not see himself as responsible, then it is easy not to care. When that happens the love that Gardner often speaks of as necessary for a person to make real contact with another is missing. Clumly tells a wonderful story, a parable of sorts, about a time he went to a local drugstore and ordered a ham on rye sandwich. When the sandwich was placed in front of him he saw that the ham was all fat and that the lettuce looked as if it had been trampled on the floor. When he told the waitress that the sandwich wasn't fit to eat, she begged off saying it's not her problem, that she just works at the counter. "*Everybody* just works here," Clumly concludes. "If the sandwiches are going to be fit to eat, somebody's got to behave as if he owned the place." (655)

It becomes the theme of the novel: If life is to be what people would have it to be, then somebody's got to behave as if he owned the place. It used to be the case that God was seen as the owner, and the people but tenants. But it seems God has less and less of a hold on the minds of people. There is a God-figure in the novel, Judge Sam White. He plays little role in the action of the story but is a presence, nonetheless. In the context of Clumly's earlier remarks to the mayor and the councilmen, one would have to say a Judge is the highest representative of that set of rules—the legal system—which shields ordinary people from a sense of personal responsibility for what happens to others caught in the jaws of the law. God, viewed in classical theistic terms, is representative of that set of theological rules which also can shield people from a personal sense of responsibility. To be saved or to be damned is a matter of

God's grace, a mystery over which mere mortals are not privy. The Judge, however, makes clear the situation is changing at the level of Batavia politics, and by metaphorical implication at the level of deity as well. When told by the fire chief, Mr. Uphill, that Clumly is no longer working by the rules in his investigation of the Sunlight Man, the Judge echoes Clumly by saying that the times are changing. He then follows up by saying, "There are no more powers, principalities, gods, demigods. No more wizards, kings. And even if I could—" (395) It is an otiose God that is shown in the person of the Judge, a God whose hands are tied. With no God to carry responsibility for how things are, and no effective Judge to carry responsibility for the civic rules of Batavia, it is left to the people to take up the challenge to act as if they own the place. Clumly and the Sunlight Man are the only two who accept the challenge. Clumly's acceptance is ultimately successful while the Sunlight Man's is not, though Clumly could never have reached the level of intuitive understanding he attains without the influence of his adversary.

Whitehead, in his *Adventures of Ideas*, argues that every civilization has within it competing sets of values. At its zenith, however, a civilization will exhibit a realized unity of values. Whether a civilization is able to maintain itself for any length of time will depend on its ability to allow fresh experimentation within this unity of values. Without experimentation the society will stagnate. Once a civilization has run its course it may then, according to Whitehead, go either of two directions. One possibility is that the civilization may slowly decay. In such a case, satire usually becomes "the last flicker of originality in a passing epoch as it faces the onroad of staleness and boredom. Freshness has gone: bitterness remains." (278) At such times there remains "the show of civilization, without any of its realities." (278) An alternative possibility is to seek novel ways of valuation, daring to think new thoughts of new unities of value. In such instances thought races well ahead of actualization as an adventure of the imagination. The physical adventure of exploration will come later. There is an inherent danger in such adventure, however. As Whitehead warns, adventurous leaps of the imagination and subsequent action will sooner or later go beyond the safe bounds of an epoch, well beyond the limits of approved rules of thought and conduct. Social dislocations and confusions are the result during these times of adventurous change. A society will preserve its vigor only so long as there is a real contrast between what has been and what may yet be, only so long as it is willing to venture beyond the safe haven of already accepted verities. "Without adventure," Whitehead writes, "civilization is in full decay." (279)

Gardner shows Batavia to be a people acting a charade of civilization, maintaining the outer forms of orderliness and kindliness, but lacking that inner dynamism which provides a society its sense of meaningfulness and purposefulness. The fact that Gardner sees so much of contemporary fiction as being dominated by cynical authors satirically smirking at modern life is an indication that, along the lines of what Whitehead writes, modern civilization is poised on the brink: it will either decay further and ultimately erode, or be revivified through an adventure of the imagination. The Sunlight Man presents just such an adventure for the people of Batavia, an adventure they perceive as a threat to the rules by which they live—or at least mimic. The Sunlight Man's approach is deeply flawed, however. Pure novelty, untied to the past or any other system of organization, is but another name for anarchy. Indeed, the Sunlight Man often refers to himself as an anarchist. At one point he claims that there is only rule or anarchy. To talk of anything between rule and anarchy as freedom is, in his mind, to speak nonsense.

The Sunlight Man shares the same tragic errors of James Chandler and Agathon: an intellectualism which devalues human emotion, human feeling, and human love. Because his earlier attempts at love were betrayed by others he has become embittered, adopting an intellectual stance which acts both as an explanation for past wrongs done to him and as a justification for his own future acts. He restates Camus's notion of the "absurd" in the form of a question: Which should be abandoned, belief in society or belief in the cosmos? Of course, the cosmos for the Sunlight Man is an unending and unyielding expanse of space containing mere physical stuff, all entirely indifferent to human striving. And while society holds out the hope of creature comfort in loving community, of active ties to other men and women, the cosmos holds out no comfort whatsoever, other than an intellectual pleasure in knowing the world for what it is. While he *wants* to believe in the former, it is the indifferent cosmos that he sees as the ultimate reality, and thus he seeks to comport his life with its wisdom rather than the pleasant illusions of human society. It comes to a head when the Sunlight Man, together with an Indian he helped escape from jail, are described as holding his aunt and nephew prisoner while they hide from the police. In conversation with his nephew, Luke, the Sunlight Man attempts to justify his beliefs about the cosmic order by comparing the universe to a machine gun which riddles all human attempts at coherence with cosmic bullet holes. We find ourselves torn apart by nature's way, then we try to rebuild our riddled world only to see it come crashing down again; as fast as we build a working society it all collapses again. The Sunlight Man has certainly seen his personal attempts to build a meaningful existence all go for naught. "You put up bird houses and cities," he tells Luke, "but cats eat the birds and cyclones eat the cities, and nothing is left but the fruitless searching." (450)

His nephew finally is able to challenge the Sunlight Man effectively, though the Sunlight Man works at not showing the others how pointed and telling Luke's words to him are. After first accusing the Sunlight Man of doing nothing but talk, eliciting from the Sunlight Man that he occasionally "acts" as well, Luke mocks the effectiveness of his actions in releasing the Indian, Nick, from jail. The Sunlight Man prefers to think of it as an act of "freeing" the Indian. But Luke pointedly criticizes his release of Nick as a vicious act. Anyone who knew Nick would know him to be vicious. Had the Sunlight Man been grounded in community, in other words, he would recognize the viciousness of his act. Instead, anarchist that he is, he feels no compulsion to learn from Nick's past. Nor does he feel any moral obligation to those who may be affected by Nick's murderous actions in the future. Luke accuses the Sunlight Man of believing anything is possible simply by saying it is, which is always the danger when one overly intellectualizes experience. The conversation takes a sudden turn when the Sunlight Man asks if Luke is afraid of him. Luke nods in agreement, and begins to explain why before falling quickly silent. The Sunlight Man finishes his thought for him, "Because I'm crazy, you were going to say." (451) Luke then launches into a description of the inhuman manner in which the Sunlight Man walks and talks. In a brief exchange the Sunlight Man asserts:

> "Suppose I say I do believe in the past? Suppose I say I once walked and talked like you?"
> "But you don't say it. You say 'suppose.' If you said it, it would be asking me to wonder what happened, what turns a human being into a monster. It would be talking as if we were both human." (452)

His nephew's criticisms have their affect on a perhaps nostalgic Sunlight Man, leaving him simply to assert that he did indeed, in his past, walk and talk like other men and women. "God's truth," he says. But he recovers enough to tell Luke not to be concerned for him, then parodies the line from Jesus about those without sin casting the first stone, all while he writes the word "Youth" among the filings on a nearby workbench. "You haven't understood," Luke concludes, "I was offering help." After a moment, the Sunlight Man, softly violent, says, "With what, boy? With *love*? Is *Love* your weapon?" (453) The Sunlight Man would say nothing more.

Luke's words—and actions—have even more of an impact than it might appear. Luke is one who sees the hypocrisy of his elders around him, and rages against the cruelty and injustice of his times. And the Sunlight Man is convinced Luke—once seasoned a bit more with life's cruel experiences—eventually will come to view the world as he does. It is not to be, as the Sunlight Man learns when Luke is forced to transport him and Nick in the back of a truck. Thinking the Sunlight Man and the Indian are in the back of his truck, Luke deliberately drives off the edge of the road and crashes. Sacrificially, Luke allows himself to be killed thinking he is taking the Sunlight Man and the Indian with him. Despite his anger and frustration with the community around him, Luke still feels a moral obligation to save it. Regardless of society's shortcomings, they are preferable to that "rough beast" slouching toward, in this case, Batavia that the Sunlight Man represents. The Sunlight Man is, for his part, prodded by Luke's death to recall some of the ideals of his own youth, and it compels him to finally see himself as responsible: "Though he didn't die in the crash, it was of course Luke's crash that killed him." (710) When the Sunlight Man goes to the police station to turn himself in he is, because of one last practical joke he plays, shot through the heart by a frightened deputy.

Chief Clumly has learned important lessons from the Sunlight Man. He has learned that rules and laws ought not to be thought of as unyielding structures, but as dynamic orderings of human value in need of change from time to time to reflect the current needs of the people. While law and order may be important, Clumly comes to believe, there is a reason why laws exist. When laws start to run counter to the very reasons why the law came into existence in the first place, then it should no longer be considered a law. Clearly, he is no longer the person who believes "a cop hasn't got opinions." (23) Still unable to articulate fully his new understanding of law and order, he tries to express himself before a civic organization in the last section of the novel. He tells those gathered that the Indian has been captured and the Sunlight Man has been killed. He speaks of his pride in his police force and the work they accomplished in pursuing the two. And while justice was served in one sense, he also wants to convey his notion that justice, in another sense, was not served. "I can't explain that if you don't see it in your heart," he tells his audience, "it's just the way it is, maybe always was and always will be." (742)

Clumly comes to know the Sunlight Man well enough to discern that the anger displayed by him is largely the result of the way others had lied, cheated and stolen from him; they had promised their love and devotion and then turned on him when convenient. The Sunlight Man then found himself tangled in a legal system which left him at the mercy of those seeking to hurt him for their own selfish reasons. Over time he grew to hate all systems which hide their arbitrariness behind ceremonies valorizing the public good. As a result of the Sunlight Man's questioning the validity of our notions of social order, Clumly has come to realize that the people who make and are governed by laws and rules must, in turn, be willing to take responsibility for how those laws and rules are carried out. In addressing his audience, Clumly says that each person lives in the hope that life will get better, despite what we see as the obvious faults within society. We may realize that life is not all that it ought to be, but we still yearn to make our lives and our community better. Then, drawing on Einstein's conception of the universe (of all things), at least as best as he could understand it, he describes the world as forever moving outwards at terrific speed, and that at its edges it can get very cold, freezing to ice. "Ladies and gentlemen," Clumly concludes, "we mustn't let that happen, I feel. I feel we must all be vigilant against growing indifferent." (743) In short, people need to start acting as if they owned the place.

It is important to note that Clumly draws on the imagery of funerals to help make his point. Funerals are spread throughout the text. We are told early that Clumly enjoyed going to funerals. In some mysterious way he could not quite fathom, he finds pleasure in the rituals associated with funerals. The generations of family surrounding the grave, the members of civic organizations present, all lend dignity to the occasion as a man's life is closed shut, "like the book in the minister's hands." (19) The funeral for the Sunlight Man's father-in-law, who had tormented the young Taggert Hodge so cruelly, is orderly and dignified. Clumly is somewhat shocked, however, by how pleased the man's relatives seem to be now that he is dead. Another funeral, for the Italian deputy murdered by the Indian during his escape, prompts Clumly to meditate on the young man's untimely end. Nonetheless, Clumly comforts himself with the thought that each of us will have to go sometime, and the funeral for his deputy was fitting: "whatever tensions, uncertainties, joys and sorrows warred in the heart, law and order were restored, and there was peace." (417) In a field beyond the cemetery Clumly could see cows laying in the field, dogs sniffing at fenceposts, and the unending ripples of tree-covered hills. Despite the intrusions of death, life goes on for Clumly and the others. Clumly feels comfortable with the rituals of funerals for, in spite of life's seeming chaos and tragedy, the funeral brings a sense of wholeness to life, and makes life beautiful.

In speaking to the civic group Clumly talks about how most people, living their lives under the shadow of societal Law and Order, are afforded funerals which honor the good lives they have lived within the community. It is right, he says, that a community honor a man's life, that all of the people who ever knew him gather to afford him that last final moment of order, that last final moment of significance to a life lived in community. He then makes note of the fact that the Sunlight Man will not have a funeral like that, and that everyone knows why. "He didn't obey the laws," Clumly tells them. "*Our* laws that we've put on the books for the benefit of all, or anyway the benefit of almost all, all of *us*, anyway." (742)

The Sunlight Man is fully open to an imaginative adventure of novel possibilities, but he completely cut himself off from those social traditions that had helped form him. In the dichotomy between a social order requiring individuals to forego personal freedom for the public good, and an unrestrained personal freedom amounting to social anarchy, he clearly opts for the latter. Clumly, at the beginning, opted for the former, but in his contact with the Sunlight Man comes to realize the importance of balancing two human needs: security and tradition on the one hand, and freedom and novelty on the other. In addition to law and order there is justice, and "justice requires imagination and a capacity for vision." (Morris, 1984:95) It requires both an appreciation for impersonal order and the capability personally to reach out to another in love, and it is just this holding of two seeming opposites in balanced tension that Whitehead speaks of as the "essence of Peace." (1967:292)

This Whiteheadian notion of "peace" will be discussed at length later, but part of what is included in the notion is a sense of the interconnectedness of things. Gregory Morris is one of the few who notes the connection with Whitehead here, but only in passing as he describes Clumly (and Gardner) as having a belief in a connected and coherent world. "It is a Whiteheadian faith in a connected, unified system," he writes. (1984:79) Unfortunately, he pursues the matter no further. Regardless, Clumly is the sort of character Gardner loves to hold up as a hero. As Daniel Laskin eloquently states it, Clumly triumphs because

> the experience has changed Clumly, has forced him to abandon his once easily held conception of law and order; the Sunlight Man has taken him on a spiritual journey. For Gardner, a man like Clumly is the most admirable kind of hero. He is an undistinguished man, a flawed person with long regrets and an uneasy feeling that his life has been wasted, his marriage a failure, his career insignificant. But in his pedestrian way—clumsy, glum, humble—he has been brave enough to submit his values to a test, honest enough to recognize their shortcomings, and strong enough to resist despair, and to embrace instead an amended view of life. (1978:36)

CHAPTER VIII:
Self-Reliance and Redemption

The 1976 publication of *October Light* preceded by less than two years the release of *On Moral Fiction*. While the latter, as already noted, caused tremendous consternation on the part of other writers and critics, resulting in direct and sometimes vicious attacks on Gardner, *October Light* is, in many respects, Gardner's finest novel. Conceived as a Bicentennial novel, meant to explore some of the foundational values that make up the American character, the novel was named winner of the 1977 National Book Critics Circle Award for fiction. There is irony in the fact that this novel presenting certain ideas through the indirect mode of fiction would be so well received, while a literary critical book which presents those same ideas in the more direct fashion of critical discourse would be so bitterly rejected. Regardless, *October Light* is a deeply satisfying novel which continues Gardner's exploration of issues related to death and guilt.

James Page, a Vermont farmer approaching his 73rd birthday on July 4th, is much like other Gardner heroes in that he is a common man seeking, in his own sometimes blundering way, to come to terms with the life that has been granted him. His life and values are based, mostly, on the rhythms and certainties of his physical environment. His is a Yankee individualism forged in the harsh realities of living off the land and enduring the radical changes of the seasons, a niggardly life forcing one to work desperately hard to support one's family. In this part of the country a person gains the respect of neighbors by making his or her own way in the world. In the land of Emerson, self-reliance is a primary virtue. As a part of the geographical and social landscape, James Page has a bedrock sense of who he is, and of what is to be valued. That his sense of values might lead him to narrow-minded and intolerant views is of no concern to him. His moral compass is sure. Indeed, it is his strong sense of what is to be valued that leads him one night to load his shotgun and shoot his sister's television set, blowing it back to a hell from which he believes it to have originated. Television is for James Page the most egregious indication of how corrupt life is becoming in the United States. It is its unending and simpering advertising, together with "its monstrously obscene games of greed," (3) that particularly irk him. How can something which shows people getting lots of money without having to work for it be of any use? It just isn't natural to his way of thinking. Besides, James concludes, "God made the world to be looked at head on." (4)

James's personal life has been as harsh as his views. One son, Ethan, died in a farm accident while a second son, Richard, ended his life by suicide. His wife, Ariah, has also died by the time the narrative begins. Indeed, James Page knew the world as one of danger and darkness. He understood "life's gravity" as he sometimes called it. Working the fields and working with animals he knows that all life is a brutish struggle, hopeless and brief, against the entropic pull of the earth. When a creature becomes ill it struggles to go on despite the ever-growing pull of the earth. And no matter how long or how gallantly that creature may strive to continue its life, its body will continue to bend lower and lower until gravity finally has its eternal say. Yes, James knows the world. It is not an altogether bleak world, however, for James Page also believes in a life of the spirit that counterbalances the entropic physical pull to the earth. Bone and meat is what the world pulls downward, he knows, while the spirit of a man is what pushes him upward and allows him to soar, if only briefly. That which is decent is what aids men and women in their struggle upward, their battle against gravity. That which is most foul, however, is not that which gives way to gravity—there is nothing inherently evil in bone and meat, after all—but rather that which evokes a false image of freedom and ascent. That is what bothers James most about television: it gives viewers the *illusion* of freedom and ascent, thus leaving men and women unprepared for the real challenges of life. In Gardner's scheme of things, that is what all "immoral" art does. As far as James Page is concerned television, along with Snoopy, Coca-Cola, the state of California, foreign cars, foam rubber, TV dinners, and other consumer goods of commercial America, are part of that "senselessly prettified life" (13) which he violently rejects.

Ideas and subsequent actions do have consequences, however, and the consequence of his shooting the television set is to chase his sister, Sally Abbott, to her bedroom, where she has been for three weeks preceding the narrative beginning of the story. James takes this rift with his sister in stride, justifying himself with the thought that he has done plenty to accommodate her since she arrived following the death of her husband, Horace. But her constant watching of television finally put him over the edge. For her part, the shooting of the television is just another example of James's bullying, and she decides she will tolerate it no longer. As the narrative opens James and Sally are intransigent, each convinced of their moral rightness and of the other's foolishness. As their conflict continues each would ratchet up the confrontation: she thinking she'll put the pressure on him by refusing to eat, and he thinking he will make it easy for her to stay in her room by locking the door from the outside. Her hunger strike isn't all it is cracked up to be, however, for her bedroom is connected to an attic filled with twelve bushels of apples to keep her going. As for his locking her in the bedroom, Sally feels she has the last laugh by locking her door from the inside. They are at an impasse.

The idea of "locking" is actually quite central to the story, for area residents refer to that time heading toward winter when the days grow shorter and shorter and nature begins its natural process of shutting down as the "locking time." After "locking time" movement is near impossible because of ice and snow; the rivers have become frozen and all of nature seems cold and dead. It is an apt metaphor for what is happening to James and Sally. They are "locked in" to their positions and unable to move. In time, their dispute becomes public knowledge. In a telephone conversation James tells his daughter, Ginny, that Sally is locked in her room. Moreover, he tells Ginny why she is locked in her room. Ginny, immediately seeing the silliness of it all, says she will be right over. That part of the conversation in which James tells of Sally being locked in her room is accidentally heard by a neighbor on a party line. "I'm not one to tell tales," the neighbor says to his wife, "but . . . if old James Page locks his sister in the bedroom, it's certain he's got some good reason." (120) Later that night, the neighbor mentions it again to some of James's friends at Merton's Hideaway, a local tavern.

James's friends have been taking note of the changing season, the sun going down earlier as fall moves toward winter. It is always a bit of a surprise to see it happening, seemingly unnatural at times, even though it has been a part of their lives every year. The sudden dwindling of daylight in October is the first persuasive proof that locking time, and then the cold and snow of winter, is coming. The growing darkness is obscurely magical to them, known "in their blood if not quite in their conscious minds." (122) The mood quickly changes after hearing of what James has done to his sister. Each of them immediately voices his support for James. Sally is seen by them as an outsider, a loafer taking advantage of James. One of the men claims James had plenty of provocation from Sally, while another offers that Sally has "strange opinions." A third, Sam Frost, adds that it's just not right for James to work as hard as he does, trying to put a little money in the bank, and then have his sister come along looking for a handout. What makes it worse, he adds, is how she has come to run his life since moving into his house, even to running his politics. Turns out Sam Frost's wife had called James earlier to help with a Republican fund raiser, and Sally told her that James was not at home, all the while with James heard yelling in the background to find out who was calling. Hearing Sam's story they all sat thoughtfully, thinking of the implications. Finally, one of them breaks the silence by offering, "He'd ought to shoot her." (123) This "hardening of heart" against Sally, this "locking in" of their views of her, is but an indication of the values endemic to the farmers of this part of Vermont. It is not that they are mean-spirited; it's just that they are very sure of what is right and what is wrong. Whether a flint-hard Vermont farmer like James Page is able to demonstrate moral growth, despite his absolutism, is one of the questions Gardner wishes to explore in the novel.

While locked in her room Sally passes the time by reading a cheap paperback book she finds on the floor. A novel, it is described by blurbs on the back cover as:

> "... *A sick book, as sick and evil as life in America ...*"
> —*National Observer*
>
> "*Deeply disturbing!*"
> —*St. Louis Post-Dispatch*
>
> "*Hilarious!*"
> —*New York Times*
>
> (15)

Titled *The Smugglers of Lost Soul's Rock*, the book becomes a foil for what Gardner believes to be truly dangerous about what he calls "immoral" art. As fiction, *Smugglers* manifests those "faults of soul"—sentimentality, frigidity, and mannered writing—that Gardner believes destroy the vivid and continuous fictional dream toward which a writer should strive. He also believes such fiction creates ultimately harmful images of reality. In other words, *Smugglers* is representative of what Gardner finds wrong with most of contemporary fiction. This novel within a novel concerns a hip group of drug-smuggling revolutionaries, headed by a Faustian ship captain named Fist, who accidentally save the life of a man, Peter, who had attempted suicide by jumping off a bridge. Other characters in this novel within a novel include a competing group of drug smugglers headed by the amoral Santisillia, a wide-eyed young co-ed named Jane who gives her all for the revolutionary cause while being used sexually by the less altruistic men around her, and an 83-year-old paraplegic ex-brain surgeon named Alkahest trying to track them all down. Ideas, with innumerable quotes from several modern philosophers as ballast, are bandied about like shuttlecocks. All but three characters—good guys Peter and Jane, and bad guy Santasillia—are killed in an orgy of violence near the end of the story. The three are left stranded on Lost Soul's Rock with B-52 bombers about to attack them when, suddenly, part of the rock on which Santisillia is standing falls inextricably into the sea killing him. Simultaneously, a flying saucer appears in the sky—a contemporary *deus ex machina*—to save Peter and Jane. And thus ends *The Smugglers of Lost Soul's Rock*.

On one level, *Smugglers* is a silly novel. On another, however, such novels have achieved critical acclaim. There are even some who argue the novel within a novel is a more satisfying fiction than the narrative about James Page and Sally Abbott. For Gardner, such a literary conclusion is precisely what is wrong with those who publicly pronounce on literary standards. As parody, *Smugglers* has been associated with the fiction of Robert Stone, Kurt Vonnegut, Thomas Pynchon, and John Barth, each of whom being a highly regarded novelist within the literary-critical establishment. (Cowart, 1983:120–21) As a device, the use of this novel within a novel allows Gardner to show how such fiction can have a deleterious effect on a reader.

Sally begins reading the book mostly for something to do. At the beginning she clearly sees the book for what it is: cheap and vulgar drugstore trash. Occasionally, after a silly incident or when she finds a couple of pages missing, she tells herself she will quit reading it. But she continues. As she begins to get more involved with the characters and the story she still views it as cheap pulp fiction, but she is becoming less distanced from it than before. Thinking of Horace, her dead husband who had surrounded himself with the "great books" of human civilization, she begins to ponder her own reading of such a tawdry novel. After an exclamation of defiance, she poses an important question: Which is worse, a pedestrian book which provides for a laugh or a smile every now and then, though it speak of impolite human activities (e.g. excretory and sexual matters), or books of memorable prose that speak in the most hushed and gloomy ways of human tragedy, with terrible warnings of the dismal future which awaits us all? "Show me Horace," she demands of her dead husband, "a book that's got insights into human nature that an eighty-year-old woman hasn't thought of!"

While in her room, the bitterness, cynicism, unfeeling brutality, and avoidance of responsibility displayed by the characters of *Smugglers* becomes a part of Sally's emotional make-up in her dispute with James. When a good friend of hers, Estelle Parks, comes to talk with her through the bedroom door, Sally justifies her intransigent position by a conscious appeal to a Walter Cronkite statement about Freedom, and an unconscious appeal to assertions from *Smugglers* about "reality and truth" (214, 155) and about our lives being scripted, as if in a book, with the end, even if happy, being defiled and corrupted when we finally reach it. Her touchstones of moral direction, in other words, are a television personality and a brutish, pseudo-philosophical paperback novel. Together, they blind her to the human endeavor of Estelle to reach out to her and help end the feud. She will not come out of her room and has become, in her own way, just as intolerant as James and his friends. Locked in as they are, neither Sally nor James is capable of reaching out to the other in love.

Estelle, along with Ginny and Lewis, James's daughter and son-in-law, come upon a plan to get Sally out of her room: they decide to bring together a number of Sally's friends, inviting them to the Page home for a party. The goal, of course, was to lure Sally from her self-imposed exile once she heard her friends in the other room. The scene is similar to others from Gardner's novels when members of a community gather and share their wisdom at a time of crisis. When there is a breach of the social fabric it affects a community wider than that of the immediate participants. Thus, it is vitally important to the community as a whole to attempt to redress the situation and reintegrate those who find themselves estranged. No less than 14 people find themselves in James Page's kitchen. Sally hears the commotion and calls out to them three times. They ignore her, hoping she will end her isolation and join in. For his part, James is uncomfortable with the sudden gathering in his kitchen. He was not a part of this conspiracy and he wants nothing to do with it. He prefers to handle Sally in his own way. Without anyone realizing it, James slips out of the house, into his truck, and drives to Merton's Hideaway to be with his friends. Those who remain at James's home begin to discuss barn-fire parties. "Barn-fire parties?" a visiting priest new to the area asks. Ed Thomas, in his rural Vermont dialect, tries to explain to the priest that whenever someone in the area loses a barn or a home to fire there is a gathering of local residents at the home of the victim. Ed's wife, Ruth, adds that first everyone works to help put the fire out and save the stored goods and livestock. Then, when it's all over, everyone heads to the home of the nearest neighbor, or perhaps even the home of the fire victim himself, for refreshments. Eventually, it turns into a party. When the priest continues to express his distaste, Ed pipes in that it's not a case of the neighbors not having any feelings. In fact, he says, it is all done for the sake of the victim as much as anyone. The priest, maintaining his aversion, nonetheless tries to act forgiving by stating a relativistic sop about people behaving in different ways in different places. Estelle, hearing the conversation, tries to excuse the priest:

> "It's just as you've said yourself, Father. It's a fragile life. One moment we're happy and wonderfully healthy, and our children are all well, and it seems as if nothing can possibly go wrong, and the next some horrible accident has happened, and suddenly we see how things really are and we cling to each other for dear life.
> "Hear, hear!" Dr. Phelps said merrily, . . . They all laughed, understanding his intent. Yet after the moment of laughter the room was unnaturally quiet, as old and insubstantial as the yellowed lace curtains, infirm as the shadows on the fireplace bricks, the whole house still as a grave. (234)

It is a shimmering truth. With the exception of the priest and the minister present, both of whom new to the area and still outsiders, it is a truth with which they are all familiar. Those hopes we have of protecting our families may be "old and insubstantial" and "infirm as the shadows," but when some "horrible accident" brings life's tragedies to our doorstep there is the community, to which one can cling "for dear life." Despite the mythology of "Yankee individualism," it is a profound sense of community which allows these rugged individuals to keep working, in hopes of securing a fruitful life for themselves and their families. The prolonged silence is finally broken by Ruth Thomas's reciting from a poem:

> And we are here as on a darkling plain
> Swept with confused alarms of struggle and flight,
> Where ignorant armies clash by night. (235)

The lines, from Matthew Arnold's "Dover Beach," capture well Estelle Parks's feelings. It leads her to recall the words of a friend of hers, a Japanese professor: "Very fragile, this world," he had said, "the tiniest rent in the veil, as we say—the tiniest disturbance of the god's sleep . . ." (236)

Gardner is contrasting the literature and aesthetic ideals of people like Ruth Thomas and Estelle Parks with that of Sally Abbott. Estelle, an English teacher who occasionally is asked how she can teach the same poems years after year, has known tragedy in her own life. It is her deep and abiding knowledge of literature which has helped her to cope, however, as is seen when she is described as contemplating Wordsworth's "Lines Composed a Few Miles above Tintern Abbey." These poems are described as having grown in importance with her, becoming even more rich in significance as each decade passes. Once, several weeks after listening to a 15-year-old boy recite the Wordsworth poem, she was having an experience of *déjà vu*—a long-forgotten memory wells up when the boy's father, many years earlier, had recited the same poem. There is a passing on of a tradition, of values that will see another generation to their obligations. The lines of the poem continue to be inspirational to her:

> For I have learned
> To look on nature, not as in the hour
> Of thoughtless youth; but hearing oftentimes
> The still, sad music of humanity,
> Nor harsh nor grating, though of ample power
> To chasten and subdue. And I have felt

> A presence that disturbs me with the joy
> Of elevated thoughts; a sense sublime
> Of something far more deeply interfused,
> Whose dwelling is the light of setting suns,
> And the round ocean and the living air,
> And the blue sky, and in the mind of man:
> A motion and a spirit, that impels
> All thinking things, all objects of all thought . . . (201-02)

By contrast we have Sally's literary model in *The Smugglers of Lost Soul's Rock*. Estelle and Ruth approach life's problems with an insight that sees the spiritually affirming interconnectedness of things, and of the need for human community. Sally instead comes to phrase her "tragedy" in the overblown melodrama of pulp fiction and pop philosophy, and her answers to life's challenges become couched in terms of the inviolate "I."

The evening ends with Ruth Thomas reciting poetry to the delight of those gathered. Even though the ostensible purpose for the gathering—the ending of the feud between Sally and James—has not been brought to a successful conclusion, it nonetheless has been deeply satisfying and meaningful for those who have come. Community values and strengths, their deep and abiding caring for one another, are reaffirmed. And, judging from how Dr. Phelps's granddaughter and Estelle's grandnephew are smiling at each other and sharing whispered thoughts, the ongoing process of community renewal has also been a part of the evening. Despite the tragedies along the way, life does go on.

For his part, James is beginning to strike a conciliatory tone with his friends at Merton's Hideaway. Explaining his feelings on the matter with Sam Frost and Henry Stumpchurch, he says that there are always two sides to an argument, and that her coming to live with him no doubt gives her a right to live her life however she wishes. When his friends resist his more thoughtful approach to Sally, he begins to defend her, saying it's not her fault that she is poor, and that she mostly does her share of work around the house. "I ought to just try and bend more," he concludes, "whole thing stotted with that television." At that, his friends begin to chuckle, recalling his taking a shotgun to it. "I *hate* that God damn television," James says.

While there, James notices some young women from Bennington College arrive. After a moment they are fawning over a man with a coarse gray beard (a thinly disguised description of Gardner himself), one of them telling the man that she has read all of his books. The man, obviously drunk, almost knocks over his chair getting up to take the girl's extended hand in both of his. The women then move on to sit with some of the local boys. James tries to hear the conversation of the Bennington girls, which mostly concerns literature and art, subjects toward which the local boys are decidedly indifferent. It does get James to thinking about literature and art, though. James includes contemporary art and literature as part of his litany of what has gone wrong in America. He doesn't spend time reading books, though he recalls buying a "comic blockbuster" (i.e. *The Smugglers of Lost Soul's Rock*) once when he'd driven Estelle and Sally to the bus station. He read a couple of sentences at the beginning, flipped a hundred pages or so into the book, and read a little more. From what he could tell, it was all about sex. He threw it into the garbage for the pigs where, unbeknownst to him, his nephew had found it and taken it into the house. What had particularly irked James was that the book was proclaimed a masterpiece on the cover. It was the kind of book people seemed to like these days, the kind of book from which one could learn about life. No doubt professors and writers would claim such books tell *the Truth* about life, but James Page considers it all hogslop, along with television. His one real question was, Where will it end? Thinking of Brazilian "snuff" films, which are pornographic movies in which the actress is actually murdered and dismembered on film, he has come to believe that "if the acting was right and the language was vile enough, people would be hard put to figure out why it wasn't art." (297)

Overhearing snatches of conversation of the Bennington girls, occasionally glimpsing the images of the television being watched by others in the tavern, James is feeling more and more like a man out of place in modern America. With a flash of anger, he recalls the party going on at his place and the sleep he is missing by being forced out of his own house. The prospect of completing the next day's chores with little sleep is unsettling. One of his friends then asks James what he is going to do about his battle with Sally. James really doesn't know at this point. The change in conversation leads his friends to begin telling him about the ways Sally has misrepresented him to others. Sam Frost tells James that Sally tricks him. James doesn't know what he means. Sam tells him about the time James put an advertisement in the local

Pennysaver for someone to help with farm chores. James had always been puzzled why no one ever responded to that ad. Sam tells him that his wife, on the same party line as James, overheard Sally telling one interested applicant that James "wouldn't consider a soul that wasn't Negro or female." (307) James's first reaction was to say she would never do such a thing. Internally, however, he was seething. She'd do it; of course she'd do it. As James contemplates the effrontery of his sister, his friend Sam continues by telling him of another incident. When the local Republican Party called James seeking contributions, Sally would tell them that he wasn't at home. But it wasn't the truth, Sam says, because his wife could here James hollering in the background. Again, James told the others she would never do such a thing. "Mebby not, mebby not," Sam demurely concedes, "Mebby the little woman heard wrong." (308) Now, James Page is mad! Racing home in his truck quite drunk, James does not plan to shoot his sister, but he does have "the fixed intention of knocking the door down and belting her one." (309) Before he can reach home, however, his truck leaves the road about a half mile from his house. The wreck is heard by those gathered at his house just as they are preparing to leave. Instead, they rush to the sound of the wreck and find James in the crotch of an apple tree with minor cuts and bruises, his teeth lost in the wreck, and full of spiteful anger. It is the new Protestant minister, Lane Walker, and a visiting friend, the Catholic priest from the earlier episode named Rafe Hernandez, who reach James while the others stand at the edge of the road looking down on the three of them.

    James has now plummeted to the depths, literally and figuratively. The two clergymen see that his truck is burning, but to them it is only a truck. To James, however, it is his entire life going up in flames. James constantly bemoans the fact that the truck wasn't even paid for, while the clergymen try to soothe him with the soporific that he is still alive, and that that is all that really counts. It does not have its intended effect. James explodes in anger at them. Here he sits in an apple tree, missing his teeth, battered, his only truck destroyed and burning, unpaid for and uninsured, his life of hard work and miserable sadness seemingly wasted, sick and old and ready to see an end to it all, and here are two strangers, clergymen, with their shiny shoes and their city clothes telling him things aren't so bad. What is flashing across James's mind is that "all that had made him once think life worthwhile was gone," (311) his wife, his two sons, his health, his hope. He thinks of how he was tempted to end his life back when he "killed" his son, but did not because he knew others were dependent on him. And these clergymen, "living off their wholly fictitious God and the fat of the land" (307) dare to laugh at him along with the others now looking down from the edge of the road, gazing at him as if he were an exhibit at a fair, all the while his life burning in front of him. Seeing a cemetery nearby, he considers those earlier generations of local folks, fools all, buried now under sod and stone who, like him, lived lives "of, for the most part, misery, lied to and cheated and teased by false hopes." (311) In short, James Page decides to shoot his sister.

Back in his house James finds, then brandishes, his shotgun and orders everyone to leave. Having voiced his intention to shoot Sally, the others are hesitant to leave her alone with him. Then, suddenly, Ed Thomas is clutching his chest in the throes of a heart attack. After Ruth Thomas and others leave to take Ed to the hospital, James is left in his kitchen with the two clergymen. He orders them to leave by the count of five, and though they make it out the door by the end of his counting James fires the shotgun anyway "for pure manic glee." (315) By this time Sally is well aware James has a gun and is threatening to shoot her. She sets up a defense for herself by rigging an apple crate above the door in such a way that it will come crashing down on anyone entering. Unbeknownst to her, James falls asleep on the commode with his shotgun at his side, held in the grips of his own drunkenness and constipation. Sally eventually turns to her book, and the wisdom of its pages in her reckoning is telling her:

> There was no one in this world, however mighty of will—her own life was proof—not capable of being robbed, or raped, or murdered, not capable of being attacked from nowhere, for no real reason, by the mindless bestiality of things—her drunken brother with his shotgun. And also there was no one not capable of slipping toward the bestial himself. (332)

She is left to ponder the gloomy thought during one of those irritating times when her novel has a gap of some pages. Gardner then makes an important novelistic transition. Sally considers for a moment submitting to James and to the example set by her husband Horace, but rejects it. She ends her train of thought with the line, "But if submission was wrong . . . ." The reader is then told that Sally looked at the page just beyond the interruption, bit into her apple, and then continued to read. The next line of the novel says, ". . . life evil." (333) Melding Sally's thoughts with the text we end with the line, "But if submission was wrong [then] life [is] evil." She sets up the conditional premise with the antecedent "if submission was wrong," but she does not know how to finish the thought. Instead, she allows her novel to finish the thought for her. And it is important to note the bite of the apple before she allows the novel within a novel to complete her thought. It is a symbol of her fall.

Apples are used throughout the text—indeed, in many of Gardner's other novels as well—as a potent symbol. It is while trapped in the crotch of an apple tree that James is at his lowest, most violent, point. The trap set for James is sprung accidentally on Ginny when she enters Sally's bedroom. The apple crate comes crashing down on her head, sending her to the hospital. When James sees his daughter is nearly killed by the crate of apples he again focuses his anger at Sally—not only for the accident, but because it now becomes clear Sally had been cheating on her fast by eating the apples. Apples are constantly being associated with anger, violence, and death. We learn early in the novel of the crates of apples in the attic which sustain Sally. Also, a coleus plant in Sally's bedroom has been slowly dying despite her best efforts. Not until James is visiting Ed Thomas in his hospital room do we learn the full story of the coleus plant. Ruth Thomas tells James that had she known he would be at the hospital she would have brought the plant book for Sally. Upon questioning, Ruth tells James that Sally has had a coleus in her room, and that it had been slowly dying for months. James registers his surprise that Sally has a coleus in her bedroom, then says matter-of-factly that the plant will die. Ruth tells him again that it is dying, but that she and Sally don't know why. It's the apples, James tells her, describing how there are apples in the attic and that plants can't live around apples. Indignant, Ruth asks why James never told this to Sally. In his best elocution, given his missing teeth, he declares, "Thee didn't athk." What Gardner is developing is a metaphoric correlation:

apples:coleus plants :: immoral fiction:humans

Just as coleus plants cannot live around apples and thrive, so too men and women cannot live around immoral fiction; just as the coleus plant is slowly withering away, so too are the sensibilities required of Sally for living a fruitful life withering away.

One of the clear requisites for community living is an acceptance of the shortcomings of others, but also an ability to come to terms with one's own faults. One way of resolving the issue is simply to reject the notion that one has faults, which is tantamount to rejecting the notion of personal responsibility for the consequences of one's actions. This is the model presented by characters in *The Smugglers of Lost Soul's Rock*, as well as by Sally once she comes under the influence of the novel. But then there are those who do accept responsibility for their actions. For them, a communally-accepted moral code may act as a justification for their responsible actions (e.g. a soldier accepts responsibility for killing another, but is sanctioned by his community to do so). But then there are those like James Page who, seeing the consequences of their responsible actions, feel guilt when the consequences are tragic, as when his son, Richard, kills himself. Coming to terms with guilt is, for Gardner's heroes, perhaps the most important, humanly significant event of their lives.

On a superficial level it is the dispute between James and Sally that constitutes the dramatic tension of *October Light*. What becomes evident, however, is that the real conflict in James is with his own sense of guilt. He has lost both his sons: the youngest, Ethan, when he fell from a ladder left standing in the barn, and the elder, Richard, when he hung himself. It was Richard who had left the ladder from which Ethan had fallen, and Sally always believed that Richard was forever being punished by James for his thoughtless act. Indeed, Richard did feel a very palpable guilt at the death of his younger brother, as did Gardner at the death of his younger brother, Gilbert. Perceived by his family—and himself—as cowardly for not standing up to James, Richard turned to alcohol to soothe his troubles. By the time of his death he is judged a drunkard by the community. In Sally's mind it is James who drove Richard to suicide. In fact, James does hold himself guiltily responsible for Richard's death. And it is that guilt that has kept gnawing at James through the years.

Ginny recalls James being very hard on Richard, but also remembers her mother saying that James loved the boy more than anyone, including himself. Once, while with his friends at the Hideaway, James has a flash of memory about the boy hanging from the rafter, his body gripped in the stillness of death. James had been unable to believe that his son could have killed himself over such a little slap. They'd had fights before, and this one seemed no different from the others. His wife led him to believe the boy was up to something, and James figured it no doubt had something to do with women. So James tried to talk to the boy. But Richard refused to speak with him about his problems. Words were exchanged, the boy called his father a bastard, then a "quick, impetuous little slap" from James. (303) Richard ran off. It seemed such a minor incident at the time, though James knew when he saw Richard hanging from that rafter that it was more fraught with pain than he had at first realized, and that his son had avenged himself in a "dead-final victory." (303) There was another flash of memory while sitting at the Hideaway, of standing by a creek, looking down at his own reflection, condemning himself for having killed his son. "*Oh James, James*" he hears, his wife's whisper in his thoughts. Angry and full of grief, tears well in his eyes. Then, just as suddenly as it had come, it is forgotten and beyond his conscious reach.

Just before visiting Ed Thomas in the hospital, and feeling guilt for his role in Ed's heart attack, James recalls another time with Richard. It was just before Richard's suicide when James took the boy to the place where James's uncle Ira had committed suicide by firing a shotgun into his mouth. He meant no harm; he was simply showing Richard the place where an important event in his life was carried out. He recalls telling Richard how all these years he has carried a snake's skull that had belonged to his uncle Ira, and how much he had cried when he found Ira's body, which leads Richard to ask what Ira was like. He was crazy, James said, and didn't talk much, but he then added that Ira was brave and one of the toughest men he had ever known. Richard then asked whether Ira's mind was clear when he shot himself. James wanted so much to reach out and touch his son at that moment, but he held back like always, confused as to why his affection for little Ginny was so easily shared while his deep love for Richard remained mute. James fingered Ira's snake skull in his pocket, thinking he might pull it out and give it to Richard. He didn't. He simply said that Ira probably thought he was clear-headed at the time.

James, standing in a hospital hallway, finds himself wishing there were a secret door which would allow Richard to come back, so that he might try and make everything right between the two of them. But there is no such door. Mistakes, once made, are final. A wisdom at least as old as Heraclitus tells us that time is like a river flowing endlessly through the universe, and that none of us can step into the same river twice. Whether it be the ladder left against the barn which led to the tragic death of his youngest son, or the story about Uncle Ira that no doubt never should have been told to Richard, mistakes are final, water under the bridge. An odd sensation goes through James as he walks toward Ed Thomas's hospital room. Fingering that snake's head he feels a gossamer sense of insight, of understanding, of wisdom. Passing a hospital wastebasket in the corridor, he pulls the snake head out of his pocket and drops it in. James is coming to terms with his own sense of guilt.

It is immediately afterwards that James enters Ed Thomas's hospital room, where the discussion about the dying coleus plant takes place. The scene is another of those gatherings of people which Gardner so often uses as a coming together of the community to give strength and comfort to one another. In the room with Ed are his wife Ruth, James, and the two clergymen from before. Feeling his mortality, Ed is reminiscing about his past experiences and, among other pronouncements, declares to James that television really isn't so bad. He also begins talking about what he will miss when he is gone. At length, using the wonderful imagery of a man well acquainted with the land, he talks of the seasons. He describes what happens to the earth, the weather, the animals, and the people during these cyclic changes until he speaks, at last, of his favorite time: the "unlocking" time, that time which some call "mud season" because of all the mud that results when the land unfreezes. He continues, saying it is the rivers that unlock next, followed by two other kinds of unlocking: the town meeting where the community comes together after being isolated during the winter, and the "sugarin" time, when farmers are back in their fields working the land and gathering syrup from the maple trees. On and on Ed goes describing in minute detail all of the changes that occur during "unlocking" season, until finally he says with a kind of joyful sadness that he will not be able to take part in it this year, at least not in the same way he has in previous years. Looking up at James, Ed asks why he is bothering to listen to all this. James, still missing his teeth, says, "Becauth, ith true." (418) Ed smiles when he hears this, and says that is what he tells his wife when she swears she can't tell the difference

Self-Reliance and Redemption 163

between a good poem and a bad one. "I explain to her only the good ones are exactly true," he says. (418)

James is in a forgiving mood in the hospital room, partly because of his own recollections and partly because of what Ed has been saying. James is going through his own "unlocking." He even tries to be friendly and helpful to the two clergymen he earlier had chased out of his house with a shotgun. Lane Walker notices James's helpful behavior, and thinks to himself that James is, in his own way, trying to make amends. While at the hospital James also visits his daughter, Ginny. His "unlocking" continues as he considers how his actions have led to his daughter being hospitalized. For the first time in years he finds himself praying. Later, he flashes a memory of the drunken writer he had seen at Merton's Hideaway, of how the writer had given him a look, one of those all-consuming looks, as if he were going to use him in one of his books. It reminds him of Norman Rockwell's use of real people. James knew some of the people in Rockwell's paintings, and also knew Rockwell intended to paint the world and the people in it the way it could be. Occasionally, he was even able to paint how things actually are. James also recalls the time he stood near Rockwell when the painter, brooding on the times, declaimed that both the country and Christianity are ill, and that he wasn't feeling all that well himself. Others present laughed, but James realized that the painter was quite serious, at least about Christianity and the country. Despite his comfortable painterly life in a sunlit Vermont village, Rockwell knew there was the devil afoot. His paintings, James thought, were done as if they "might check the decay—decay that, in those days, most people hadn't yet glimpsed." (424)

Driving home from the hospital James is asked by his grandson to tell the story about Parson Dewey and the hero. James complies, recounting how Ethan Allen, after the improbable victory in the battle of Fort Ticonderoga, attends church the following Sunday. The parson of the church, during the morning prayer, thanks God for the victory at Fort Ticonderoga. Later in the prayer Parson Dewey again gives thanks to God for the victory, eventually saying all credit for the victory goes to Almighty God. Finally, Ethan Allen can stand it no more. Rising to his feet, he interrupts the prayer to ask if the parson would please remind God that he and his Green Mountain boys had been there as well. It is a basic principle of which James needs to remind himself: We, in our actions, help create the kind of world in which we live. We are not powerless in establishing the kinds of relations and communities we want. In that sense, if God is creator then we are God's co-creators. We must take responsibility for the results of our actions and, when necessary, do what is needed to redress the conflicts that invariably arise.

Sally has won the war, though she hardly realizes it when it happens. James simply tells her Ed Thomas thinks televisions are wonderful, especially for elections, which is something James had never thought about. Then, mentioning to Sally that Ed does not look well, Sally is out in the hall inquiring for further details about Ed's condition. In passing, she says Ruth Thomas at least would know what is happening to Ed, rather than the mystery that surrounded the death of her own husband, Horace. James is surprised to hear there is any kind of mystery about Horace, whereupon Sally reminds him that the front door to their home was left open that Halloween night Horace died. She'd always figured some child had just gotten a Halloween treat and that before he could close the door he had his heart attack. Sometimes, though, she wonders whether someone *meant* to frighten Horace, and whether as a result of that fright he had had his heart attack. If that were the case, then surely that person would have seen Horace staggering in pain, would have gone for help of some kind. James, while Sally tells her story, becomes more and more agitated until Sally finally asks him what is wrong. He tells Sally that she never told him about the open door. Alarmed, she says she told the police. "But you never told *me*," he yells at her.

Sally's account, together with other pieces of information he already knew, forces on James the realization that it was Richard who had frightened Horace, causing his heart attack and death. It was this act, and the resultant burden of guilt, that Richard had carried through the years—a burden he was forced to hold secretly to his own breast. James makes for the living room where the family photograph albums are kept. The aging family pictures remind him that there was a time when life had been good. Indeed, life is good, as Ed Thomas understands more clearly than ever now that he is in a hospital dying. He also remembers the time his wife approached him about Richard, saying the boy is in need of help. "It's something he's done . . . five years ago." (428) James asks his wife what it is, but she says Richard has to be the one to tell him. The conversation never takes place. When Richard approaches him the next day James, thinking it must be a problem with a woman, demands to know what Richard has done. It was then that Richard had called him a bastard, then followed by laughingly saying, "I'd die first." (429) James slapped him, and Richard skulked off, first to get drunk and then to hang himself.

James now knows that his son had reason to be afraid of telling him, for James would have forced Richard to confront Sally out of a sense of moral duty. Now, having the recent experiences with Sally, Ed Thomas, and others in the community, he is seeing it all quite differently. He is now recognizing something his wife and son already knew: his notion of truth had been very narrow-minded and punitive, and that he had been a fool. Because of his narrow-minded intransigence, Ariah too had gone to her grave full of guilt at having told James of Richard's "sickness" from a five-year-old incident. As for Richard, it wasn't revenge on his father that led him to commit suicide, but a five-year burden of guilt over what had started as a childish Halloween prank. He was 20 at the time, a man as society judges such things, but a man who had been told all his life that he was cowardly. That night he had frightened his uncle to death, and believing what others had said about his cowardice, he ran off and left his uncle to die. James's wife, near death herself, has some final words for him: "Oh James, James." His recollection of her words has darted in and out of his memories over the years, and he was only dimly aware of their significance. Only now does he see those final, intimate words to him as a benediction: her forgiveness of his actions as well as her own.

The final section of the novel finds James working near his barn with "the unlocking of his heart" continuing. (432) He has a surprise visitor as a black bear looking for honey confronts him. The two stare at each other for some time, then the bear turns toward the honey, ignoring James. He reaches for his shotgun, takes aim at the bear, but suddenly points the gun to the sky and fires. The startled bear races off into the woods. Trying to explain to his son-in-law why he didn't shoot the bear James says he clearly heard the bear say something: "Oh James," the bear had said, "James." Like Fred Clumly and Henry Soames, James Page has changed during the course of the novel. In not shooting the bear he demonstrates two areas of change. First, he has learned he cannot dominate every situation by simply imposing his rock-hard sense of New England propriety; he must be accepting of aspects of life that are not to his liking. Second, in not shooting the bear he also demonstrates an acceptance of the forgiveness extended him by his wife. Caught up in a value structure which posits the rugged individualist as morally good, James has not been in a position to even recognize his wife's gift of forgiveness, much less accept it, until the end of the novel. Before, when his wife's dying words would come to mind, he would immediately repress the thought. In not shooting the bear he is allowing that which points to his guilt to forever remain a part of his conscious life. Further, he transcends the limitations of his New England ethos to accept forgiveness for the tragic errors of his past. He knows the role he has played in causing suffering and death, and he feels the guilt of it, but he is now able to continue in his life without succumbing to it. It is a notable human achievement.

October Light is a masterful novel presenting a variety of characters and plot twists that allow for the gaining of several perspectives on the issues being addressed. Clearly, Gardner wants to present a variety of images having to do with the stories we tell ourselves about ourselves, and how these stories affect our lives. There are stories that belittle our lives, like the novel within a novel, and the images James gives Richard about his being a coward. Indeed, Sally slowly is transformed by the brutish cynicism of *The Smugglers of Lost Soul's Rock*, and Richard acts out the image provided him by running away when Horace needs his help. But there are also positive stories to tell of human life and endeavor, whether well-recognized poetry like that of Wordsworth or the down-to-earth ruminations of a truth-teller like Ed Thomas. Many of the characters, especially James by the end, manifest the values and perspectives of those images. These are stories and images that present not a Pollyanna world of unending happiness and glee, but a world of possibilities where barns do burn down and sons do commit suicide and friends do have heart attacks. Nevertheless, it is a world which presents opportunities for creativity and a deeply satisfying sense of purpose in our lives. The importance of community is again valorized by Gardner; it provides support when a barn burns down, or a son commits suicide, or a friend has a heart attack. A community can also intensify life's pleasurable experiences. A necessary ingredient for a healthy community, however, is communication.

Many of the conflicts and tragedies of *October Light* have their genesis in a lack of communication. Sally's coleus plant is dying because neither the problem nor the cure is being communicated. A crucial fact for James's understanding of why Richard killed himself comes too late because the fact is never communicated, thus forcing the young man to bear an unbearable guilt. For that matter, Richard's suicide is, in part, a result of an inability to communicate with his father. The main action of the novel, the dispute between James and Sally, is largely an exercise of missed communication. In a sense, the tragic consequences of missed communication is an indictment of those forms of individualism which have as their most desirable human image that of a person able to stand on his own two feet, unaffected by the acts of those around him, independent in thought and action, beholding to no one. While the image has an attraction in our culture it also carries a price. It leads to isolation, and more easily to the sort of "locking" or "hardening of heart" that occurs in *October Light*. A community is strengthened to the extent members of that community are able not only to *speak* of their own values and opinions, but actively to *listen* as well while others speak of their values and opinions; it is strengthened when its members work at molding the lives of others, but also by allowing their lives to be molded. A community is also strengthened by its acknowledgment, usually through formal and informal rituals, of the importance of a shared life together—both as a source of joy and pride, and as a source of strength and sustenance. James Page comes to realize the truth of the matter. In his gaining of wisdom he is approaching that dispassionate apprehension of life's fullest possibilities, which is that novel harmony of feeling which Whitehead speaks of as "peace."

CHAPTER IX:
Death, Guilt and Ritual Beginnings

Death is the preeminent theme in all of Gardner's fiction. Why this is the case probably has to do with the accidental death of his brother, as Lifton's work on survivors clearly suggests. The omnipresence of death in his novels, as well as the guilt harbored by nearly all of his main characters, leads Gardner to explore the reality of death and the volatile emotions associated with guilt. In Gardner's world, death and guilt lead to social strife of one sort or another. How these conflicts threaten the ongoing life of a community—not to mention the life and well-being of the individual in the midst of the conflict—is another area Gardner explores. One way such conflicts may be addressed in our social lives is through ritual activity. Anthropologists have long noted the use of ritual in effecting a resolution to social conflicts, thus preserving the social structure. The next two chapters will set a cultural context for Gardner's emphasis on death and guilt in his writing. They will also look at his fictional use of ritual in addressing issues of social conflict, as well as the use of ritual in establishing a sense of social identity.

In openly confronting the reality of death, guilt, tragedy, and the "thousand natural shocks that flesh is heir to," Gardner is similar in approach to the ideas of Martin Heidegger, who argued a man should live an "authentic" existence by being open to his own death. William May provides a nice context for this idea in his essay, "The Metaphysical Plight of the Family." May identifies three attitudes toward God in the "western" religious tradition: the man of faith, the Titan, and the philistine. The man of faith, May posits, lives in awe of God and dreads God's sacred power, while the Titan is the metaphysical rebel who defies the deity. The philistine is the person who avoids God by fleeing from God's presence. May goes on to argue that contemporary attitudes toward death are comparable to earlier attitudes toward God, which is to say contemporary attitudes toward death are ones of either dread, revolt, or flight. May suggests the writings of Heidegger and Albert Camus exhibit each of these three postures.

Camus, particularly in *The Rebel*, describes modern men and women as in metaphysical rebellion against death. This rebellion is largely a result of what Camus has referred to as the "absurd," the recognition of that disrelationship between a man or woman crying out for coherence and meaning in life, and the heavens answering with the cold and stony silence of anonymous dissolution. Given the absurd, one can either dumbly succumb to the universal physical pull toward extinction, or by an act of the human will impose meaning in the face of ineluctable death. Hence, Camus sees heroism in men and women resisting the "natural" order of things through their own choices and actions. It may be that death is an enemy threatening men and women, and that it cannot be defeated. Nonetheless, Camus insists that death be fought and resisted if we are to affirm our humanity. Heidegger, in his notion of "authenticity," speaks of both an avoidance of the reality of death as well as its acceptance. In point of fact, most men and women seek through artifice to remove thoughts of sickness, aging and death to the edges of their conscious experience. By being involved in a myriad of economic, political, social, and religious activities, men and women manage to maintain dynamic images of themselves, thereby repressing knowledge of their own ultimate end. Such people, in Heidegger's view, lead inauthentic lives of self-evasion. By contrast, Heidegger suggests a healthier, more authentic approach is to recognize oneself as a being-unto-death. While such a recognition is hardly easy and never pleasant, May agrees with Heidegger on this point, saying one must experience the "dreadfulness of death" in order to come to an authentic understanding of oneself. (53) He goes on to suggest that one's relationship to death is not like other possible relations. Rather, he argues that one's "authentic relationship to death is the touchstone of authenticity in all other relations." (53)

Gardner is in essential agreement with the ideas of Camus and Heidegger as presented here. What Gardner detests are those who take the ideas of thinkers like Camus and Heidegger, cast them in the gloomiest of lights, and thereafter strike the pose of the literary intellectual cynically championing a nihilistic world of meaningless—indeed farcical—human thought and action. It is these *poseurs*, generally encountered either in the graduate school seminar or on the cocktail party circuit, and most distressingly encountered in contemporary fiction read by a wide public, that Gardner comes to despise. May, in his essay, also alludes to those who misinterpret Heidegger, saying their "dark thralldom with the 'negative,' in the sense of the menacing and destructive," results in a romanticizing of violence and destruction. (54)

What is particularly striking in May's essay is the interpretation he gives to Dostoevski's "Grand Inquisitor," that seeming power-seeker described by Ivan to his brother Alyosha in *Brothers Karamazov* as threatening a newly-returned-to-earth Christ with *auto-de-fé* for endangering the well-being of the people. In May's hands, the Inquisitor is an arch-humanist, with a great and abiding love for the people in his care. Rather than a villain, as other interpretations regard him, the Inquisitor gives people miracle, mystery, and authority in order for them truly to have safe haven. He accepts responsibility for the people and cares deeply for them. As May writes, there are only two realities in the world of the Grand Inquisitor: a passionate love for all his people and the unrelenting torment from which he attempts to protect them. But the Grand Inquisitor, of course, has a secret which the insightful Alyosha guesses—he does not believe in God. Indeed, it is the secret May suggests is at the center of contemporary families, and it constitutes their metaphysical plight. God is dead! If May is right, it means families today find themselves in exactly the same predicament as the Grand Inquisitor:

> Parents assume that there are only two realities in the world: their love for their child and the suffering from which they want, with their money, their advice, their urgency, and their moral support, to protect their own. They are keenly aware of all those catastrophic possibilities that lie in wait for their children—a Mack truck bearing down the highway, a skidding motorcycle, bad grades, a mediocre college, a disastrous love affair, a rudderless career, a bad marriage, and middle-age ennui. As conscientious parents, they operate as though the powers that are decisive in the universe could not possibly do anything in and through the suffering of their children. They alone bear the burden of succor, wisdom, and counsel. They take upon themselves the responsibilities of a savior-figure; and, of course, because they cannot do a very good job of being saviors, they are filled with apprehension as they cope with their children. What an anomaly it must be for a child to see his parents attend a church or a synagogue and yet betray, by the worry across their faces, their great secret fear that God is dead! (51)

The situation of parents is not exactly that of the Grand Inquisitor, however. The Inquisitor is in metaphysical rebellion against death, resisting the forces of entropy in the name of a humanity seeking meaningfulness in life. He does so fully in the knowledge that he is isolating himself from the rest of humanity. It is because of the ultimacy of death, the reality of which he keeps secret from the people, that he is isolated. May suggests that the ordinary parent manifests a combination of resistance and avoidance in protecting his children, for not only does he deceive like the Grand Inquisitor, but he also seeks to self-deceive. He tries to hide the tragic side of life and thereby create a safe world for his children, and then he tries to convince himself that he can live in that world too.

Avoidance of death in modern culture is exhibited in a variety of ways, not the least of which is the growing tendency to isolate the old, the sick, and the dying from public view. Philippe Ariès has chronicled the changing attitudes toward death, evolving as they have from the elaborately prepared deaths officiated over by the Church to the family-oriented deaths choreographed by the dying person surrounded by generations of family and friends in his final moments. Implied in these deaths of an earlier age is the transition from this life to another. With the "death of God," and concomitant belief that nothing exists beyond the grave, death becomes more and more secretive. Ariès notes that modernity and the development of sophisticated medical practice leads to relatives not sharing with a dying person just how sick he really is. He goes on to say the original motivation for lying to the dying person

> was the desire to spare the sick person, to assume the burden of his ordeal. But this sentiment . . . very rapidly was covered over by a different sentiment, a new sentiment characteristic of modernity: one must avoid . . . the disturbance and the overly strong and unbearable emotion caused by the ugliness of dying and by the very presence of death in the midst of a happy life, for it is henceforth given that life is always happy or should always seem to be so. Nothing had yet changed in the rituals of death, which were preserved at least in appearance, and no one had yet had the idea of changing them. But people had already begun to empty them of their dramatic impact; the procedure of hushing-up had begun. . . .
>
> Between 1930 and 1950 the evolution accelerated markedly. This was due to an important physical phenomenon: the displacement of the site of death. One no longer died at home in the bosom of one's family, but in the hospital, alone. (1974:86–87)

Hospitals and nursing homes, while in their own way of benefit to their clientele, nonetheless serve to remove from sight those who would bring to the consciousness of others the reality of death. Out of sight, it may be said, out of mind.

May also notes certain demographic trends that have distanced the nuclear family from grandparents with the same effect of restricting a child's experiences of aging, sickness, and death. Indeed, grandparents seem more and more to be placed outside the nuclear families of their children and grandchildren. This trend may have to do with the fact that grandparents, growing more and more dependent on others as they age, act to remind "those in the fullness of their powers rather too vividly of their own imminent eclipse." (1975:59) This tendency to isolate grandparents from the nuclear family contrasts sharply with the attitudes of other cultures in which the aged command respect and are looked to for their wisdom. Though aging, and perhaps sick and dying, they are still seen in other cultures as having value, and as having something to offer their communities, including the children. The Church has also played a role in this attitude of avoidance when it comes to death, May argues. He cites reports of church members saying they have never heard a sermon in which the minister confronts the question of their own dying. In May's view, such ministries have betrayed the message of Christianity. To avoid preaching about death, he believes, is to preach with "the profound melancholy of men who have separated the church from the graveyard." (60) Such preachers act as if there were two Gods, one presiding over all those cheerful Sabbath activities of the church, and the other holding sway over car wrecks and wife-beatings and hospital bleedings. This manichean split restricts God to the sunny side of life, while allowing for a separate "Dark Power," about whom one never speaks, to handle everything in the end.

There is an ideal toward which May points, however. The "Grand Inquisitor" is a creation of Ivan Karamazov, and as such is a character in a story in which Ivan expresses his own intellectualized rebellion against death. But Alyosha, Ivan's brother to whom the story of the Grand Inquisitor is told, exemplifies a different approach to death. A deeply religious monk, Alyosha gives a sermon near the end of the novel at the site where a young boy was killed by other children. As May sees it, Alyosha take his stand at the very spot where the young boy was persecuted and killed. There, on that killing ground, Alyosha gives a sermon in which he acknowledges both the cruelty of those boys who had done the killing and the searing pain of the dead boy's father. But he goes on to say that despite the death, and in the midst of the world's weight in pain and suffering, he and the boys and the father are all bound together as one community. Dostoevski, May argues, thus suggests another way of dealing with death other than avoidance or deception: in the midst of the killing fields "it is possible for men to remain human, to remember, to grieve, and even to rejoice." (60)

This is the model Gardner would also present in his fiction. Indeed, his career as a writer has been one of presenting to a reading audience the reality of death and guilt so it may be openly addressed. In this public confrontation with that which tends to be hidden in our everyday lives Gardner is, like Heidegger, advocating a clear recognition on the part of men and women that people do die, that their actions sometimes lead to the deaths of others, that guilt seems an ever-present reality in their lives, and that they, too, one day will die. But unlike those who cite the same facts as justification for their nihilism, Gardner ardently proposes that a clear recognition of the power of death and guilt in human life can be the impetus for a deep and abiding wisdom, a sense of "peace" which sees the totality of life—its benevolence as well as its cruelty—as a glorious time full of meaningful human possibilities. In addition to advocating a clear recognition of the reality of death and guilt, Gardner also upholds the importance of a person's maintaining ties with the larger community. The saddest of Gardner's characters are those isolated not only from family and friends, but from the ideals and ordinary practices of the communities in which they live. Sometimes this isolation is self-imposed, as when one removes himself from the ethos of a community by adopting a different, usually overintellectualized, set of values (e.g. the Sunlight Man, Agathon, Peter Mickelsson) or is brought down by a paralyzing sense of guilt (e.g. Mickelsson, James Page, Henry Soames). Actually, these characters are not so much isolated as they become "strangers."

Robert Lifton's analysis of "survivor guilt," which prudent judgment would suggest is applicable to Gardner's life, demonstrates how guilt can lead to one's thinking he is contaminated and impure, not worthy of being a part of the community. To feel ashamed, to feel one is bearing the judgment of an entire community upon oneself—whether that judgment be accurate or not—is a difficult burden for even the strongest and most confident individual to bear. On the positive side, however, when a person feels guilt it implies for that person an acceptance of the efficacy of certain societal or personal norms. It is in recognizing that these norms exist and are efficacious, and in further recognizing that one has violated or fallen short of them, that the stage is set for the possible reintegration of a person into the community despite feelings of guilt and shame. Indeed, this is the import behind Lifton's remark that guilt and shame may suggest "an evolutionary function of guilt, its importance for human ties in general and for maintaining individual responsibility for *sustaining* other's lives." (1987:237) To feel guilt implies the need to be part of a community. Peter Mickelsson, despite his intellectual posturing and self-perception as an independent thinker, feels himself continually burdened by guilt. But rather than a burden, it may have been what helps save him. What becomes clear for the reader is that notwithstanding Mickelsson's intellectualized perception of himself, he nonetheless harbors a deep-seated desire to be an accepted part of his community and, in fact, is desperately in need of others in his life.

Ritual activity is a primary vehicle by which Gardner seeks to exhibit the ingrained feelings, emotions, and dispositions that give members of a community a sense of identity. Ritual is also a means by which he depicts the social and personal transitions of individual members of a community. In Gardner's fiction, ritual activity becomes the principle means by which people's need for each other is expressed and the value of community is demonstrated. In the process Gardner not only depicts formalized rites (e.g. weddings, funerals), but also attempts to point to those unconscious—or not yet conscious—modes of ritual sensibility that Ronald Grimes refers to as "ritualization" and Fred Clothey, more skeptically, calls "proto-ritual." It is not that Gardner expressly seeks to offer readers a better understanding of ritual. Rather, he simply provides an accurate depiction of a variety of human lives which, as a matter of course, involve describing both the efficacy and the full range of ritual activity.

Ritual's efficacy, it is argued by some, lies in its effecting both social control and social change. Particularly instructive in looking at Gardner's fiction is the work of Victor Turner, who emphasizes the role of ritual in conflict situations, those irruptions in the social fabric which, if left to fester, might permanently destabilize a community. Turner's "general approach has tended to direct attention to the individual as an entity controlled by group processes." (Bell, 1992:172) In particular, Turner has described these crises as a "social drama" which typically has four phases of publicly observable action: (1) a *breach* of social norms or expectations, (2) a *crisis* in which the breach reaches a dangerous dimension threatening the stability of socially accepted structures or norms, (3) juridical or ad hoc attempts at *redressive action* in order to end the crisis leading, if successful, to (4) a *reintegration* of the offending parties in the disturbed community as it takes stock of itself. (Turner, 1975:37–42) The battle between James Page and his sister Sally can be seen as a novelistic representation of Turner's "social drama." Indeed, Gardner's fiction often raises questions about the role of the individual vis-à-vis the community in which he lives. As Turner states it:

> After all, the ritual symbol has, in common with the dream symbol, the characteristic, discovered by Freud, of being a compromise formation between two main opposing tendencies. It is a compromise between the need for social control, and certain innate and universal human drives whose complete gratification would result in a breakdown of that control. Ritual symbols refer to what is normative, general, and characteristic of unique individuals. Thus, . . . symbols refer among other things, to the basic needs of social existence . . . and to shared values on which communal life depends. (Turner, 1967:37)

In *Beginnings in Ritual Studies* Ron Grimes adopts a taxonomy by which ritual activity may be divided into six categories: ritualization, decorum, ceremony, liturgy, magic, and celebration. (35–51) These are not hard and fast demarcations, but fluid. As sensibilities or ritual modes they can coexist, several being present in a ritual event. For example, a fiesta can simultaneously involve celebration, liturgy, ceremony, and magic. Grimes is helpful in two ways; he provides a vocabulary by which to articulate distinctions between various modes of ritual activity, and he strongly advocates the notion that ritual has its beginnings in the preconscious somatic life of a people. This latter notion is a corollary to the work of Langer and Whitehead, in that each stresses the importance of preconscious experience. Adopting Grimes's terms, we can say Gardner's fiction primarily depicts the ritual modes of ritualization, decorum, magic, and celebration. The remaining two— ceremony and liturgy—are present in Gardner's fiction, but not to the extent of the other four. In fact, ceremony and liturgy represent much of what Gardner means when he uses the term "religion,"[1] and as such he tends to identify ceremony and liturgy with the societal *status quo*. It happens that Gardner thinks of ceremony and liturgy more narrowly than does Grimes, and thus is too quick to identify ceremony and liturgy with those aspects of community life which are stultifying. Grimes provides a far more sophisticated and nuanced perspective on the value of ceremony and liturgy in the ritual life of a community, including, contrary to what Gardner might think, the role ceremony plays in validating changes within a society. As a novelist, Gardner is more interested in exploring that which gives a sense of identity to an individual, as well as exploring the transitions and changes that occur with individuals and communities. Thus he emphasizes those ritual modes of sensibility which pervade one's most basic physiological activities (i.e. ritualization and decorum) as well as one's sense of transcendence and playful self-expression (i.e. magic and celebration).

To begin, Grimes is critical of approaches to ritual that are done "from the top down," from highly liturgical rites to the less formal, thus giving the impression of ritual being essentially civilized and sophisticated. He argues that we are mistaken when we immediately assume ritual must always have to do with "ultimacy, sacredness, awe, sacrifice, or eternality," each of which ties ritual to a religious tradition. (36) To do so, he suggests, is to "disincarnate ourselves from our own bodies, our own present, and our own ordinariness." (36) In order to focus attention on those somatic elements of ritual Grimes speaks of *ritualization*, which he describes as a term adopted by ethologists to describe the kinds of repeated and seemingly choreographed gesturing and posturing of animals, typically consisting of a series of movements which have no obvious pragmatic purpose. This leads him to suggest that ritualization occurs as a necessary part of human life for reasons ecological, biogenetic, and psychosomatic. "We cannot escape ritualization," he writes, "without escaping our own bodies and psyches, the rhythms and structures of which arise on their own. They flow with or without our conscious assent; they are uttered—exclamations of nature and our bodies." (36–37) Grimes's notion of ritualization has strong affinity with Whitehead's notion of causal efficacy. There is absolutely no indication Gardner was aware of Grimes's work in ritual—indeed, the timing of Gardner's death with the advent of Grimes's published career suggests the near impossibility of influence—but he was aware of Whitehead's notions of "causal efficacy," that bodily flow of feeling that has, at best, only a possibility of being raised to consciousness.

For Whitehead, consciousness is a relatively narrow aspect of experience, dependent upon antecedent experiences in the dim world of vague physical feeling. Whitehead often speaks of two primary modes of experience: causal efficacy and presentational immediacy. In contradistinction to the "pure mode of presentational immediacy," which is Whitehead's term for the vividness of experience as organized and presented by means of the five senses, he writes in *Process and Reality* of the vague physical feelings of causal efficacy, sometimes referred to as bodily efficacy:

> [W]e feel *with the body*. There may be some further specialization into a particular organ of sensation; but in any case the '*withness*' *of the body* is an ever-present, though elusive, element in our perceptions of presentational immediacy. . . . This component feeling will be called the feeling of bodily efficacy. It is more primitive than the feeling of presentational immediacy which issues from it. (311–12)

He makes essentially the same point in language less technical than that of *Process and Reality* when, in *Adventures of Ideas*, he writes of the error of valorizing presentational immediacy over causal efficacy, much as Grimes criticizes ritualists who valorize as ritual only the most sophisticated of rites over ritualization. After Whitehead takes notice of the mistaken assumption that our communication with the outside world is limited to the five sense organs, particularly the eyes, he goes on to suggest another mode of communication between the outside world and the conscious experience of an individual. "The living organ of experience," Whitehead writes, "is the living body as a whole. Every instability of any part of it—be it chemical, physical, or molar—imposes an activity of readjustment throughout the whole organism. In the course of such physical activities human experience has its origin." (225)

Whitehead makes the point that presentational immediacy has been valorized as the *sine qua non* of human experience, largely because of its vividness in presenting the world as organized by the sense organs. It is a "thin" experience, however, for it can say nothing of the past or the future. In Whitehead's system an experience in the pure mode of presentational immediacy is contemporaneous with and causally independent of an actual occasion. This is why Hume, with his sensationalist doctrine of human perception assuming presentational immediacy to be the *sine qua non* of human experience, is forced to argue that since one cannot perceive causation it cannot empirically be shown to exist. For example, Hume would argue that while a man blinks when a light is flashed there is no demonstrated causal relationship. One cannot in a sensory way "feel" causation, and since such feelings are all a person can know, we cannot have knowledge of causation. Hume's explanation is to point to the association of blinking with flashes of light and argue it is "habit" that explains the phenomenon. But Whitehead makes a telling point when he asks how it is that Hume can know a "habit" but not a "cause." Whitehead believes we have here a perfect example of "applying the test of presentational immediacy to procure the critical rejection of some doctrines, and of allowing other doctrines to slip out by the back door, so as to evade the test. The notion of causation arose because mankind lives amid experiences in the mode of causal efficacy." (175)

Process thought advocates an expansion of the concept "experience" as moderns have come to use it, for process seeks to include the sorts of preconscious activity that Whitehead, Langer, and Grimes speak of as a legitimate mode of experience. Presentational immediacy is, according to Whitehead, a development of high-grade actual occasions resulting in vividness that is subsequent to causal efficacy, which is the interactive processual world of experiencing actual entities, a world producing feelings that are vague, uncontrolled, and heavy with emotion. Causal efficacy, according to Process thought, has a sense to it of being derived from the immediate past, and of being passed on to an immediate future. Emotionally, it gives one a sense of "belonging to oneself in the past, passing into oneself in the present, and passing from oneself in the present towards oneself in the future." (178) This coherent, emotionally felt self is a bringing together into one localized actual occasion the varied and vague feelings of many past actual occasions, then to be passed on to be experienced by future actual occasions. "This is our general sense of existence," Whitehead concludes, "as one item among others, in an efficacious actual world." (178) Thus, it is the vague, physically felt experience of causal efficacy which gives a rhythmic sense of past, present, and future. The sense of being one actual entity in a nexus of perpetually perishing actual entities is a part of the conceptually vague experience supplied by causal efficacy. Experience in the pure mode of presentational immediacy in high-grade occasions has quite different characteristics in that they are distinct, definite, controllable, and prone to be used for immediate, conscious enjoyment.

The interaction of the two, causal efficacy and presentational immediacy, results in what Whitehead calls "symbolic reference," a concept we will explore momentarily. For now, a productive way to think of their interaction is to say that we first encounter and experience the world through the mode of causal efficacy, while we adjust our experiences in the mode of presentational immediacy.

Whether it be Grimes's "ritualization" or Whitehead's "causal efficacy," each seeks to bring to the foreground an ineffable realm of human experience which, though often overlooked, is the generative ground of later, more public, conscious human experience. As such, each investigates similar realms of human preconscious activity. Langer's concept of "entrainment" has a similar focus on that "unconscious appreciation of forms" that is "the primitive root of all abstraction, which in turn is the keynote of rationality; so it appears that the conditions for rationality lie deep in our pure animal experience." (*Philosophy in a New Key*:89) Gardner's work testifies to an acceptance of this wider concept of human experience as including preconscious somatic activity. Though he is, as a writer, in the very difficult position of attempting to articulate that which is "beyond words," Gardner does point to intuitive, preconscious levels of experience in his characters.

In addition to the many references to characters "sensing" another's mood, or "feeling" the presence of another before seeing them, Gardner takes more direct note of this vague bodily flow of feeling in *The Resurrection* when, for example, he speaks of James's initial reaction to the painting by Emma Staley. One part of him—the sophisticated intellectual part—laughs at the amateurish landscape, while another part of him

> felt a sudden, surprising unrest, a vague, ardent thirst for the past, for wilderness, for freedom, for heaven knew what—a paradoxical sense of intense dissatisfaction with himself and, at the same time, a kind of vaulting joy. He stood perfectly still, his head on one side, his eyes closed to slits, and he explored what he felt, the sensation he would have said he'd outgrown and forgotten long ago. (52)

It is a level of experience that is always present with James, but takes the occasion of standing before Emma Staley's painting to bubble up to the surface of consciousness, though in his intellectual sophistication he doesn't know quite what to do with his feelings. What is particularly noteworthy with the experience is that these vague physical feelings connect him to his own past, which is something experiences in the pure mode of presentational immediacy do not do. It takes a character with the spiritual sickness of Horne to come closer to an understanding of the matter when he tells James that one doesn't simply open one's eyes to God's creation, passively receiving impressions on the blank slate of their mind, and then suddenly be moved to change one's life. Either one is able to see or is not able to see "by virtue of a health or sickness deeper than consciousness." (149)

Agathon speaks of feeling contrary emotions which, like music, he wishes he could feel more intensely "not with my mind but with my body." (63) Dorkis speaks of being so attuned physically to life that one can "ride it, like a bird." (47) This notion is repeated in *The Sunlight Dialogues* when, in one of his dialogues with Clumly having to do with the disparity between the order of the conscious human mind and the order of the universe, the Sunlight Man speaks of acting with the gods, of being so attuned physically to life that one's unconscious actions are an expression of human experience and knowledge. He uses the example of a soldier who, in attacking, gives up his personal will to live and simply gives himself over to the immediacy of the moment. Describing it in almost mystical terms, he suggests that at such moments the soldier "becomes" the hill, the night sky, the position he is attacking, as "he ducks, spins, turns as the gods reach down to duck him, spin him, turn him." (462) While it may be a question of science what is really happening, for the soldier it is a sensual act. "The mind grows large and irrational, one suddenly knows things impossible to know." (463) The most obvious examples of Gardner's use of preconscious experience in the life of his characters is from *Mickelsson's Ghosts*. Two episodes have already been cited: that of the mute girl shouting for her father to stop when Mickelsson is threatened with death, and that of the coed who did not consciously know when another subject was being electrically shocked but whose body, as measured by "cardiograph, encephalograph, rapid-eye-movement tapes, and so forth," did know. (371) There are also the oft-mentioned dim feelings on the part of Mickelsson of a presence in his house, and of his inability to consciously understand what it signified, though some more primitive part of him would come alert at such times. The tone is set in the novel by Mickelsson's quoting of several philosophers:

> "Great truths are felt before they are expressed," says Teilhard de Chardin. "Like great works, deep feelings always mean more than they are conscious of saying," says Camus. Or Ralph Waldo Emerson: "Every man's life is a solution in heiroglyphic to those inquiries he would put. He acts it as life before he apprehends it as truth." (31)

What Grimes, Whitehead and Langer in their scholarship, and Gardner in his fiction, all suggest is that the patterns within which men and women live—whether they be philosophical patterns of thought, linguistic patterns of language, ritual patterns of activity, or patterns of aesthetic sensibility—are physiologically grounded, and only later are they socially validated. Which is to say, we do not simply assent intellectually to our patterns of behavior, but rather emerge into patterns of life which, at their best, are consistent with our somatic selves. The danger each points to is a tendency of men and women intellectually to construct "top-down" theories of philosophy, language, ritual, and aesthetics which impose conceptual patterns that are not reduplicated in our somatic lives.

Grimes speaks of *decorum* as a natural outgrowth of ritualization which has its beginnings in our civic and social lives. Grimes maintains that when a society uses the instinctual gestures and postures of ritualization in order to regulate social interaction, the result is decorum. "When our patterning, indirection, and repetition become part of a system of expectations to which we are supposed to conform," he writes, "we have passed from ritualization to decorum." (39) As social beings men and women are constantly engaged in decorous behavior, including the ways we shake hands or nod heads toward each other, the phrases we use in speaking to each other, how and whether we stand, sit, smile, or cross our legs. Decorum within a society covers behavior that usually is not consciously recognized until it is suddenly no longer present, as when one is in the presence of a "rude" person, or in a foreign culture. There is a sense in which just as ritualization is psychosomatically unconscious behavior, decorum is socially unconscious behavior. (41) Grimes goes on to note that decorum carries with it a slight cultural "ought," as in "one ought to behave" properly. What sanctions are imposed for violations of decorum usually are little more than being "ignored, snubbed, gossiped about, or frowned at." (40) A measure of the cultural weight of decorum is that it "is enforced socially, not religiously, legally, or psychobiologically." (40) Decorum, then, can include all those voluntarily agreed upon conventions which act as a kind of social glue bonding a community of men and women together.

In describing the interaction of characters in his fiction Gardner does, in a myriad of ways, describe the decorous behavior which allows one to feel a part of, or estranged from, a group. James Page, in *October Light*, shows through a variety of mannerisms and colloquialisms that he is a part of the group at Merton's Hideaway that make up his friends. Indeed, the larger community in the area has shared behaviors which help hold it together as a community. Despite the fact James destroys Sally's television and locks her in her room he is still seen as a part of the community, as expressed in his decorous interactions with neighbors and friends. The same is true of Sally. The "outsiders" in the novel— those who do not share in the decorum of the community and are not an integral part of their society—are the Bennington College coeds and the writer at Merton's Hideaway, all of whom maintain their own decorum as part of a "college community," and the newly arrived priest and minister who, for example, have difficulty understanding the supportive intent behind barn-fire parties.

Gardner's most isolated characters are those who, for whatever reason, cease decorous behavior. Agathon is an affront to nearly all the citizens of Sparta at the time of his arrest because of his constant belching, farting, and intemperate speech. Simon Bale in *Nickel Mountain* sees a "higher truth" than that expressed in his community's decorous acts. The Sunlight Man is another example, as he goes out of his way to violate decorum. James Chandler in *The Resurrection* allows his intellectualism to reflexively discount social decorum, though when he visits the Staley sisters and engages in the socially-accepted decorum of the community "it surprised him that he should find it so extremely enjoyable to play this game of empty forms, communion as pure gesture." (55–56) In Gardner's novels decorum is the warp and woof in which characters move and live their lives.

CHAPTER X:
Magic, Celebration and Novelty

When Grimes speaks of *magic* he does not, as moderns are wont to do, use it in a pejorative way. Rather, he is referring to those rituals with a pragmatic intent seeking a desired change. When speaking of magic a listener will often think in terms of a so-called "primitive" society's ritual attempts to, for example, manipulate the gods in order to assure rain for their crops or to assure the cyclical reconstitution of their cosmos. Indeed, as Grimes uses it, such rituals are in the mode of magic. But magic refers to much more. He argues that magical thinking is integral to modern therapy and modern sexuality, as much as primitive healing and fertility rituals ever were. Advertising, too, is full of magical thinking. "People deny that they believe in magic," Grimes writes, "but ingest this pill and use that shampoo expecting 'somehow' (the cue for magical transcendence) to become what they desire." (47) Whereas ritualization and decorum are, respectively, psychosomatically and socially unconscious ritual behavior, an integral part of magical ritual behavior is a *conscious* desire on the part of ritual enactors to achieve a change of some kind. Its ritual performance is within a transcendent frame of reference as ritual enactors seek to bring about some modification in their prosaic lives.

As has been noted, Gardner uses gatherings of members of a community as a device for presenting the hard-earned wisdom and solidarity of a people. These occasions usually mark a time of magical attempts to bring about a change in an individual or a group. Everything from the Vermont "barn-fire parties" to the Batavia musical recitals of the Staley sisters are magical occasions when people gather in anticipation of personal and communal change. According to Grimes, the force of a magical mode of ritual activity is "in its use of desire as a major contributing factor in causing hoped-for results." (46) Often, these gatherings in Gardner's novels center around music, which was so much a part of Gardner's own youth. A particularly instructive example is Gardner's autobiographical story "Come On Back," in his collection *The Art of Living*. The story is told by a narrator remembering an experience from his youth. Called "Buddy" or "Bud" by his family (as was Gardner when a young boy), the story describes the boy's first attendance at a *cymanfa ganu*, an annual gathering of Welsh men and women to sing songs from their native country. When the boy asks his Uncle Charley what *cymanfa ganu* means he is told it is a Welsh word meaning to "come on back"—an invitation on one level to "come on back to Wales" while on another level an invitation to "come on back" to one's deepest sense of him or herself. There are a number of squabbles and family arguments among Buddy's relatives leading up to the songfest. Uncle Charley, for example, is depressed after having been permanently injured in a farming accident; he believes himself to be a useless drain on the family's limited resources. Buddy's father is critical of the ever-gloomy grandmother—the "Angel of Death" as he calls her—leading to an argument with Buddy's mother. And all of the relatives try to have their say on how best to bring Charley out of his doldrums. Buddy was always fond of his Uncle Charley, partly because it was his Uncle Charley who told him what "Buddy" means in Welsh. "Means 'the poet,'" his uncle said. "They used to set great store by poets, back in Wales. Only second to kings—maybe not even second. Same thing, kings and poets. Different kinds of liars." (234)

Attending the *cymanfa ganu* Buddy stays next to his uncle, and when he realizes the words to the songs are all in Welsh his uncle tells him to simply sing what he sings. Once the organ begins to play the room becomes focused. Everywhere people are standing up. Buddy's father and Uncle Charley help him to stand up on a chair. Then, "like a shock of thunder that made the whole room shake, they began to sing." (235) Those gathered have little need of songbooks, and couldn't have read them anyway what with their heads lifted to the rafters, projecting their voices to the roof. As Welsh choruses typically do, the people sing in numerous parts, creating a full and rich harmony. Not a weak voice among them, "the river of sound could use it all." (236) And Buddy is able to join in among them, lifted up by that gathering of voices, and borne along by the music's aged structure. It seems mystical to Buddy, "our bones and blood that sang, all heaven and earth singing harmony lines, and when the music broke off on the final chord, the echo that rang on the walls around us was like a roaring Amen." (236) Buddy continues to sing hymn after hymn, feeling himself so caught up in the moment that he even feels himself at one point to be floating among the beams, looking down on the congregation. In fact, his father held one of his hands, anchoring him, while his Uncle Charley held the other.

Looking at them, Buddy could see their beaming faces, and their tears. By engaging in this ritual songfest those with roots in Wales renew their deep and abiding sense of identity as Welshmen; they have a solid sense of themselves and their place in the cosmos. As well, they are lifted up by the music and in a metamorphosed moment transcend their particularity, their foibles, their petty squabbles, and merge together with a force they experience as greater than themselves. As a sort of aesthetic alchemy, the conflicts of Buddy's household dissolve and are transmuted into a far richer and emotionally far more satisfying unity of feeling. They are changed, as reflected in their interactions afterward.

The tragedy of the story is that Uncle Charley commits suicide. Attending a *cymanfa ganu* he experiences a perfection that is denied him in his ordinary day-to-day life. In a proleptic passage earlier in the narrative the grandmother claims singing to have always been Uncle Charley's downfall. When Buddy asks what she means by that, she tells him that while singing has its place, a person can start to believe that what he experiences while singing with a choir is how the world ought to be. What a profound disappointment it is when he comes down out of the clouds. "It's a terrible disappointment," the grandmother concludes. (222) Grimes notes that magic, as well as other ritual modes, can take pathological forms. Such is the case with Uncle Charley, his family recognizing that he is too much under the spell of the emotions generated by the songfests. For the other characters, a *cymanfa ganu* is a magical period of time in which the vicissitudes of life are bracketed, a moment in which they seek to be strengthened, thus allowing them to return to the give and take of their prosaic lives, the challenges and disappointments that are so much a part of their daily existence.

"Come On Back" ends with family and friends gathered to console one another, reminding themselves of what Uncle Charley had meant to them. They share memories of Uncle Charley, and acknowledge that the festivals will never be the same without him. Some express how unfortunate it is that Uncle Charley never married and had children, thinking that might have made the difference in his life. As the conversation dies out, the silence seems the final benediction for Uncle Charley. Then a farmer sitting in a corner clears his throat and begins to sing. Slowly, tentatively, others begin to join in. Aunt Kate slips over to the piano and begins to play. "On the carpet, one after another, as if coming to life, their shoes began to move." (239)

Another description of a gathering occurs in *Nickel Mountain* when a number of residents gather in Henry's diner in hopes of celebrating the first rain in many months. Their optimism, despite a lengthy draught, is buoyed by a prediction by an Indian named Nick Blue that rain would come this night. He had been right in the past, and farmers in the area want to believe he will be right again. As the evening passes and the hour becomes late, however, it is increasingly clear that there will be no rain. Henry, still in the throes of guilt at the death of Simon Bale, comes into the diner with his son in tow. There is a sense in which the draught is emblematic of Henry's situation. Just as the draught upsets the normal rhythms and patterns of the local farming community, so too is Henry paralyzed and unable to act while caught in the grips of his guilt. (Butts, 1988:39) Callie realizes it is important for Henry to be in the diner with his friends, and also knows how foolish they will all feel once they understand the silliness of their naive optimism. But more importantly, she realizes in a flash of intuition the source of much of Henry's wordless rage:

> [T]hey were going to see they'd made fools of themselves, that any dignity they thought they had was a word, empty air, and to act on the assumption that they had any rights in this world whatever, even the rights of a spider, to survive, was to turn themselves into circus clowns, creatures stuffed with old rags and straw who absurdly struggled to behave like human beings and who, whether or not they succeeded, were ridiculous. (253)

All his life Henry simply wanted the world to reflect his moral intuition of what the world ought to be. Instead, he had been isolated nearly all his life and saddled with a heart whose physical strength was no match for the heartfelt love he wanted to share with others. And this night, again thwarted by the heavens, he is asking the ongoing question: "Why?" Why do the strivings of men and women so often meet with universal indifference?

Approaching midnight, those in the diner begin to shuffle, speak of having to get home, and ask what they owed for their food and drink. Henry will not hear of it. He tells one of his customers that everything is on the house, and then extends it to everyone. "Tonight it's all on me," he tells them. (254) None wanted to accept his offer at first, but it is soon clear that Henry is a man possessed. Yelling as if angry, Henry tells them it is his birthday and asks Callie to give everyone cake. He then orders everyone in the diner to sing "Happy Birthday" to him. Despite Callie's loud whisper telling him to stop, Henry raises his arms and yells for them to begin singing. More out of shock than anything else, they begin to sing. Magically, the mood shifts as they sing, and tears start to form and stream down the face of one of the customers. Soon, everyone in the diner is singing, breaking up into harmony. Even George Loomis is "more or less singing." (254)

When midnight comes only Henry, Callie, and George Loomis are left in the diner. The others have returned to their families. What follows is the section described earlier[1] when George is given an opportunity to unload his own guilt for his part in the accidental death of the Goat Lady. Leonard Butts is exactly correct in saying Henry's insistence that everyone gathered "sing 'Happy Birthday' to him seems to unite them in a small cluster of defiance against the apparently indifferent forces of nature. . . . This small catharsis is welcomed by those who experience it, and it allows them to carry on, assured that they are not alone in the world." (1988:39–40) George Loomis is given an opportunity to tell Henry and Callie of the accident with the Goat Lady, and thereby share in the strength of the community in exorcising his guilt. Instead, he chooses to remain silent, thus continuing his isolation.

To sing "Happy Birthday" is, in many if not most cases, an empty ritual performance repeated as a matter of decorum on a person's birthday. But on this occasion, the ritual is pregnant with magical significance as those gathered reconstitute their world, reaffirm their reliance upon one another, and renew their sense of meaningfulness. George Loomis cannot share in the event, however. His guilt has left him far more crippled than have his physical wounds from Korea and the farming accident. Though lost on George, the evening does prove to be enormously redemptive for Henry. Realizing how pitiable George is in his isolation, Henry signals his reemergence as a man with moral responsibilities, a man needing to control his eating and thereby continue to live for his wife and son, as well as for the wider community. The episode ends with the narrated information that during the night, while they were all sleeping, the heavens opened up and it began to rain.

Ritualization, decorum, and magic are all interwoven throughout Gardner's fiction, helping to define a community and an individual's place within a community. The use of ritual in his fiction also allows

Gardner as an artist to bring to a reader that vivid and continuous dream that is, in his view, the goal of all serious fictional art. John Gardner was a child of his times, however, and knew that the literary reflexivity of our post-modernist age mitigates against a reader simply abandoning himself to a text. No matter. He still insists on the importance of the artist being proficient enough in her craft to engage the reader. If the art of fiction is performed technically well, and maintains a vision of moral seriousness, reflexivity in and of itself is not a problem. Grimes can help explain why this is the case.

In differentiating the modes of ritual sensibility Grimes reserves *celebration* as his sixth and final category. He distinguishes celebration from magic by noting that while magic tends to be achievement oriented, celebration tends to be expressive and ludic. Echoing the work of Roger Caillois and Robert Neale, he points out that magic is "ritualized work" while celebration can be characterized as "ritualized play." (48) Because rituals of celebration are expressive they are closely related to the arts, and their " 'as if' quality, like that of good fiction, must be at once convincing and specially framed." (48) Carnivals are celebratory rituals, as are fiestas, feasts, dancing, music-making, and other similar activities. In moving toward these sorts of activities men and women begin to detach themselves from the ordinary day-to-day matters that require a more pragmatic approach, thus allowing for experimentation and reflection on their structured lives, which is to say they begin to play.

Robert K. Johnston, in a doctoral dissertation, writes extensively on the concept of "play." After citing a number of theologians and philosophers on the subject, he integrates their ideas in describing play:

> I would understand play as that activity which is freely and spontaneously entered into, but, which once begun, has its own design, its own rules of order, which must be followed so that the play activity may continue. The player is called into play by a potential co-player and/or play object, and while he is at play he treats his fellow-players and/or his play "things" as personal, creating with them a community that can be characterized by "I-Thou" rather than "I-It" relationships. This play has a new time (a playtime) and a new space (a playground) which function as "parentheses" in the life and world of the player. Ongoing life comes temporarily to a standstill in the mind of the player and his world's boundaries are redefined. Play, to be play, must be entered into without outside purpose; it cannot be connected with a material interest or ulterior motive, for then the boundaries of the playground and the limits of the

> playtime are violated. But though play is an end in itself, it results, nevertheless, in several consequences. Chief among these are the joy and release, the personal fulfillment, the re-membering of our common humanity, and the presentiment of the sacred which is experienced by the player in and through the activity. One's participation in the adventure of playing, even given the risk of injury or defeat, finds resolution at the end of the experience, and one's ongoing life is re-entered in a new spirit of thanksgiving and celebration. The player is a changed individual, his life having a new largeness beyond the workaday world. (55–56)

Johnston, later in the dissertation, seeks to articulate a fuller understanding of Christian worship by inviting his reader to substitute the word "worship" for the word "play" in the foregoing description. For our purposes, I would invite the reader to substitute the concept of "reading fiction" as explicated by Gardner for the concept of play in Johnston's description, thus rendering:

> I would understand the reading of fiction as that activity which is freely and spontaneously entered into, but, which once begun, has its own design, its own rules of order, which must be followed so that the reading activity may continue. The reader is called into reading by a potential story-teller and/or story, and while he is reading he treats his author and/or his story as personal, creating with them a community that can be characterized by "I-Thou" rather than "I-It" relationships. This reading of fiction has a new time (virtual time) and a new space (virtual space) which function as "parentheses" in the life and world of the reader. Ongoing life comes temporarily to a standstill in the mind of the reader and his world's boundaries are redefined. The reading of fiction, to be the reading of fiction, must be entered into without outside purpose; it cannot be connected with a material interest or ulterior motive, for then the boundaries of the virtual space and the limits of the virtual time are violated. But though the reading of fiction is an end in itself, it results, nevertheless, in several consequences. Chief among these are the joy and release, the personal fulfillment, the re-membering of our common humanity, and the presentiment of the sacred which is experienced by the reader in and through the activity. One's participation in the adventure of reading, even given the risk of injury or defeat, finds resolution at the end of the experience, and one's ongoing life is re-entered in a new spirit of thanksgiving and celebration. The reader is a changed individual, his life having a new largeness beyond the workaday world.

This substitution of "reading" for "play" might seem facile and lead to awkward phrasings. Some of the awkwardness, however, is due to parts of Johnston's description being overstated. For example, it seems an unreasonable standard to insist that in order for an activity to be play it "must be entered into without outside purpose." Think of Kant's second statement of the Categorical Imperative, to the effect that one ought not to treat other men and women as a means *only*. His intent rests on that last word. Of course we will treat other men and women as means toward an end. How else would human commerce be possible? However, given the fact we do and will continue to use others as a means toward an end, nonetheless we ought not to treat others *exclusively* as a means toward an end. Similarly, engaging in play or reading a novel can reasonably have an outside motive. One might choose to play a game in order to relax, for example. Or, one might read the novels of John Gardner with the clear intent of writing a book which may, in turn, be published. But—if personal witness may be allowed—that does not necessarily mean the experience of reading Gardner's novels is any less playful and fulfilling. What is important, as Johnston, Huizinga, Caillois, Grimes, and others have noted, is that play and the reading of fiction ought not to be dominantly or exclusively motivated by outside interests.

Despite these minor misgivings, Johnston's description is deeply provocative and helps to identify similarities between play, worship, the reading of fiction, and celebration. Another similarity that Johnston does not specifically address is the invitation to reflexivity that is endemic to these activities. Each form of these activities is bound by sets of rules and expectations, which can, in turn, lead to the questioning of the foundational bases of these rules and regulations. And there is the rub! When one questions the rules of a game, asking "Why do we do it this way?" one doesn't get very far before hearing answers along the lines of, "That's simply the way we do it." There is no bedrock, metaphysically-fixed basis for the rules. Whatever compulsion one might feel to follow the rules is a voluntary adherence, whether consciously or unconsciously. On one level, a person gives up their freedom; on another level, that person is allowed to play and enjoy community with others.

If, however, one concentrates solely on the metaphysical bases of the rules and regulations, the absence of demonstrable bases apart from voluntary adherence quickly leads to a conclusion that the rules and regulations are manifestly absurd. There is no metaphysical justification for this particular rule or that particular regulation. It is rather like Viola in *The Resurrection* watching the Chandler girls playing their version of "Simon Says": because she cannot understand the efficacy of the rules Viola sees their game as completely absurd. There is always the danger, if reflexively caught up in the rules and regulations, that one might "break" the rules and thus end the game. It happens all the time on playgrounds during pick-up basketball games. When the rules are no longer in place, either a new set of rules are developed in order to allow play to continue or play comes to an end. Indeed, there is a sense in which the current popularity of "metafiction" and literary "deconstruction" is a kind of "breaking" of the rules of reading literature. When the rules and conventions of reading fiction are, with a critically reflexive consciousness, "deconstructed," then readers influenced by such an approach may no longer know quite what to do with literary texts, no longer know quite how to play the game of reading.

This is part of Gardner's objection to contemporary trends in fiction. Robert Coover, for example, can write intellectually entertaining fiction in which he seeks to turn fictional forms against themselves in order to highlight the "fictiveness" of reading. In doing so, Coover is forever playing tricks on readers, leading them to believe certain events are happening before pulling the literary rug out from under them, in effect saying to his readers, "What fools you are for believing what is written here." It isn't long before the reader begins to distance himself from Coover's text. One might still get a good laugh—Coover is entertaining, after all—but after being tricked several times the reader, now quite wary, hesitates to willingly suspend his disbelief, to echo Coleridge, and thus denies himself the experience of that vivid and continuous dream about which Gardner so often speaks.

But the difficulty has to do with more than just games and literature. One might also extend the questioning of the metaphysical bases of rules and regulations covering games to a questioning of the most basic cultural assumptions of one's personal and social life. It has been done, and those asking such questions in a critically reflexive manner often reach the conclusion that the rules and conventions governing our very lives are also manifestly absurd. Existentialists, particularly Nietzsche and his heirs, and contemporary post-modernist thinkers have done just that, eroding that foundational grounding upon which modern western cultural assumptions have been based. These thinkers will often speak of social, economic, and political structures as so much *bricolage* built up around some unquestioned—indeed unquestionable in the eyes of most—assumed starting point which is beyond dispute. To proceed to question and de-legitimize these cultural archimedian points is to make all structures of thought and action manifestly absurd and rip away that which allows a group of men and women to see themselves as an identifiable community. Fictional representations of those whose reflexivity leads to a de-legitimization of cultural assumptions and isolation from others are Antoine Roquentin, the protagonist of Sartre's novel, *Nausea*, and Camus's eerily anomic Meursault, protagonist of the aptly titled *The Stranger*.

Gardner understands the force of such an approach, and it is that part of him which reflexively recognizes the "groundlessness" of social rules and regulations that leads him to describe himself as "a kind of bohemian type.... I hate people who are always obeying laws that they don't understand." (Edwards, 1977:43) But he also believes a valorization in intellectual circles of a critically reflexive consciousness can lead to the utter undoing of the social life of men and women, and it is that concern which emotionally and intuitively guides him to write "moral" fiction exploring issues of freedom and responsibility, the individual and the community, in a twentieth-century post-modernist world. It is that part of him which declares himself to be "a kind of New York State Republican, conservative.... I really believe firmly, you know, gotta obey the laws, what's going to happen to the society if we let the anarchists take over?" (Edwards, 1977:43) For Gardner, fiction is the arena which engages both sides of his personality, the arena in which his doubts and questions may be expressed. But it is also an arena in which those doubts and questions are ultimately contained by the very forces of rule and custom that are being questioned. In this sense Gardner's use of fiction is like Grimes's concept of celebration.

Grimes describes celebration as "social and metaphysical fiction." (1982:49) Elsewhere, Grimes notes René Girard's dictum that "violence is the heart and secret soul of the sacred." (Girard, 1977:31) Thus Girard seeks to argue that religion, and more precisely religious rituals, seek to contain and control violence so as to protect a society from the destructiveness of unbridled violence. Grimes insists Girard tells only "the terrible half of an important truth." (1982:229) For Grimes, ritual not only contains and prohibits, it also instantiates and embodies a positive image of and for the celebrants. That is to say, "[p]ublic festivity can contain the lifeblood of a group, city, or culture, and if it does, such festivity simultaneously and symbolically makes of the many, one blood." (229) This "social and metaphysical fiction" in which celebrants engage

> is not the same as lying or wishful thinking, because a fiction draws culture into its wake. Its object is not merely to reflect the cultural status quo, but to transform it in a moment of specially concentrated time. Such a moment can quickly be dragged back into the social system or even co-opted by other ritual processes such as ceremonial ones. . . . Rituals and dramas can be either a substitute for, or prelude to, the actions they symbolize. Celebration is that ritual moment in which such enactments actually effect what they symbolize. They are not practice for some more real kind of action, say, pragmatic or economic action, nor are they sublimations for some remembered or more desirable action. In a celebratory moment the ritual action is a deed in which the symbols do not merely point, mean, or recall, but embody fully and concretely all that is necessary for the moment. (230)

This captures Gardner's sense of what he believes fiction to be when it aspires to engage a reader in a vivid and continuous dream involving moral seriousness. The writing and reading of fiction, in other words, is for Gardner an activity which may lead to festive moments in which readers/celebrants are offered a vivid and continuous image of themselves that symbolically makes of them "one blood." These are but moments, however. Readers/celebrants must eventually disengage from the "fiction" and re-enter the secular world. In a provocative passage of which Gardner would surely approve as applying to fiction as well, Grimes writes of the efficacy of such celebratory moments:

> Even when rituals are culturally creative and for a moment accomplish what they signify, entropy is a fundamental law; therefore, whatever is achieved ritually begins to erode in the very moment of its success. Consequently, we repeatedly pay the high cost of spilled symbolic blood as we await receptively the moment in which a celebration can make of us one blood. A public celebration is a rope bridge of knotted symbols strung across an abyss. We make our crossings hoping the chasm will echo our festive sounds for a moment, as the bridge begins to sway from the rhythms of our dance. (230–31)

These festive moments are important for another reason as well. Celebratory occasions are usually marked by periods of time in which the normal rules governing the interaction of people are suspended.

These can be times of sexual license, status reversal, clowning, and other acts normally proscribed. It is this release from the normal expectations of social behavior that helps generate the celebratory moment, that period of play in which dominant social structures of thought and action are superseded by a "communitas," to use Turner's term, that is "spontaneous, immediate, concrete." (Turner, 1975:274) Released from these socially dominant structures, celebrants have a window of time in which novel possibilities may be thought and perhaps acted upon. Thus, these periods of time can be the genesis of new structures of thought and action. In speaking of how rituals and fiction might be "culturally creative" it will be helpful to take a closer look at both Turner's work in the area of ritual, especially as regards his concept of "liminality," and a corollary concept in process thought which Whitehead refers to as "novelty."

As was stated in Chapter I, Clifford Geertz tends to emphasize only the more ceremonial aspects of ritual, and thus he tends to accentuate only that mode of ritual sensibility which reinforces the status quo. He is correct as far as he goes, but he gives short shrift to those aspects of ritual activity which lead to personal transformation and societal change. Victor Turner is far more adept at identifying transformative aspects of ritual. In his influential essay, "Betwixt and Between," contained as a chapter in *The Forest of Symbols*, Turner makes his own distinction between religious activity that is ceremonial and that which is ritualistic. Ritual is a term he believes more fitting when used to describe religious behavior having to do with social transitions, while ceremony is best reserved for that religious behavior allied with social states. "Ritual is transformative," Turner concludes, "ceremony confirmative." (95) The additional distinction being made is that between social "states," which represent the existing politico-legal structures of a society, and social "transitions," which mark individual and/or social changes within a society. Drawing then on Arnold Van Gennep's work on rites of passage, Turner explores that transitional phase of rites of passage which is termed the *liminal* stage.

Taken from the Latin *limen*, meaning threshold, Turner speaks of the liminal period in traditional rites of passage as that period of time when an initiand is no longer what he was and not yet what he will be. Such a person, caught for a period of time "betwixt and between" those cultural demands defining both his former and future self, temporarily is free from normal social expectations and constraints. Typically such rites have to do with inexorable natural events like birth, death, puberty, etc. Because societies tend to view that which does not fit neatly within concepts available to them as ritually unclean, there is a perceived danger present in initiands during this liminal phase. What is a not-boy-not-man? What are twins? What are sea-dwelling creatures that have neither scales nor fins? In certain cultures each of these is atypical and resists conceptual definition, and is therefore seen as dangerous and unclean. Thus societies seek to separate and control those individuals who are in a liminal phase of transition.

Seen from the perspective of the larger community as a potential source of danger, liminality may, in fact, act to subvert the accepted beliefs of a community. But Turner wants to be clear in saying liminality is also, in its way, a source of positive structural assertions as well as "a realm of pure possibility whence novel configurations of ideas and relations may arise." (1967:97) Those neophytes caught "betwixt and between" during the liminal phase of a rite of passage are encouraged, if not forced, to "think about their society, their cosmos, and the powers that generate and sustain them." (105) Thus, liminality may be thought of as a period of reflection on the world and one's place in it. Another way of looking at it is to say that during the liminal period initiands are allowed to "play" with those structures of thought and action that govern their former and future social life. Thus, this liminal period can be the genesis of creative novelty leading to changes of perception, thought, and action once the initiands return to their community and take up their new social responsibilities. This is how, using Whitehead's terms, a society's cultural inertia toward conserving the status quo is able to avoid triviality by ingesting creative novelty into its cultural forms. Turner states the matter succinctly and well:

> [I]n order to live, to breathe, and to generate novelty, human beings have had to create—by structural means—spaces and times in the calendar or, in the cultural cycles of their most cherished groups which cannot be captured in the classificatory nets of their quotidian, routinized spheres of action. These liminal areas of time and space—rituals, carnivals, dramas, and latterly films—are open to the play of thought, feeling, and will; in them are generated new models, often fantastic, some of which may have sufficient power and plausibility to replace eventually the force-backed political and jural model that control the center of a society's ongoing life. (1977:vii)

When speaking of "liminal" periods, Turner generally refers to traditional societies and rites of passage. He reserves the term "liminoid" for those "betwixt and between" events that occur along the margins of the political and economic structures of post-industrial societies; liminoid events include "theater, ballet, film, the novel, poetry, music, and art." (1978:253) As such, liminoid phenomena "are plural, fragmentary . . . , experimental, idiosyncratic, quirky, subversive, utopian, and characteristically produced and consumed by identifiable individuals, in contrast to liminal phenomena . . . , which are often anonymous or divine in origin." (1978:253) Liminoid genres like fiction can be seen as threats to "the axioms and standards of the *ancien régime*," (1975:14) because they proffer alternative visions which may act to subvert the dominant structures of thought and action. Just as traditional societies seek to contain and control the dangers present in liminal activities, so too do post-industrial societies seek to contain and control those liminoid activities which challenge accepted norms of behavior, i.e. censorship.

Whitehead's philosophy of organism has as one of its central tenets the notion of *creativity*, a concept of which Gardner is clearly aware. Creativity within a processual metaphysical system is Whitehead's answer to the philosophical problem of "the one and the many." Building on the concepts of "actual entity," "prehension," and "subjective aim," creativity is introduced by Whitehead as "the universal of universals characterizing ultimate matter of fact." (1978:21) As such, creativity is the principle by which the many discrete entities that exist disjunctively in the universe "become one actual occasion."(21) This notion of creativity, by which the many become one complex unity, is dubbed by Whitehead the principle of *novelty*. As Whitehead writes:

> The ultimate metaphysical principle is the advance from disjunction to conjunction, creating a novel entity other than the entities given in disjunction. The novel entity is at once the togetherness of the "many" which it finds, and also it is one among the disjunctive "many" which it leaves; it is a novel entity, disjunctively among the many entities which it synthesizes. The many become one, and are increased by one. (1978:21)

In the foregoing passage from *Process and Reality* Whitehead describes the physical theory behind process thought. As such, novelty is a constant of each actual occasion, for each actual occasion is, in its subjective immediacy of the moment, an integration, in an act of concrescence, of past actual occasions, thus bringing about a "new being." But novelty also refers to the capability of high-grade actual occasions to subjectively bring about change and modification. In process thought low-grade actual occasions (e.g. stones, tables, etc.) essentially mirror their past actual world and manifest negligible novelty, while high-grade actual occasions (e.g. animals, human beings) are able to prehend their past actual world in an act of concrescence by which novel conceptual forms are integrated and creatively advanced into an intensely felt harmony of satisfaction. High-grade actual occasions, being more complex entities often with specialized modes of organizing experience, namely those physical senses which make up experience in the pure mode of presentational immediacy, manifest novelty to a much higher degree than do low-grade actual occasions.

Previously, reference was made to the fact that the interplay between presentational immediacy (that vivid experience as organized through the physical senses) and causal efficacy (that area of vague visceral feeling which is foundational and antecedent to presentational immediacy) result in what Whitehead calls "symbolic reference." In higher phases of experience, Whitehead argues, prehensions derived from these two modes of experience are integrated into a unity of feeling. This unity deriving from two distinct yet interrelated modes of experience is achieved by a subjective form laden with "emotion and purpose, and valuation, and causation" selecting out congruous elements of the two modes and unifying them into an integrated harmony of satisfaction. (19) This brings an element of originative freedom to experience, but also introduces the element of error. When speaking of human perception what is really meant, according to Whitehead, is experience in the mixed mode of symbolic reference, which has as its basic characteristic that it is interpretive.

In high-grade occasions like human beings this originative phase is very marked. We are able imaginatively to conceive differences. Thus our physical experiences may be conceptually reorganized in an act of reversion, thereby allowing physical experience to be compared with an imaginative realization in the realm of pure possibility. For example, one might visit a white house in hopes of buying it, and compare the physical experience of that house with an imaginative realization of that same house with gray vinyl siding. Or, one might watch the television news and hear of a world caught up in violence and hatred, yet imaginatively conceive of a world of peace and harmony. These conceptions are mere possibilities, but are nonetheless conceptual feelings which are available to be taken up by a percipient occasion and integrated in an act of concrescence into an intense unity of feeling. Whitehead refers to this stage of unity in a moment of subjective immediacy as an attained "satisfaction." Indeed, satisfaction is the goal, the telos, the final cause, toward which men and women as percipient occasions move in seeking more intense unities of feeling. Satisfaction is the bringing together in one percipient occasion the many varied past actual occasions of experience, both physical and conceptual, in one novel unity, a harmony of feeling.

Because men and women, as high-grade actual occasions, have available to them the imaginative use of conceptual feelings, many possibilities may be elicited for consideration. Those which are positively prehended may then act as a prod in bringing about the reality of that which was formerly but a conceptual possibility. Men and women, in experiencing that novel unity of feeling that is satisfaction, may act on that novel vision in such a way as to bring about change in the future. Having attained a novel vision of a white house with gray vinyl siding, for example, one might then act to bring it about; having conceived a world of peace and harmony one might then help to make the conception a reality. When Whitehead describes this aspect of human experience he adopts the term *superject*. Tied up with this notion of a "superject" is the pragmatic assertion, based on what empirically is but a belief, that those ideas we conceive, together with the actions we initiate, will affect the future. To the extent one's thoughts and actions replicate that which is valorized within a community it will tend to strengthen that community. However, an ever-changing world of process demands novel thoughts and actions lest the society as a whole drift toward triviality and irrelevance. Whitehead captures the sense of this ongoing need for balance between both cultural tradition and cultural revision at the end of his book, *Symbolism*:

> No elaborate community of elaborate organisms could exist unless its systems of symbolism were in general successful. Codes, rules of behavior, canons of art, are attempts to impose systematic action which on the whole will promote favourable symbolic interconnections. As a community changes, all such rules and canons require revision in the light of reason. The object to be

obtained has two aspects; one is the subordination of the community to the individuals composing it, and the other is the subordination of the individuals to the community. . . .

It is the first step in sociological wisdom, to recognize that the major advances in civilization are processes which all but wreck the societies in which they occur:—like unto an arrow in the hand of a child. The art of free society consists first in the maintenance of the symbolic code; and secondly in fearlessness of revision, to secure that the code serves those purposes which satisfy an enlightened reason. Those societies which cannot combine reverence to their symbols with freedom of revision, must ultimately decay either from anarchy, or from the slow atrophy of a life stifled by useless shadows. (87–88)

Turner's work in ritual process, particularly his description of liminal phenomena, speaks of a ritual time and space in which novel alternatives to those structures dominant in a given society may be conceptualized. Whitehead's work speaks more to the mission of novel alternative visions, suggesting their necessity for the psychological and social health of men and women. John Gardner very much sees the role of literature, as well as the other arts, as engaging men and women in such a way that novel visions leading to intense unities of feeling might then lead to a creative advance by individuals and, by implication, by the communities in which they live. Literature has clearly been a means by which Gardner, as an artist, has elicited a variety of conceptual feelings about death and guilt for exploration. Thus, art may be viewed as Gardner's ritual manner of presenting novel perspectives on death and guilt which will be for him personally—and he hopes for readers as well—helpful in understanding a world in which death and guilt exist.

Gardner's use of the liminoid character of fiction is but one way he uses ritual activity. He is not unique in that regard. In considering Grimes's category of celebration, in showing its similarities with concepts like games, worship, and the writing of fiction, and then in indicating how each of these activities allow a person to distance herself from the dominant structures of society, thereby allowing for the reflexive questioning and alternative visioning of that society, no real distinction is made between Gardner and other artists. They all use these "margins" of modern society to provide alternative visions which, superjectively, may lead to changes in individuals and their communities. However, Gardner seeks to separate his fiction from the work of other contemporary writers, particularly from those he believes abet only cynical and nihilistic alternative visions in their fiction. If technically gifted, these other writers—he thinks particularly of Sartre—may have a profound, and to his mind dangerous, influence on readers. These other writers, in Whitehead's words, are more than happy to fearlessly revise societal structures, but they do so without a commensurate reverence for "society's symbols," thus risking societal decay from anarchy. In Gardner's view, a novel alternative vision today means an alternative vision to the "dream" articulated by those contemporary writers who abdicate what he believes to be the artist's responsibility to provide "visions worth trying to make fact." (Gardner, 1978:100) Gardner wants to be technically proficient as an artist, thereby providing a vivid and continuous dream in which the reader might, for a playful celebrative moment, believe. It is here Gardner has a second use for ritual. By accurately depicting the myriad ways men and women interact, including the omnipresence of ritual activity in their lives, Gardner uses ritual as one means of engendering that vivid and continuous dream in the reader.

Gardner's consistently believable use of ritual activity fleshes out that vivid and continuous dream allowing the reader to engage fully the hypothetical situation of the novel to see if the vision expressed there is "commensurate with 'our deepest sense of ourselves.' " (Gunn, 1971:27) The question then is: A dream of what? What becomes clear for the reader familiar with the corpus of Gardner's published work is that the vision one finds expressed in his fiction—the vision, in other words, he would have the reader dream—is of "peace."

CHAPTER XI:
Whitehead, Gardner and Peace

In *Adventures of Ideas* Whitehead maintains that any successful civilization requires the virtues of Truth, Beauty, Adventure and Art. Each of these elements lend zest to a society as it creatively advances toward its future in turbulent pursuit of its destiny. Whitehead believes a fifth element is required, however: "I choose the term 'Peace' for that Harmony of Harmonies which calms destructive turbulence and completes civilization. Thus a society is to be termed civilized whose members participate in the five qualities—Truth, Beauty, Adventure, Art, Peace." (285)

By *Truth*, Whitehead simply means the conformation of appearance to reality. In fact, truth has only to do with appearance because reality simply exists, and it would be foolish to ask whether reality is either true or false. Appearance, being the result of conformal feeling of the congruent elements of the two pure modes of experience (i.e. presentational immediacy and causal efficacy), is always a matter of interpretation and is thus subject to error. As such, sense perceptions are only appearances, not reality. Nonetheless, when a person sees the light from a star in the north sky that experience is true. It is an appearance in the immediacy of the present, however, of a reality that is a past actual occasion. Indeed, the appearance of the star in the subjective immediacy of a percipient occasion may be of a reality that no longer exists—at the moment of the true appearance to a percipient occasion it may have become a dead star in reality.

For non-human animals sense-perception is the final end of experience. But for men and women another type of truth, even more vague and indirect, is available. Whitehead terms this "symbolic truth," and an example would be languages. In language there is an indirect truth relation between reality and the appearance as symbolized by sounds or marks on a piece of paper. This indirect form of truth requires some conditioning on the part of the users of language—an acceptance of the agreed upon conventions by the users of the language, as Wittgenstein would say—in order for an appearance to be conveyed and adjudged true or false. An aesthetic form like literature is unique in that it conveys both objective meaning and subjective form. But Whitehead does not limit himself to considerations of just literature. "Music, ceremonial clothing, ceremonial smells, and ceremonial rhythmic visual appearances, also have symbolic truth, or symbolic falsehood," he writes. "In these latter instances, the conveyance of objective meaning is at a minimum, while the conveyance of suitable subjective form is at its height."[1] (249) It is because the truth of a proposition has to do more with appearance rather than reality that Whitehead has said: "It is more important that a proposition be interesting than that it be true." (244) However, he quickly amplifies this statement by adding, "a true proposition is more apt to be interesting than a false one." (244)

In his chapter on *Beauty* Whitehead identifies two senses of the term: (1) that harmony of realized unity of feeling that is an actual occasion's satisfaction, and (2) those parts of the objective content of an occasion that contributes to the perfection of subjective form in future occasions. The former accents how each percipient occasion, though conditioned by the immanence of its past, has the freedom to spontaneously instantiate a novel harmony of feeling. The latter emphasizes an occasion's production of perfections of novel harmony as a datum to be prehended by future occasions, and thus includes the work of artists. Beauty, as conceived by Whitehead, can also lead to social disharmony. Being finite individuals, we often are forced to dismiss alternative novel visions because of the pragmatic realities of one's social world, thereby acknowledging a discord between one's novel harmonies of perfection (i.e. beauty) and the world as given. The presence of discord, occasionally referred to as "evil" by Whitehead, poses a risk for a society, but can also be a positive moment engendering renewed intensities of feeling. As Whitehead explains: "even perfection will not bear the tedium of infinite repetition. To sustain a civilization with the intensity of its first ardour requires more than learning. Adventure is essential, namely, the search for new perfections." (258)

A possible response to these discordant feelings is what Whitehead calls "anaesthesia," the repressing and ignoring of discordant alternatives to the world as given. The general result of anesthesia is that the society tends to regress into triviality and irrelevance. Another possible response is to readjust the relative intensities of these incompatible visions, thereby taming them in such a way as to derive the congruent elements of each. This would be a compromising of discordant feelings that would attain a temporary social harmony, but at the expense of lost novelty. Yet another alternative is to allow for an introduction of a third, novel system that would be relevant to both the inharmonious systems. This alternative is tantamount to a radically creative advance in civilization that Whitehead warns "all but wreck the societies in which they occur." (1985:88) They are the "paradigm shifts," to use Kuhn's term, that lead both to disharmony and dislocation, but also may lead to novel insights and renewed intensities of feeling resulting in more complex unities of satisfaction.

When Whitehead turns to the subject of *Art* he seeks to integrate the concept of truth with the dynamics of harmony and discord that he maintains is endemic to the notion of beauty. Whitehead insists on the importance of truth for the promotion of beauty. Acknowledging truth is "various in its extent, its modes, and its relevance," he proceeds to argue that the truth that inheres in great art

> is that truth-relation whereby Appearance summons up new resources of feeling from the depths of Reality. It is a Truth of feeling, and not a Truth of verbalization. The relata in Reality must lie below the stale presuppositions of verbal thought. The Truth of Supreme Beauty lies beyond the dictionary meanings of words. (266–67)

Thus, Whitehead argues, art integrates beauty and harmony in such a way that the felt intensity of feeling has its genesis at some intuitive level of experience. "This intuition," he writes in a different context in *Religion in the Making*, "is not the discernment of a form of words, but of a type of character. It is characteristic of the learned mind to exalt words. Yet mothers can ponder many things in their hearts which their lips cannot express." (65) Julius Bixler takes note of this argument in his essay on Whitehead's philosophy of religion:

> The senses simplify, and it is well for us to seek simplicity; but we should distrust it when it is found. Reflective thought, which puts experiences into words, has also its danger of over-simplification. Language is a tricky instrument which does only partial justice to our deepest intuitions. The prominent facts of consciousness are the superficial facts; those that are important are on the fringe. Therefore we mistakenly criticize the mystic when he attaches importance to experiences he cannot explain. Some experiences are significant in the highest degree, even though it takes us a long time to tell what they are significant of. The present enthusiasm for the scientific method in religion is thus based on a misconception. Art and poetry offer nearer analogies since,

like religion, they direct us to the inarticulate and incommunicable quality of the vivid flash of insight. (1951:506–07)

In his *Adventures of Ideas* Whitehead defines art as "purposeful adaptation of Appearance to Reality." (267) He then proceeds to say that the perfection of art has but one goal: Truthful Beauty. Without truth, Whitehead believes art lacks "massiveness," or weightiness. Without beauty, whatever truth may be present in a work of art sinks to triviality. "Truth matters," he says, "because of Beauty." (267) In his chapter on art Whitehead also speaks of the human body as being an instrument for the production of art. It is in this aspect of his work that his ideas are quite similar to Grimes's emphasis on the somatic role in ritual. In an important passage from *Adventures of Ideas* Whitehead speaks of what he believes to be the biogenetic origins of art: "Art is a message from the Unseen. It unlooses depths of feeling from behind the frontier where precision of consciousness fails. The starting point for the highly developed human art is thus to be sought amid the cravings generated by the physiological functionings of the body." (271)

By *Adventure* Whitehead simply refers to the ongoing evolutionary search for new perfections and more complex unities of satisfaction. Individuals and societies can become so tied to a single structured way of thought and action that the harmony achieved becomes stale and trivial. Given the Whiteheadian assumptions of Process thought, the desire for change on the part of individuals and societies is deeply rooted. No civilization becomes great by simply replicating its past. Rather, each embraces an adventurous spirit which, though risking pain and dissolution, often will result in greater cultural achievements and novel intensities of feeling as it seeks even more complex unities of satisfaction. Thus it happens that societies and individuals come and go, and the most intense feelings of an epoch's accomplishments and joys, as well as its disappointments and sorrows, are superseded in the often turbulent, but necessary, ongoing process of life.

Gardner is certainly aware of the classic *Adventures of Ideas*, and his own ideas about art and civilization are very much in agreement with Whitehead's. Gardner will quickly acknowledge that truth, in any sort of perfectly objective sense, is impossible. Being finite individuals, men and women are constantly required to interpret their world, to understand as best they are able the ways in which what they say and do will conform appearance to reality. The characters in his novels make mistakes and are generally prone to error; several characters may have quite differing perspectives on a subject. Each is trying to approach truth as best he or she can, but it is always but an approach. It is this aspect of his novels that Dean McWilliams, adopting the ideas of the Russian theorist M. M. Bakhtin, examines in his book on Gardner. It is why he believes the author refuses a monological acclamation of one perspective over all others, opting instead for a dialogical exploration of several competing perspectives. But Gardner is also aware of the presence of evil in the world, that discord which, in turn, can lead to destruction. At the same time he recognizes that discord and destruction can be the impetus to greater insights and intensities of feeling. Gardner's world is one in which death and guilt are ever present, and can lead to despair and an unbridled cynicism. Lifton's work with survivors suggests that Gardner's guilt over the death of his younger brother may have been the prod—Gardner calls it a psychological wound—that drives him not toward despair and cynicism, but toward a more comprehensive understanding of the world.

One idea that seems to have been rejected early on is a naive rendering of classical theism, such that tragic events are caused—or at least allowed—by a good God in order to fulfill some indiscernible plan. Rather, Gardner seems quickly to have come to his mother's position in counseling him after the accident: "I told Bud, *Nobody* could have stopped that cultipacker except God, and He doesn't work that way. He doesn't interfere. When a big thing of nature hits you it hits you, and there's nothing that can be done to interfere." (P. Gardner, 1984:235) Process thought is an intellectual alternative which appeals both to Gardner's basic religious intuition, as well as his need for a conceptual schema by which to understand why the world is as it is. In seeking this conceptual understanding, Gardner envisions a world in which men and women together seek "for positive ways of surviving, of living," and for a world in which "life is better than death." (Ferguson, 1979:47–48) Gardner's depiction through his novels and his short stories of a diverse world of competing and sometimes contradictory interests, a world in which tragedies do occur, but also a world in which individuals may, in their originative freedom, achieve intense feelings of harmony and of emotionally satisfying purposefulness, is a Whiteheadian vision of truthful beauty.

In literature, and to a lesser extent in music, Gardner believes he is able to present to a reader a vivid and continuous dream of truthful beauty. His fiction strives to present a vision attuned with a reader's deepest sense of himself, to use Gunn's phrase, and thus reach into that intuitive realm of human experience summoning up "new resources of feeling from the depths of Reality." (Whitehead, *Adventures of Ideas*: 266–67) Such an aesthetic vision has the value of creating new conceptual feelings which may then be positively prehended and integrated in novel intensities of feeling on the part of a reader. When a fiction is technically ill-conceived, or when lacking in truth or beauty, it may be negatively prehended by a reader, which is to say the fiction is relegated by a reader to irrelevancy. By contrast, that art which meaningfully depicts "truthful beauty" is that which is most likely to be integrated into a reader's novel intensities of feeling in its subjective immediacy, thus allowing for the attainment of a final satisfaction that is likely to be deeply gratifying.

Literature, being on the margins of the dominant economic and political structures, has a role to play in making a society adventuresome. Gardner's most severe critics attempt to say he is a moral conservative trying to maintain the status quo. As already noted, these critics are seeking rhetorical advantage and their comments are hardly to the point. The fact is, Gardner wants to acknowledge the importance of traditional modes of thought and action while at the same time advocating a constant review and, if necessary, revision of those same modes of thought and action. His major fictional heroes—Fred Clumly, James Page, Henry Soames—are all forced to take a hard look at their habitual ways of thinking and acting, with the result that each undergoes quite remarkable changes. They are open to adventure, to that search for novel perfections. The characters in Gardner's novels that are most sad are those unable to change, unable critically to reassess their habitually accepted ways of thinking and doing.

A short story that perhaps best exemplifies Gardner's adherence to a Whiteheadian perspective is "The Art of Living," which is the title story of a collection of Gardner's short stories that include "Redemption" and "Come On Back." The story concerns a cook named Arnold Deller, another of Gardner's simple folk heroes who tries, given his limitations, to understand his world. A cook at a small Italian restaurant in upper New York State for more than twenty years, he has recently lost his son in Vietnam. As the narrative opens he has befriended a group of young motorcycle enthusiasts who fancy themselves Brando-esque "outsiders," rebels too cynically hip to accept the world being handed them by their elders. But their "hipness," as the narration by one of the motorcycle youths, Finnegan, makes clear, is a charade. They are "really just a bunch of greaser kids in second-hand black jackets," Finnegan admits, "fighting pimples, hanging around, waiting to get drafted and shot at." (244) The 1960's was a time of social chaos as people questioned the effectiveness of those modes of thought and action that had, in earlier generations, created and maintained harmony. Arnold Deller, knowing a thing or two about the ways of the world, and less prone to the violent reactions of youth, offers his wisdom to the bikers:

> Listen, the world's in chaos, right? . . . War, revolution, students rioting, police rioting, drugs and promiscuity . . . Let me tell you something: it will pass. Nobody believes that, nobody thinks about afterward—hell no!—but let me tell you, *it will pass!* After the world-wide glorious high there's going to be a crash like the world never dreamed of. Things will be changed, even here, in a backwater hick-town like this one, but whatever the world's like afterward, we're gonna be stuck with ourselves again—ourselves! . . . The thing a person's gotta have—a human being—is some kind of center to his life, some one thing he's good at that other people need from him, like for instance, shoemaking. I mean something ordinary but at the same time holy, if you know what I mean. Very special. Something *ritual*—like, better yet, cooking! (250)

This leads Arnold to philosophize: he characterizes human beings as "super-apes" with brains so big that they are no longer attuned to the ways of the body. What animals know by instinct simply doesn't register with human beings, anymore. We are oblivious, Arnold tells his charges. After noting that humans are social animals desiring to run in packs, Arnold then asserts that humans have a war instinct. "Any animal can fight," he tells the boys, "but human beings are serious about it." (253) He attributes the level of violence to which humans engage to the fact that human babies take so long before they can be left on their own. In the meantime, the parents have to protect the baby until he can walk and talk, until he can learn to make fire, to hunt and to cook. For this reason it is not enough to simply knock off an enemy every now and then. "You gotta clean out that forest, make the whole place safe. So the baby that survives is the one with the parents that are the best at holding grudges, the ones that are *implacable*." (253) Parents learn to love each other for the sake of the baby, Arnold insists, and learn to love other relatives, and friends and neighbors—even dead relatives, friends and neighbors—because it all helps to raise the baby. But there always remains an unmitigated hatred of the enemy, the outsider, the threat to their child. This is all well and good so long as humans stay in isolated conclaves, but what happens, he asks, when former enemies try to live in the same town, on the same block? When that happens, Arnold tells them, people have to retrain their instincts. Institutions are developed, courts and governments, in order to figure out how best to live together without killing each other again. There are even stories that are developed that honor the fathers and grandfathers of "those other guys," who happen to be the same people who were killing and saying terrible things about your father and grandfathers. "That's when you've gotta use your head," Arnold insists, "Love by policy, not just instinct. That's the Art of Living. Not just instinct; something you do on purpose. Art!" (254)

Arnold continues by insisting that the value of art is that it is able to create strong emotional feelings that allow people, despite their former differences, to come together as a community. He ends with a final tribute to the efficacy of art, saying that what an artist does is make things no one asks to be made or perhaps even wants to be made. But the artist makes it anyway. Then, once people have it in their hands or hear it or see it, once the art object is in front of them, they want to keep it, or take it home with them, or have it on display at some museum. "That's what it's all about," Arnold says. "Making life startling and interesting again, bringing families together, or lovers, what-not." (257)

As the story develops Arnold tries to convince the boys to help him prepare a special Chinese dish called Imperial Dog, which his son had written him about before his death. It calls for the killing and preparation of a black dog. The young motorcyclists resist, as does Angelina, the granddaughter of the restaurant's owner. In time Angelina begins to understand that Arnold wants to prepare the meal as a way of remembering his son, and eventually she asks the help of Finnegan in securing a dog. It happens. When Arnold kills the dog late at night in the restaurant's kitchen, Finnegan and his friends are horrified. Arnold revels in the moment, however, seeing it as the exact opposite of that anonymous preparation of artificial food that has become the staple of

American diets, an acceptance of which has led to men and women acting like sheep, leading trivialized lives of empty harmony. Disturbed by what is happening, Finnegan explodes: "Arnold, . . . you're crazy!" (269) There are two reasons why Finnegan is mad. For one, it bothers him that when his friend Rinehart, who is Arnold's son, sat down to that meal of Imperial Black Dog and then writes home to say how he felt at one with generations of dead Asians, that those same Asians would have killed him in an instant and used the pages of his Bible for their own profane purposes. Secondly, it angers him that Arnold now wants to be at one with those same Asians, all to be with Rinehart once again. All Finnegan can see is that Rinehart is dead, as will they all soon be. So what's the point? To Finnegan, Arnold's attempt to re-create the special Chinese meal that his son had written him about is ludicrous.

Arnold makes no attempt to defend his act as "good" or "right," but simply claims he is an artist acting in covenant with another culture's artistic tradition. Finnegan is holding on to his traditional ways of thinking and acting, not seeing the preparation of Imperial Dog as an attempt to "love by policy" those who have previously been considered the enemy—in this case, those who have killed his friend Rinehart. Arnold is choosing to promote an advance of creative novelty such as would honor his art, his son, and those of a culture that had killed his son. As Arnold argued earlier, what is important in art is its results. Does the object made by the artist—an object perhaps people did not want to have made, as indeed Finnegan did not—make life startling and more interesting once again? Does it bring together families? Lovers? The answer is provided as Arnold, his three daughters who have arrived at the restaurant, Finnegan and his friends, and Angelina sit down to the meal. Angelina's father, who arrives unexpectedly on the scene and is aghast by what is happening, refuses to join and leaves the restaurant. Finnegan thinks to himself that Angelina's father is the one who had been right, "sane and civilized from the beginning." (273–74) But he also notices that the man's "walk was oddly mechanical, and the way he shook his head when he looked back at us from the door, it was as if under his hair he had springs and gears." (274) Angelina's father refuses to be open to the novelty of adventure, and is described in the text as a sort of "mechanical man" replicating uncritically his society's traditional modes of behavior. For those who remain, the dinner takes on ritual dimensions, though there is, for Finnegan, no sign of the thousands of dead Asians, nor of Rinehart. Nonetheless, it *felt* as if they were all present, "maybe even more there if there's no such thing in the world as ghosts, no life after death, no one there at the candlelit table but the few of us able to throw shadows on the wall." (274) This celebratory moment, this artistic instant of "truthful beauty," brings a novel intensity of feeling for those gathered. It allows them to transcend their traditional modes of thought and action in such a way that an even more complex satisfaction, a novel harmony that is greater than any previously felt harmony of satisfaction, is adventurously sought and achieved. The story ends with those gathered exchanging toasts. After the last is delivered, the reader is informed that "in the darkness beyond where the candles reached, Rinehart nodded, and a thousand thousand Asians bowed from the waist." (274)

David Hall has written an intriguing study of culture using Whiteheadian categories. Titled *The Civilization of Experience: A Whiteheadian Theory of Culture*, Hall posits a basic analogy between Whitehead's metaphysical theory and civilization. Examining the process model he notes "[t]here are three principle stages in the growth of an occasion of experience, internally considered: datum, process, and satisfaction." (33) That is to say, there is a datum, an already existent occasion that in its moment of achieved satisfaction perishes, either to be taken up again and objectively immortalized in a subsequent occasion or dismissed into irrelevancy. In addition to a datum to be experienced there is the act of concrescence in which a subsequent occasion prehends that datum along with other past actual occasions into its own subjective immediacy. Then there is that moment of an actual occasion as it attains an intensity and harmony of feeling that is its final satisfaction, thence to perish and serve as a datum for future occasions. Using Whitehead's five characteristics of a civilization, Hall then argues that Truth and Beauty are *data* to be experienced, Art and Adventure are the *process* by which a civilization experiences, and Peace is the final *satisfaction* toward which a civilization strives.

In *Adventures of Ideas* Whitehead refers to *Peace* as a "Harmony of Harmonies which calms destructive turbulence and completes civilization." (285) In speaking of the "calm" of peace he is not speaking of an absence of feeling but of a "positive feeling which crowns the 'life and motion' of the soul." (285) While qualifying his remarks with the disclaimer that it is ineffable, he then describes peace as an expanding of feeling such that a person experiences a "deep metaphysical insight, unverbalized and yet momentous in its coordination of values." (285) One of its benefits is the removal of stress as one no longer is driven by an acquisitive preoccupation with self. Once one attains peace, life is lived outward and one feels "a grasp of infinitude, an appeal beyond boundaries." (285) Peace, in other words, is the gaining of a perspective that includes the self but also transcends the self. One might fully enjoy the dynamics of truth, beauty, art, and adventure as expressions of the ego, imposing value in its own desire to attain more complex and intense unities of satisfaction. Of course, one's egoistic desires may be thwarted, or may come into conflict with another's egoistic desires, or may lead to great joy in victory or great suffering in defeat. This is why there is turbulence endemic to egoistic strivings for truth, beauty, art and adventure. Peace is the more distanced perspective that inverts the relative egoistic values of the self and intuitively grasps the reality of a permanence interweaved in the flux of process. It is, as the line from Wordsworth's poem quoted by Estelle Parks in *October Light* says, "a sense sublime / Of something far more deeply interfused." It is essentially a religious vision: that fine action is valued in the nature of things. Though we be finite individuals, never knowing fully and completely the truth of the matter, peace is the "faithing" insight that one's actions will serve the needs of a future which is congruent with a basic order in the universe:

> The order of the world is no accident. There is nothing actual which could be actual without some measure of order. The religious insight is the grasp of this truth: That the order of the world, the depth of reality of the world, the value of the world in its whole and in its parts, the beauty of the world, the zest of life, the peace of life, and the mastery of evil, are all bound together—not accidentally, but by reason of this truth: that the universe exhibits a creativity with infinite freedom, and a realm of forms with infinite possibilities; but that this creativity and these forms are together impotent to achieve actuality apart from the completed ideal harmony, which is God. (Whitehead, *Religion in the Making*:115)

God, as described by Whitehead, ought not to be identified with that of classical theism. Rather, in Process thought God has affinity with the Platonic concept of *Eros*, which lures creation forward. God, in Process thought, acts as an "initial aim" lending subjective form to an occasion, thus acting as a datum available to be integrated in an occasion's final satisfaction. Peace is the intuition that fine action exemplifies God's aim at perfection, thus participating in the ongoing creative advance toward that transpersonal vision of harmony, that final intensity of feeling that is an achieved satisfaction, that "harmony of harmonies," that recognizes all is right and proper and in its place. This intuition is described in *Adventures of Ideas* as a matter of faith "where reason fails to reveal the details," (285) and is always penultimate given our finite natures. Such a vision incorporates tragedy as a necessary element. Indeed, peace understands the ebb and flow of experience, and of the alternating rhythm of harmony and disharmony that is the mark of living individuals and societies. Peace includes the intuition that disharmony and its consequences are an essential aspect of the nature of things, rather than disappointment and tragedy being merely a matter of personal and social shortcomings. Individuals and societies cannot simply stand still. This is why Whitehead maintains that no civilization can remain vibrant through an indefinite reiteration of a perfected ideal. It is in such cases that "anesthesia" will always set in. "Apart from surprise," Whitehead writes, "intensity of feeling collapses." (286) This is why acts of "Decay, Transition, Loss, Displacement belong to the essence of the Creative Advance." (286)

Disharmony is required in order to set the stage for freshness and renewed zest for life, emanating in novel harmonies of perfection. He continues:

> As soon as high consciousness is reached, the enjoyment of existence is entwined with pain, frustration, loss, tragedy. Amid the passing of so much beauty, so much heroism, so much daring, Peace is then the intuition of permanence. It keeps vivid the sensitiveness to the tragedy; and it sees the tragedy as a living agent persuading the world to aim at fineness beyond the faded level of surrounding fact. Each tragedy is the disclosure of an ideal:— What might have been, and was not: What can be. The tragedy was not in vain. (286)

This intuitive insight that is peace is reserved for men and women who have experienced tragedy in their own lives. Thus youth, by the very fact of their youth, have an extraordinarily difficult time grasping the concept. Indeed, in *Adventures of Ideas* Whitehead defines youth as lives not yet touched by tragedy. Thus, a person's youth is not a peaceful time in Whitehead's view. For one, when a youth feels despair it tends to be felt as overwhelming. This is so because youths do not yet have experiences of having survived disasters of one kind or another. This is one reason why suicide is an especially troublesome issue with adolescents. "The short-sightedness of youth matches the scantiness of its experience," he writes. (287) But another aspect of youth is the ability to embrace whole-heartedly an ideal, like Unferth in Gardner's *Grendel* embracing the virtues of the hero in his effort to kill the monster. Youth can grasp, intellectually, the notion of a transcendent ideal. But it is only with the experience of tragedy—of seeing their intellectual ideals battered, abused, disregarded or otherwise rejected, and friends and loved ones destroyed in the service of an intellectual ideal—that a man or woman becomes capable of experiencing viscerally that transcendent vision of ultimate harmony that is peace.

The end of the matter: peace is the acceptance of the world and of the nature of things. Integral to peace is the notion that men and women can act in such a way as to make a difference in the world in helping to bring about greater and more complex realizations of harmony. This is to recognize the superjective character of an actual occasion; one's actions may transcend self-satisfaction and serve as a model for future occasions in their search for novel intensities of feeling. One lives for others. Sometimes our attempts fail, however, and the failure is a tragedy. But tragedy simply means the attempt at a greater and more complex realization of harmony is not attained, *not* that it is unattainable or unworthy of being attained. This is one of the basic differences between Gardner and those writers with whom he most ardently disagrees. Gardner believes they would have the reader accept the notion that any attempt at harmony and meaningfulness is just so much puttering about until our appointed time at the grave. By contrast, Gardner believes that peace, informing the art of literature's vivid presentation of truthful beauty, leads to readers being "powerfully persuaded that the focal characters, in their fight for life, have won honestly or, if they lose, are tragic in their loss, not just tiresome or pitiful." (Ferguson, 1979:48) As he writes elsewhere:

> That art which tends toward destruction, the art of nihilists, cynics, and merdistes, is not properly art at all. Art is essentially serious and beneficial, a

> game played against chaos and death, against entropy. It is a tragic game, for those who have the wit to take it seriously, because our side must lose; a comic game—or so a troll might say—because only a clown with sawdust brains would take our side and eagerly join in.
>
> . . . Art asserts and reasserts those values which hold off dissolution, struggling to keep the mind intact and preserve the city, the mind's safe preserve. Art discovers, generation by generation, what is necessary to humanness. (1978:6)

Gardner's novels depict conflicts among a variety of characters, but also show how some of these same characters are transformed. In the process, Gardner expresses a general approach to life that incorporates the Whiteheadian notion of peace, that acceptance of the world and the nature of things—including tragedy—that intuits a permanence immanent in the flux of experience. All of his protagonists either are facing death or are suffering from guilt at having been the cause of another's death. Those able to confront death and guilt openly, rather than avoid them in an act of anesthesia, are those most likely to embrace the fuller vision of life that peace affords. They are the ones able to invigorate their communities and act, superjectively, as models to guide and nurture others seeking to make their way in the world. They, like Dorkis in *The Wreckage of Agathon*, are the one's able to "accept in peace" horror and tragedy as an ineluctable element in the nature of things. Those characters unable to embrace death and guilt as essential elements in the creative advance toward novel harmony are the ones in Gardner's novels who find themselves isolated from their communities; occasionally they choose suicide.

Peter Mickelsson at one point near the end of *Mickelsson's Ghosts* displays an intellectual understanding of this aspect of peace. In the midst of his own guilt and sorrow, Mickelsson is "[l]ike an old man watching his grandchildren crying their hearts out in childhood's immeasurable, brief sorrow, he felt not anger at the bitterness of life or dismay at his inability to help, but only cool sympathy, a guarded Boethian amusement." (523) But at this point it is only an intellectual acceptance, for a moment later he is on the verge of killing himself. What is still required is the intuition that fine action is needed, acts which superjectively make a difference in helping others find their way in life. It comes to pass that Mickelsson does just that near the end of the novel when, contrary to earlier episodes when he refused calls for his help, he rushes to the aid of one of his students who, in the flush of her youth, believes her boyfriend's betrayal to be the worst possible tragedy life can offer. Drawing on his gained wisdom, his more clarified intuition of peace, he tries to turn her "tragedy" into a more accepting vision of a world in which betrayals—and worse—will continue to happen, but a world also full of possibilities to be realized.

James Chandler, in *The Resurrection*, also comes to the aid of a youth at the end of the text, in an attempt to allay Viola's crushing sense of guilt after she tragically, because of her unwise decision to visit James, allows her senile aunt to wander from her home to her death. From his more mature perspective, with a wisdom now aware of a permanence immanent in the changes and tragedies of life, he counsels her: "No harm. It's done us no harm." (232) His insight into the world, his vision of peace, occurs just previous to his reaching out to Viola to help her: "It was not the beauty of the world one must affirm but *the world*, the buzzing blooming confusion itself. He had slipped from celebrating what was to the celebration of empty celebration." (229) Each finite vision of the world is a vision of beauty, realized in a perfected novelty of satisfaction. But it is always a finite vision of beauty, to be superseded at a future time. Having attained a transpersonal intuition of peace, Chandler comes to realize that the valorization of any one vision of beauty as ultimate is to miss the reality of the world—the processual world, the buzzing blooming confusion itself. His final act is to reach out to Viola, superjectively, to allay her intense feelings of guilt, thus freeing her to pursue life.

James's more intuitive wife, Marie, interrupts a conversation among some friends, a discussion about the "truth" of contemporary art, with the declaration: "This is much truer." (155) Her interjection directs all of their attention to what is playing out before them:

> All three of them looked at the same time, as if perfectly understanding her, at the miles of gray-green, dwarfish trees, the cliffs to the right, . . . What Chandler, at least, had seen that instant was Death, wheeling and howling, and two little girls in red coats running down the path toward them, laughing. Marie sat like the Buddha, her legs out like sticks, her red hands resting tranquilly on her enormous belly. Her face was full of light. (155)

James Chandler is fond of saying, "Life goes on." But it is usually a cliche coming from him. For Marie, life does go on even in the midst of her husband's death. She attends Elizabeth Staley's piano recital—a death of its own as it will be the last recital given—as her husband breathes his last. There are three daughters, and she is now responsible for them. Life, indeed, does go on, full of tragedy, but also full of promise.

James Page is forced by circumstances to take a hard look at himself. He is forced to see how his actions have indirectly led to the death of his son and to suffering for the rest of his family. It is a terrible burden of guilt he must carry by the end of the novel. But he is able to bear it because he comes to accept the forgiveness long offered him by his wife, Ariah. Formerly, he had tried to repress his feelings of guilt in an act of anesthesia, but by the end he embraces his guilt as that tragic element that is present in all of life. It is his wife as superject that James integrates into a novel harmony of satisfaction. In accepting his wife's forgiveness, he is finally able to forgive himself, and others.

Fred Clumly is, at the beginning of *The Sunlight Dialogues*, an officious servant of the law. As such, he merely replicates the modes of thought and action dominant in his community. Indeed, he doesn't question the laws of the town, but merely carries them out. Then, influenced by the Sunlight Man, he begins to rethink his uncritically accepted beliefs. He, more than any other, is willing to risk adventure in seeking to resolve the disharmony all about him into a novel harmony of satisfaction. At one point near the end of the text a psychiatrist gives Clumly a psychoanalytic image of man:

> According to Jung life is like the daily course of the sun. . . . You rise out of the unconsciousness of babyhood . . . and you learn who and what you are in youth, reacting with the world, and you build more and more consciousness, you think you can judge everything, meet all demands. But at a certain point you learn that the more you learn the more you'll never know! You begin to shrink back from thought . . . and you flee forward to the unconsciousness of senility. (664)

Clumly had always led a life of deference to authority, so it is an occasion to be noted when, some time later, Clumly rejects the image of man presented by the authority, the doctor. In thinking about the stages of life mentioned by the psychiatrist, Clumly realizes that he is in that twilight stage himself, "no longer fit for the world." (668) But he also knows that this would not be the case in other cultures, Indian and

African cultures he had read about, nor in the cultures about which the Sunlight Man had been lecturing him. In those Mesopotamian cultures old people were the guardians of the law and of the mysteries. Rather than old age being a slippage into unconsciousness, it was seen as simply the next stage in life's long progress. The point being, old age is an aspect of progress, not regress. To borrow that Jungian image of life being like the rise and fall of the sun, Clumly comes to believe that "in that final stage the sun carried all it had known before, all its intellect and activity, but now surpassed mere intellect and activity, surpassed mere propagation, mere earning, mere things of nature, and rose to the things of culture, to civilization." (668)

Fred Clumly refuses to accept the role of "old man" assigned him by his culture. Rather, he chooses to express the wisdom attained in his adventure with the Sunlight Man to a civic organization at the end of the novel. There, he lectures them on the need for each to care for all. Despite the seeming civic chaos surrounding them, his advice is to reach out in love and forgiveness, and to take responsibility for the world they inhabit and would bequeath to future generations. The final chapter with his comments to the civic group has a chapter heading with a quote from Berthold Brecht: "Darum, ich bitte euch, wollt nicht in Zorn verfallen Denn alle Kreatur braucht Hilf von allen." (739) [Therefore, I pray, tend not toward ruinous anger, for each of us needs help from all.] He ends his talk with a benediction meant for each person present, but also for the Sunlight Man, for good Samaritans, and for bad ones, too, "for of such is the Kingdom of Heaven." (745)

Henry Soames, in some respects, is the best example of a man inspired by a vision of Whiteheadian peace. Fully expecting his own absurd, meaningless death at any moment at the beginning of *Nickel Mountain*, he becomes instead a man seeking to live and, as superject, be a model by which his son might be nurtured and grow in wisdom. He has always been aware of the ultimate power of nature, but not in the sense of fearing nature. Henry's acceptance of the inevitability of death is remindful of Gardner's passage in *On Moral Fiction* about a terrible truth artists must address: "life does not care about any of us: by our existence we may celebrate and intensify the moment, but we're as expendable as frogs." (191) Henry knows he is expendable, but by the end of the novel he also has an intuitive faith in a permanence immanent in the comings and goings of human lives which make whatever sacrifice he may make for his wife and son—and for the larger community—of worth. While he lives he can play a role in giving his wife and son a zest for life, a zest for adventure, in their own attainment of novel satisfaction. In the Whiteheadian notion of peace it is all right and proper:

> "Life goes on," Henry said sadly, and the words filled him with a pleasant sense of grief. He thought of his own approaching death, how Callie and Jimmy would be heartbroken for a while, as he'd been heartbroken when his father died, but would after a while forget a little, turn back to the world of the living, as was right. (304)

Perhaps the finest expression of peace in Gardner's fiction is from *The Resurrection*. It occurs near the end of the novel when Chandler is fighting the pain and nausea caused by the leukemia:

> More than "in the world but not of the world" (he wrote). More than Platonic. The wisdom of old people when, as sometimes happens, old people chance to become wise. To whom the death of a child is tragic but tolerable, as it is not to us. In whom no trace of self-pity remains. Who are not overly grieved by tragedy in life, and not because they have no commitment, no interest in the central figure of the tragedy, but because, having loved repeatedly, having survived by the skin of their teeth many times, just as those who love them will, despite their own wish, they can give of themselves unstintingly, fully prepared to pay back all they have spent. To see life's beauty whole implies at once the ardent desire to look and the necessity of backing off. (204)

Gardner not only presents images of peace in his fiction, but his life as an artist is one embodying the notion of peace. He has faced tragedy in his own life, and is able to find in Process thought concepts by which to comprehend his personal tragedy. As an artist he shares with readers his own emotional and spiritual crises, and thus allows his art to serve, superjectively, as a model by which they might entertain a "virtual life" of thought and action. In striving to be technically competent and morally serious, Gardner is allowing readers a dream of peace which may be integrated into their own novel attainments of satisfaction. Art, for Gardner, is a ritual embodiment of truthful beauty by which he might explore the terrible, though fruitful, role death plays in the lives of men and women. His art, then, is an adventurous dream—a vivid and continuous dream—of peace. His art is a dream of fine action that is valued in the very nature of things and that nurtures future generations into a life of zestful adventure.

The appropriateness of death, viewed from a Whiteheadian perspective, is at the heart of James Chandler's thoughts near the end of *The Resurrection* when he suddenly thinks of that last line in Wallace Stevens's *Sunday Morning*. Though evocative more than discursive, the poem does touch on the intuition of peace. The poet speaks of death being the creative ground of beauty, and hence the fulfillment of human dreams and desires, while Gardner speaks of death as a "wound" which prods him toward a deeper understanding of the world and our place in it. Death is certainly seen as a troubling and tragic end, but when one attains the quality of peace—that wisdom which intuits a permanence immanent in nature's flux—we come to see death less as a metaphysical insult and more as a fitting end to our lives as we approach our own journey "downward" towards the darkness.

Gardner's is essentially a religious vision, but not of the treacly kind. Gardner's vision is passionate, visceral, and sheds tears. Yet it is also hopeful, and thankful, and mindful of future generations which will face the same questions and doubts as have we in our modern age. He wouldn't want it any other way. When all is said and done, however, despite whatever tragedies life has in store—whether it be the accidental death of a younger brother, soured love affairs, strained relations with colleagues, colon cancer, or ending one's life smeared along a curving Pennsylvania road under a motorcycle—when all is said and done life is good. And more importantly, as several of his characters say at one time or another, life goes on. Loved ones die; life goes on. We feel guilt because of our actions; life goes on. Newspapers chronicle unending human brutality; life goes on. And life is good. Tennyson captures this idea in section 37 of *In Memoriam*:

> My own dim life should teach me this,
>   That life shall live for evermore,
>   Else earth is darkness at the core,
> And dust and ashes all that is;
>
> This round of green, this orb of flame,
>   Fantastic beauty; such as lurks
>   In some wild poet, when he works
> Without a conscience or an aim.

> What then were God to such as I?
>   'Twere hardly worth my while to choose
>   Of things all mortal, or to use
> A little patience ere I die;
>
> 'Twere best at once to sink to peace,
>   Like birds the charming serpent draws,
>   To drop head-foremost in the jaws
> Of vacant darkness and to cease.

Tennyson sometimes referred to this lengthy poem, dedicated to a close friend of his who had died as a youth, as "The Way of the Soul." A.C. Bradley's comments about the poem is pointedly fitting for Gardner as well, noting as he does that the poem marks

> a journey from the first stupor and confusion of grief, through a growing acquiescence often disturbed by the recurrence of pain, to an almost unclouded peace and joy. The anguish of wounded love passes into the triumph of love over sorrow, time, and death. The soul, at first, almost sunk in the feeling of loss, finds itself at last freed from regret and yet strengthened in affection. . . . The world, which once seemed to it a mere echo of its sorrow, has become the abode of that immortal Love, at once divine and human, which includes the living and the dead. (Ball, 1959:954)

NOTES

Introduction

1. "He's making a shrill pitch to the literary right wing that wants to repudiate all of modernism," is a sample of Barth's attitude. See Singular, 1979, and Barth's "How is Fiction Doing?" in *New York Times Book Review*, December 14, 1980.

Chapter One

1. I continue to be amazed at how often I hear this in informal conversation, though I have yet to see anyone make the assertion in print.

Chapter Two

1. As he tells it, Gardner had tried over and over again to get published, all to no avail. Finally, with the manuscripts of *The Resurrection, The Wreckage of Agathon,* and *Grendel* in a shopping bag, he took a chance by personally going to see David Segal at New American Library. Segal was aware of who Gardner was; William Gass had recommended to him that Gardner's work be given a reading. However, Segal was not quite prepared for what came through the door. Having just motorcycled into town, and dressed in his black motorcycle leathers, Gardner plopped the shopping bag full of manuscripts on Segal's desk and said, "Mr. Segal, I'd like you to read these novels. . . . Now!" Segal began to read while Gardner stood over him. After two or three pages Segal looked up and said, "Mr Gardner, I can't read your fiction while you're watching," at which time Gardner left. While he doesn't recommend this as a way to approach editors, and later was to say he was embarrassed by the affair, the fact is that the next morning Segal told Gardner that he was accepting all three of the manuscripts for publication. (*On Becoming a Novelist*:105–06)

2. "Bellow's novels," Gardner writes in *On Moral Fiction*, "come off in the end as sprawling works of advice, not art." (93) Barth's fiction is "all but unreadable—arch, extravagantly self-indulgent, clumsily allegorical, pedantic, tiresomely and pretentiously advance guard, and like much of our 'new fiction' puerilely obscene." (95) Updike, Gardner claims, "worries no more about his characters and his readers than does Rabbit about his women." (99) Pynchon "will die of intellectual blight, academic narrowness, or fakery." (94)

3. This is a key phrase that clearly impressed Gardner. As will be seen, he uses it in several of his novels.

4. See Chapter I, pages 26ff.

5. "Thoughts [concepts] without content [percepts] are empty, intuitions [percepts] without concepts are blind," from Kant's *Critique of Pure Reason.* (1965:93)

Chapter Two, cont.

6. See Chapter II, p. 37.

Chapter Three

1. For a detailed schematic of the zodiacal pattern see Larsen's "The Creative Act: An Analysis of Systems in Grendel," in *John Gardner: True Art, Moral Art* edited by B. Mendez-Egle and J. Haule. (1983:44)

Chapter Four

1. Compare this with Lifton's remarks concerning the "death imprint" in Chapter I, pages 12–13.

Chapter Five

1. Barth has written, Gardner's "making a shrill pitch to the literary right wing that wants to repudiate all of modernism." This and other comments from Barth are referenced in Introduction note 1.

Chapter Seven

1. Essentially, Gardner claims a quality of mind which gets him into trouble. He claims to remember passages word for word, and later thinks he made them up himself. See the Ferguson, et al. interview and the Suplee interview in Chavkin's *Conversations with John Gardner*, pages 160–61 and 284.

Chapter Nine

1. See Chapter I, page 25.

Chapter Ten

1. See Chapter VI, pages 129-30.

Chapter Eleven

1. It is in this area of his thought that Whitehead may have had his greatest influence on Susanne Langer. One can see in his approach a precursor of Langer's distinction between *discursive* and *presentational* symbols. For a brief review of Langer's ideas see Chapter II, pages 35–39.

BIBLIOGRAPHY

Works by John C. Gardner

The Art of Fiction. New York: Vintage Books, 1985.

The Art of Living and Other Stories. New York: Ballantine Books, 1983.

Grendel. New York: Vintage Books, 1989.

In the Suicide Mountains. Boston: Houghton Mifflin Company, 1977.

Mickelsson's Ghosts. New York: Alfred A. Knopf, 1982.

Nickel Mountain. New York: Ballantine Books, 1975.

October Light. New York: Alfred A. Knopf, 1977.

On Becoming a Novelist. New York: Harper Colophon Books, Harper & Row, 1985.

On Moral Fiction. New York: Basic Books, Inc, 1978.

The Resurrection. New York: Ballantine Books, 1966.

Stillness and Shadows. New York: Alfred A. Knopf, 1986.

The Sunlight Dialogues. New York: Ballantine Books, 1972.

The Wreckage of Agathon. New York: E. P. Dutton, 1985.

Secondary Sources

Ariès, Philippe. "The Reversal of Death: Changes in Attitudes Toward Death in Western Societies." Valerie M. Stannard, trans. In *Death in America.* David E. Stannard, ed. Philadelphia: University of Pennsylvania Press, 1975.

———. *Western Attitudes Toward Death*. Patricia M. Ranum, trans. Baltimore: The Johns Hopkins University Press, 1974.

Baker, Will. "A Personal Memoir." *MSS*. A special tribute edition to John Gardner. Vol. IV, No. 1, 2, Fall (1984):288–93.

Ball, John, ed. *From Beowulf to Modern British Writers*. New York: The Odyssey Press, Inc., 1959.

Begiebing, Robert J. *Toward a New Synthesis: John Fowles, Norman Mailer and John Gardner*. Ann Arbor, MI: UMI Research Press, 1989.

Bell, Catherine. *Ritual Theory, Ritual Practice*. New York: Oxford University Press, 1992.

Bixler, Julius Seelye. "Whitehead's Philosophy of Religion." In *The Philosophy of Alfred North Whitehead*, Paul Arthur Schilpp, ed. Vol. III of The Library of Living Philosophers. LaSalle, IL: Open Court, 1951.

Butts, Leonard. "John Gardner: A True Artist." *MSS*. A special tribute edition to John Gardner. Vol. IV, No. 1, 2, Fall (1984):282–87.

———. *The Novels of John Gardner: Making Life Art as a Moral Process*. Baton Rouge: Louisiana State University Press, 1988.

Camus, Albert. *The Rebel: An Essay on Man in Revolt*. Anthony Baker, trans. New York: Vintage Books, 1956.

Chavkin, Allan, ed. *Conversations With John Gardner*. Jackson, MS: University Press of Mississippi, 1990.

Clothey, Fred W. *Rhythm and Intent: Ritual Studies from South India*. Bombay: Blackie & Son Publishers PVT LTD, 1983.

Collingwood, R. G. *The Principles of Art*. New York: Oxford University Press, 1958.

Cowart, David. *Arches & Light: The Fiction of John Gardner*. Carbondale, IL: Southern Illinois University Press, 1983.

Dean, William. "Whitehead's Other Aesthetic." *Process Studies*. Vol. 13, No. 1 (1983):104–112.

Douglas, Mary. *Purity and Danger*. Boston: Routledge & Kegan Paul, 1980.

Edwards, Don and Carol Posgrove. "A Conversation with John Gardner." *Atlantic Monthly*. Vol. 239, May (1977): 43–47.

Ferguson, Paul F. et al. "John Gardner: The Art of Fiction LXXIII." *Paris Review*. Vol. 21, Spring (1979):36–74.

Ford, Jeffrey. "John Gardner." *MSS*. A special tribute edition to John Gardner. Vol. IV, No. 1, 2, Fall (1984):261–66.

Gardner, Priscilla. "A Conversation with Priscilla Gardner." *MSS*. A special tribute edition. Vol. IV, No. 1, 2, Fall (1984):232–41.

Geertz, Clifford. *The Interpretation of Cultures*. New York: Basic Books, Inc., Publishers, 1973.

———. *Local Knowledge: Further Essays in Interpretive Anthropology*. New York: Basic Books, Inc., Publishers, 1983.

Girard, René. *Violence and the Sacred*. Patrick Gregory, translator. Baltimore, MD: The Johns Hopkins University Press, 1977.

Grimes, Ronald. *Beginnings in Ritual Studies*. Lanham, MD: University Press of America, 1982.

Gunn, Giles B., ed. *Literature and Religion*. New York: Harper & Row, Publishers, 1971.

Hall, David L. *The Civilization of Experience: A Whiteheadian Theory of Culture*. New York: Fordham University Press, 1973.

Harvey, Marshall L. "Where Philosophy and Fiction Meet: an Interview with John Gardner." *Chicago Review*. Vol. 29, Spring (1978): 73–87.

Higgins, Joanna. "John." *MSS*. A special tribute edition to John Gardner. Vol. IV, No. 1, 2, Fall (1984):294–314.

Holmer, Paul L. *C.S. Lewis: The Shape of His Faith and Thought*. New York: Harper & Row, Publishers, 1976.

Howell, John. "The Wound and the Albatross: John Gardner's Apprenticeship." In *Thor's Hammer*. Jeff Henderson, ed. Conway, AR: University of Central Arkansas Press, 1985.

Hume, David. *An Inquiry Concerning Human Understanding*. Indianapolis: The Liberal Arts Press, Inc, 1955.

———. *On Human Nature and the Understanding*. New York, NY: Collier Books, a Division of Macmillan Publishing Co., Inc, 1962.

Johnston, Robert K. *Theology and Play: A Critical Appraisal*. Diss. Duke University. Ann Arbor: UMI, 1974.

Jones, W. T. *A History of Western Philosophy*. New York: Harcourt, Brace and Company, 1952.

Kant, Immanuel. *Critique of Pure Reason*. Norman Kemp Smith, trans. New York: St. Martin's Press, 1965.

Kaufmann, Walter, ed. *Existentialism from Dostoevsky to Sartre*. New York: New American Library, 1975.

Konner, Mel. "John Gardner." *MSS*. A special tribute edition to John Gardner. Vol. IV, No. 1, 2, Fall (1984):176–97.

Kort, Wesley. *Moral Fiber: Character and Belief in Recent American Fiction*. Philadelphia: Fortress Press, 1982.

———. *Narrative Elements and Religious Meaning.* Philadelphia: Fortress Press, 1975.

Langer, Susanne K. *Feeling and Form.* New York: Charles Scribner's Sons, 1953.

———. *Mind: An Essay on Human Feeling.* Vol. I. Baltimore: The Johns Hopkins University Press, 1967.

———. *Mind: An Essay on Human Feeling.* Vol. II. Baltimore: The Johns Hopkins University Press, 1972.

———. *Mind: An Essay on Human Feeling.* Vol. III. Baltimore: The Johns Hopkins University Press, 1982.

———. *Philosophy in a New Key.* Cambridge, MA: Harvard University Press, 1957.

———. *Problems of Art.* New York: Charles Scribner's Sons, 1957.

Larsen, Elizabeth. "The Creative Act: An Analysis of Systems in Grendel." In *John Gardner: True Art, Moral Art.* Mendez-Engle and Haule, eds. Edinburg, TX: Pan American Univ., 1983.

Laskin, Daniel. "Challenging the Literary Naysayers." *Horizon.* Vol. 21, July (1978): 32–36.

Lawrence, Nathaniel. "The Vision of Beauty and the Temporality of Deity in Whitehead's Philosophy." In *Alfred North Whitehead: Essays on his Philosophy.* George L. Kline, ed. Englewood Cliffs, NJ: Prentice-Hall, Inc, 1963.

LeClair, Tom and Larry McCaffrey, eds. *Anything Can Happen: Interviews with Contemporary American Novelists.* Urbana, IL: University of Illinois Press, 1983.

Lifton, Robert Jay. *The Broken Connection: On Death and the Continuity of Life.* New York: Simon and Schuster, 1979.

———. *Death in Life: Survivors of Hiroshima*. New York: Random House, 1967.

———. *The Future of Immortality*. New York: Basic Books, Inc., Publishers, 1987.

———. "The Sense of Immortality: On Death and the Continuity of Life." In *New Meanings of Death*. Herman Feifel, ed. New York: McGraw-Hill Book Company, 1977.

Lowe, Victor. *Alfred North Whitehead: The Man and His Work*. Vol. II: 1910-1947. J. B. Schneewind, ed. Baltimore: The Johns Hopkins University Press, 1990.

———. "Whitehead's Metaphysical System." In *Process Philosophy and Christian Thought*. D. Brown, R. James and G. Reeves, eds., Indianapolis: Bobbs-Merrill Educational Publishing, 1971.

MacIntyre, Alasdair. *After Virtue: A Study in Moral Theory*. Notre Dame, IN: University of Notre Dame Press, 1984.

Maier, John R. "Mesopotamian Names in The Sunlight Dialogues: Or MAMA Makes It to Batavia, New York." *Literary Onomastics Studies*. Vol. 4 (1977):33–48.

May, William. "The Metaphysical Plight of the Family." In *Death Inside Out*. Peter Steinfels and Robert M. Veatch, eds. New York: Harper & Row, Publishers, 1975.

McWilliams, Dean. *John Gardner*. Boston: Twayne Publishers, A Division of G. K. and Co, 1990.

Morace, Robert A. and Kathryn VanSpanckeren, eds. *John Gardner: Critical Perspectives*. Carbondale, IL: Southern Illinois University Press, 1982.

Morris, Brian. *Anthropological Studies in Religion*. Cambridge, England: Cambridge University Press, 1987.

Morris, Gregory. *A World of Order and Light: The Fiction of John Gardner*. Athens, GA: The University of Georgia Press, 1984.

Natov, Roni and Geraldine DeLuca. "An Interview with John Gardner." *The Lion and the Unicorn*. Vol. 2, No. 1 (1978):114–36.

Price, Lucien. *Dialogues of Alfred North Whitehead*. New York: A Mentor Book, The New American Library, 1956.

Riley, Judas. "Welcome to the Endless Mountains." *MSS*. A special tribute edition to John Gardner. Vol. IV, No. 1, 2, Fall (1984): 267–69.

Ritchie, A. D. "Whitehead's Defense of Speculative Reason." In *The Philosophy of Alfred North Whitehead*. Paul Arthur Schilpp, ed. Vol. III of the Library of Living Philosophers. LaSalle, IL: Open Court, 1951.

Sartre, Jean-Paul. *Nausea*. Lloyd Alexander, trans. New York: New Directions Publishing Company, 1964.

Schwartz, Sheila. "A Student's Memoir," *MSS*. A special tribute edition to John Gardner. Vol. IV, No. 1, 2, Fall (1984):253–60.

Sherburne, Donald W. *A Whiteheadian Aesthetic*. New Haven, CT: Yale University Press, 1961.

Singular, Stephen. "The Sound and the Fury Over Fiction." *New York Times Magazine*. July 8 (1979):13–15, 34, 36–39.

Stokes, Walter E. "God for Today and Tomorrow." In *Process Philosophy and Christian Thought*. D. Brown, R. James and G. Reeves, eds., Indianapolis: Bobbs-Merrill Educational Publishing, 1971.

Titus, Harold H. *Living Issues in Philosophy*. New York: American Book Company, 1964.

Turner, Victor. *Dramas, Fields, Metaphors: Symbolic Action in Human Society*. Ithaca, NY: Cornell University Press, 1975.

———. *The Forest of Symbols*. Ithaca, NY: Cornell Paperbacks, Cornell University Press, 1967.

———. *The Ritual Process*. Ithaca, NY: Cornell Paperbacks, Cornell University Press, 1977.

Turner, Victor and Edith Turner. *Image and Pilgrimage in Christian Culture*. New York: Columbia University Press, 1978.

Tylor, Ralph. "John Gardner: The Novelist Critic Finds Most of Today's Fiction Puny." *Bookviews*. Vol. I, May (1978):6–9.

Whitehead, Alfred North. *Adventures of Ideas*. New York: The Free Press, a Division of Macmillan Publishing Co., Inc, 1967.

———. *The Function of Reason*. Boston: Beacon Press, 1958.

———. *Modes of Thought*. New York: The Free Press, a Division of Macmillan Publishing Co., Inc, 1968.

———. *Process and Reality*. New York: The Free Press, a Division of Macmillan Publishing Co., Inc, 1978.

———. *Religion in the Making*. New York: The World Publishing Company, 1960.

———. *Science and the Modern World*. New York: The Free Press, a Division of Macmillan Publishing Co., Inc, 1967.

———. *Symbolism: Its Meaning and Effect*. New York: Fordham University Press, 1985.

Wigler, Stephen. "Gardner's Ghosts." In Allan Chavkin, ed., *Conversations With John Gardner*. Jackson, MS: University Press of Mississippi, 1990.

INDEX

Abraham and Isaac 104, 106
"absurd" 49, 141, 169–70
actual entity (actual occasion) 52–53, 97
Adventures of Ideas (Whitehead) 30, 56–57, 90, 103, 140, 178, 203, 206
After Virtue (MacIntyre) 105–06
Allen, Ethan 163
analytical philosophy 48, 102, 110
Aries, Philippe 172
Aristotle 104
Arnold, Matthew 154
Art of Fiction, The 25, 27, 33, 42, 60, 100
"Art of Living, The" 208–12
Art of Living and Other Stories, The 3, 10, 18, 185
atmosphere 59

Bakhtin, M.M. 5, 207
Barth, John 3, 32, 99, 151, 223, 224
Barthelme, Donald 2, 32
Begiebing, Robert 62
Beginnings in Ritual Studies (Grimes) 176
Bellow, Saul 32, 223
Beowulf 1, 22, 62, 65, 73–74
Bergson, Henri 103, 110
bibliotherapy 19–20
Bicentennial 147
Bixler, Julius Seelye 38, 205–06
Bly, Robert 114
Bové, Paul ix
Bradley, A.C. 222
Bratt, James D. ix
Brautigan, Richard 32
Brecht, Berthold 219
Brothers Karamazov (Dostoevski) 171
Burns, Heidi ix
Butts, Leonard 86, 92, 189

Caillois, Roger 190, 192
Cambridge School 36
Camus, Albert 49, 50, 141, 169–70, 182, 194

Cassirer, Ernst 36
Chaucer 99, 133
Chavkin, Allan 224
Clothey, Frederick ix, 29, 175
Coleridge, Samuel Taylor 193
Collingwood, R.G. 82
"Come On Back" 18, 185–87
community 25, 29–30, 57, 63, 74, 79, 85, 87–88, 104, 106, 108–09, 111–12, 113–14, 116, 123–25, 129–31, 142, 145, 152–55, 162, 166, 174–75, 185–89
Coover, Robert 2, 193
Cowart, David 1, 32, 62
Curran, Ron ix
cymanfa ganu 17–18, 186–87

de Chardin, Teilhard 182
de Man, Paul 89
death 169–74
Deconstruction 193
DePauw University 22
Descartes, René 45–46, 54
Dewey, John 36
dialogical fiction 5, 207
Dibble, Terry ix
Donahue 60
Dostoevski, Fyodor 171, 174
Douglas, Mary 137
"Dover Beach" (Arnold) 154
Dr. Ruth 60
"dream" 4, 29–30, 33–35, 41

eisteddfods 17
Emerson, Ralph Waldo 147, 182
entrainment 56, 180
Erickson, Jon ix
Existentialism 21, 48–50, 87, 111, 135, 193

Fear and Trembling (Kierkegaard) 104
Ferguson, Paul F. 224
Freddy's Book 3, 6–7
Frost, Robert 131

funerals 131, 144–45

Gardner, Gilbert 10, 16
Gardner, John C., Jr.
 accident with Gilbert 10, 11, 13, 16, 160, 207, 221; art 21, 27–28, 42, 62, 66, 68, 73, 154, 156, 201, 215–16, 220–21; college years 22; colon cancer 2, 221; divorce 2; "faults of soul" 42–45, 151; fictional themes 2, 4–5, 11, 59, 117, 133, 147; guilt 10, 13–14, 16, 24, 30, 128; his death 1, 221; moral fiction 3, 14, 20–21, 26, 42, 71, 99, 148, 150–52, 201; music 17–19, 24, 185–89; narrative elements 60–62; narrative voice 63, 100; plagiarism 2, 99, 133; religion 25–30, 59; suicide 15; teaching 32; Welsh background 17–19; woundedness 4, 6, 10–11
Gardner, John Sr. 17
Gardner, Priscilla 10, 16, 17, 31, 207
Gardner, Susan 10
Gass, William 20, 35, 41, 223
Geertz, Clifford 26–29, 41–42, 196
Girard, René 194
"Grand Inquisitor, The" (Dostoevski) 171, 173–74
Grendel 1, 7, 22, 62–75, 96, 215, 223
Grimes, Ronald 29, 175–77, 179–80, 182–83, 185, 187, 190, 192, 194, 201, 206
Guest, Edgar 138
guilt 107–09, 115–17, 128–31, 160, 162, 164–65, 188–89, 216
Gunn, Giles 208

Hall, David 212
Heidegger, Martin 50, 101, 169–70, 174
Heisenberg, Werner 89
Helfand, Michael ix
Heraclitus 101, 162
heroism 70–71
Higgins, Joanna 32

Hillel 97
Holmer, Paul 34
Howell, John 10
Huizinga, Johann 192
Hume, David 46–47, 178–79
Husserl, Edmund 50

Image and Pilgrimage in Christian Culture (Turner) 78
In the Suicide Mountains 6, 15, 111–12

James, William 37
Janzen, J Gerald ix
Jehovah's Witnesses 127
Jesus 97, 143
Johnston, Robert K. ix, 190–92
Jones, W.T. 45

Kant, Immanuel 47, 54, 192, 223
Kaufmann, Walter 48
Kierkegaard, Soren 73, 104, 106
Konner, Mel 31
Kort, Wesley 59, 61

Langer, Susanne 6, 35–40, 51, 54–56, 176, 179–80, 182, 224
Larsen, Elizabeth 224
Laskin, Daniel 146
"Library Horror, The" 40–41
Lifton, Robert J. 6, 12, 23, 62, 128, 174–75, 207, 224; conceptual schema 12, 20, 62; contamination 12, 14; death imprint 12; psychic numbing 12, 15–16, 19; survivor guilt 12, 13–14, 174; symbolic immortality 23–25
liminality 78–79, 196–98
"Lines Composed a Few Miles Above Tintern Abbey" (Wordsworth) 154–55
Lord's Prayer 96–97
Lowe, Victor 53
"lure for feeling" 66, 89, 107

MacIntyre, Alasdair 105

Malamud, Bernard 3
May, William 169–74
McWilliams, Dean 5, 207
Meland, Bernard 52
metafiction 61, 193
Mickelsson's Ghosts 3, 11, 99–118, 181–82, 216–17
Miller, Tracy ix
monological fiction 5
Mormons 101, 113
Morris, Gregory 86, 97, 117, 145–46

National Book Critics Circle Award 147
Nausea (Sartre) 49–50, 194
Nickel Mountain ix, 1, 11, 119–32, 183, 188–89, 219–20
Nietzsche, Friedrich 108, 193
Novels of John Gardner, The (Butts) 92
"novelty" 79, 89, 196, 198–200
Nutter, Chapin ix
Nutter, Laura ix
Nutter, Zadok William 7

objective immortality 53, 109
October Light 2, 11, 61, 119, 128, 147–67, 183, 213, 218
On Becoming a Novelist 11
On Moral Fiction 2–4, 10, 20–21, 32–33, 62, 68, 71, 99, 147, 219, 223
Oppenheim, A. Leo 133
Orbach, Alex ix

"peace" 7, 30, 57, 71, 96, 111, 124, 131, 145–46, 167, 174, 202, 212–22
pilgrimage 77–79
Plato 22, 103–04
plot 60–62
postmodernism 89, 193–94
"prehension" 53, 96
Process and Reality (Whitehead) 51, 57, 73, 89, 178, 198
Process thought 7, 30, 51–57, 66, 72–73, 83, 101–02, 110–11, 117, 130, 177–80, 198–201, 203–06, 212–15

Pynchon, Thomas 2, 32, 151, 223

"Redemption" 3, 9–10, 12–17, 19–20, 23, 25, 208
religion 4, 6, 25–27, 30, 72–73, 94, 101, 103, 113, 127–28, 134–35, 139–40, 169, 176, 194, 207, 213, 221
responsibility 138–40, 143, 144, 160, 164
Resurrection, The 1, 11, 51, 62, 77–88, 114, 127, 180, 183, 193, 217–18, 220–21, 223
ritual 6–7, 25, 28–30, 38, 39–40, 59, 62, 87, 122–25, 144–45, 167, 175–77, 180, 182–83, 185–90, 194–98, 201–02
Roberts, Robert C. ix
Rockwell, Norman 163

Sartre, Jean-Paul 22, 42, 49–50, 57, 67, 194, 202
Schwartz, Sheila 32
Science and the Modern World (Whitehead) 47
"Second Coming, The" (Yeats) 134, 143
Segal, David 1, 223
shema 96–97
Singular, Stephen 223
"Smugglers of Lost Soul's Rock" 61, 150–52, 155, 156, 158, 166
Stein, Gertrude 44
Steinbeck, John 43
Stevens, Wallace 221
Stevenson, Robert Louis 35
"Stillness" 6
Stillness and Shadows 3, 6, 13, 71–72
Stone, Robert 151
"Stopping By Woods On a Snowy Evening (Frost) 132
Stranger, The (Camus) 194
subjective aim 53–54, 56
Sunlight Dialogues, The 1, 99, 119, 133–46, 181, 218–19
S.U.N.Y. Binghamton 100

Suplee, Curt 224
Symbolism (Whitehead) 200

tabula rasa 79
Tennyson, Alfred 221–22
tone 59–61
truth 89, 93, 96–97
Turner, Edith 78–79
Turner, Victor 30, 39, 78–79, 123, 175–76, 196–98, 201

Updike, John 3, 32, 223

van Gennep, Arnold 78, 196
Vienna Circle 36
virtue ethics 105–06
Vonnegut, Kurt 32, 151

Wetzel, C. Robert ix
Whitehead, Alfred North 6-7, 22, 30, 36, 38, 47, 51–57, 59, 66, 72–73, 79, 83, 89–90, 92, 96, 103, 110, 130, 137, 140–41, 146, 167, 176–80, 182, 196–202, 203–06, 212–15, 224
Wiest, Walter ix
Wigler, Stephen 59
Williamson, Clark ix
Wittgenstein, Ludwig 102, 110, 203
Wordsworth, William 73, 154, 166, 213
Wreckage of Agathon, The 1, 11, 22, 62, 77, 88–97, 216, 223

Yeats, William Butler 134

zodiacal pattern in *Grendel* 63

MODERN AMERICAN LITERATURE
New Approaches

Yoshinobu Hakutani, General Editor

The books in this series deal with many of the major writers known as American realists, modernists, and post-modernists from 1880 to the present. This category of writers will also include less known ethnic and minority writers, a majority of whom are African American, some are Native American, Mexican American, Japanese American, Chinese American, and others. The series might also include studies on well-known contemporary writers, such as James Dickey, Allen Ginsberg, Gary Snyder, John Barth, John Updike, and Joyce Carol Oates. In general, the series will reflect new critical approaches such as deconstructionism, new historicism, psychoanalytical criticism, gender criticism/feminism, and cultural criticism.

Peter Lang Publishing
Acquisitions Department
516 N. Charles St., 2nd Floor
Baltimore, MD 21201